This book is not a work of fiction.
The names portrayed in it are the work of the
author's imagination. The characters and incidents
in it are true. Any resemblance to actual persons,
living or dead, events or localities is entirely on
purpose.

www.onetruekev.co.uk

This paperback edition 2024

For Squirrel, G Man, Ricky Organ, Hopalong, and The Chemist

Here's to making it out the other side alive.

Special thanks to the quiz machine in Bar XS

Without a chance meeting at it, none of this would have happened.

<u>Introduction</u>

An introduction of sorts, what to expect

This is a friendly notice, if you are easily offended by bad language, have a sensitive disposition, or no patience for inappropriate behaviour, then its best that you close this book now, or turn off your e-reader, and just generally fuck off, as you will hate this book, and most of those poor people that appear in it.

Hello to everybody else now that we have got rid of the wimps, religious freaks, do-gooders, and spineless, safe space seeking pussies that inhabit other worlds today, my name is Squirrel, and I'm going to be your guide through this book, your narrator as you will.

Now I'm not actually a physical squirrel, and obviously my real name isn't Squirrel, which would be a fucking stupid name now, wouldn't it? My real name isn't important here, in fact no one has a real name here, everyone has a nickname or a nom de plume in this world, maybe not at first, when they are on the periphery of what is going on, but certainly they do once they are important enough to get a mention. All the names have been changed.

To protect the innocent.

To protect the guilty too.

In fact to protect the ignorant, the idiots, the foolish and the brave, to protect them all from themselves and from others who may want revenge, no one has their own name. They only have the nickname given to them by me, as I am the arbiter of all the names in this world.

Not all names are good or logical, mainly because I am not always good or logical, some make perfect sense at a point in time, but not down the line as circumstances change, but by then it is too late, once they have been given their name it doesn't get changed – well one did, but that is part of the story, so we will come back to that – else it would be far too difficult to keep track of who is who (as if it won't be anyway).

This world doesn't exist anymore, its star rose suddenly, shone brightly for a period, before fading away, bearing the occupants of its world off to other places, but while it did exist, it was the best world ever.

The name of this world was "Number 8, Scarisbrick Avenue", which itself had its own nickname – Chez Didsbury. It was a world that had originally been made for four inhabitants, but which ended up permanently housing five, and had a whole host of other inhabitants over the twenty-one months it existed.

In that world we were the famous five, we were the oceans, though thankfully we weren't the dodgy boy band – well apart from…no, no, I'll come back to that later as well, too many spoilers up front would make an even bigger mockery of this book than me writing it is going to, so no more tangents in this introduction.

I was going to try and concentrate my rambling sentences to only the time spent in that world, but it would be amiss of me to do so, and therefore for all you wonderful people to miss out on how we ended up in that world.

The world of Chez Didsbury came into being in September 2002, and came to an end in May 2004, but this story starts a year before Chez Didsbury came into being, and with Squirrel being the story guide here, it begins somewhat unsurprisingly with Squirrel, and his arrival in Manchester, late in the summer of 2001.

This story of that world is told over twenty years after all the events upon it happened, and therefore, despite some copious notes being made at the time, some of the recollections may be a little bit hazy now. The other thing is that there may well be some embellishments made along the way as well. Not that the latter matters, that's all part of the artistic license involved in the writing of this book.

It comes in two parts, the build-up before moving into Chez Didsbury, and the first six weeks or so living there. Then comes part two, where everything is lifted lock, stock, and one lazy barrel, from the e-zine thing I did at the time. The style therefore may be all over the place.

So now that you've sat through the obligatory boring intro, it's time to get into the reason you are all here, the main story, so without any further ado, let's not stand on ceremony, let's start the show.

Part 1 – Dredged From Squirrel's Memories

All the following chapters are put together from what Squirrel remembers, there were no notes, no pictures, no documentation, just his memory, and where that is a bit patchy, then from his sick twisted imagination.

Tuesday 28th August 2001 – Squirrel arrives in Manchester

When Squirrel had woken up on that Tuesday morning, the day after the August Bank Holiday, he had no idea where he was going to end up that evening. In fact Squirrel had no plan of anything.

All that Squirrel knew was that he had made a monumental mess of his life, and one way or another everything was going to be coming home to roost that day.

So Squirrel did what only people at the end of their rope (and were chickenshits) could do, he ran away. Leaving his family, his wife, his job, and everything else in his life behind. Taking only the bare minimum with him, insomuch that that included what he was wearing, a change of clothes, some personal documents, and his wallet. Squirrel left the door keys, the car keys, his phone, and a pitiful excuse for a note in the car, took what he was taking and went to the bus stop.

From there Squirrel went into the centre of the city and dropped his work keys off through the doors of the office, knowing they were closed for an additional day after the Bank Holiday, and not wanting to take anything that might remotely belong to anyone else with him. After he had heard the keys land with a thump on the plush lined carpet behind the entrance to the office, he turned tail and headed to the bus station.

Squirrel arrived at the bus station not knowing where to go. He had ruled out four large cities as being unfeasible, due to the chances of bumping into people who knew him, or the cost of living there. That left quite a few other large cities as potential targets, somewhere he could go, and be anonymous, hidden away in the vast numbers of others wandering around these metropolises.

Squirrel felt like time was of the essence, he needed out of this city before anyone tapped him on the shoulder and asked what the hell he thought he was doing. There was no answer to that question; he was winging it big time with no chance of explanations.

Looking at the departure boards gave Squirrel hope, there were numerous National Express services out of there in the next half an hour or so. Top of the departure board was a coach to Newcastle, somewhere he knew nobody, and certainly big enough to disappear, but as Squirrel wandered over to the ticket window, the departure time changed, the Newcastle coach was going to be delayed by nearly an hour, far too long for him to hang around this bus station with eyes on the various doors looking out for people to come and drag him back to the lives he had screwed up.

Just under Newcastle on the departure board was Manchester, it was only a couple of minutes after the original Newcastle departure time, and if anything was even more ideal, Squirrel still didn't know anyone who lived there, it was a bigger city, and the accent was somewhat more understandable as English. He finished the short walk to the ticket office and bought a single one-way ticket to Manchester.

Once the ticket had been bought, Squirrel found a dingy corner to stand in for the short wait for the coach to arrive, out of the way of prying eyes, or random passers-by. The coach pulled in, and he got on, showed his ticket to the driver, and found a seat a few rows in, threw his bag in the overhead compartment, and slumped down into his seat, his heart rate reducing as other passengers got on, and the departure time came around. When the door to the coach closed, and the driver pulled away from the stand, Squirrel's heart rate was low enough for him to drift off to sleep for a bit.

The coach stopped for a scheduled break for twenty minutes at Leeds coach station. Squirrel took the opportunity to stretch his legs and have a toilet break. The coach station they had pulled into was next to a market, and realising that he had come on such a permanent journey with such a minimal wardrobe, Squirrel took the opportunity to get some cheap additional changes of socks, underwear, and t-shirts. He just made it back to the coach on time for the onward journey.

Squirrel had only been to the outskirts of Manchester before, and then only the once for a wedding reception for one of the in-laws. He had no idea of what the centre of the city would look like, or where he would end up. When the coach pulled into the Lever Street coach station, all that he knew when he got off the coach was that he needed to find tourist information.

Squirrel got off the coach, and wandered around looking for some kind of indication of where he could go. In the corner of the coach station was a Manchester city centre map, and he was in business. He took his time getting his bearings, and worked out his route to the tourist information office from the map using the least turns possible, as he didn't know where he would find another map. He could have asked people for directions, but Squirrel wasn't a people person, especially people he didn't know, and not when sober.

It was further than it looked on the map, and Squirrel felt like he was taking his life in his hands when he made his way across the tram tracks in the city, he was too busy looking out for road names, and cars on the road to notice the almost silent tram come up behind him. The horn made Squirrel jump, and he decided that for once in his life, walking on the pavements might be a good plan.

The tourist information office was massive, and there were lots of people milling about inside. Now that Squirrel was here, he wasn't sure what he was looking for. He was going to have to bite the bullet and ask for help, and went over to queue at one of the available kiosks. The couple in front of him were Spanish, or at least they spoke Spanish, they could have been from any number of countries really.

Squirrel wasn't paying attention to them poring over a map with the "information officer," as they circled various places. He was having various thoughts bounce round in his head as to what he was doing in a strange city, starting life all over at the age of thirty-one. He was still pondering this, as the Spanish couple left and was brought back to the here and now by the information officer asking how she could help.

Squirrel explained he had arrived in the city that day, and wanted as cheap a bed and breakfast establishment as possible whilst he looked for more permanent accommodation and a job. The information officer didn't ask for any other details, or want to know why he was in Manchester. She probably had this kind of request on a regular basis. She went onto her computer and got some names and prices of places. She advised Squirrel to head towards Fallowfield, and gave him directions back to the bus station he had passed on the way to the tourist information office, the numbers of buses that would take him there, and the stop to get off at.

Squirrel got her to write the information down, took the piece of paper from her and he was on his way. He had been given the names and prices of three bed and breakfast places on Wilmslow Road; The Wilmslow, The Willowbank, and The Drop Inn, of the three, The Drop Inn was the cheapest at only twenty-three quid a night.

Squirrel didn't know how long it would be until he could get a job, and therefore how long it would be until he got paid for any work. He had some money from his last wages at the job he had just walked out from without any notice, but not enough that he could ignore being as frugal as he could be until he got employment. It didn't matter to him if The Drop Inn was the biggest shit hole in the western world, if it had a bed he didn't care.

The Drop Inn – Part One

Upon arrival it was obvious that The Drop Inn wasn't the most salubrious establishment going, but it certainly wasn't the biggest shit hole in the western world. It was a sprawling pub at the front, with a little cloakroom style reception to the bed and breakfast rooms tucked into the corner towards the back of the main building, just visible if you knew where you were looking, once you went into the pub through the main doors.

Squirrel hadn't seen it though as he didn't have a clue what he was looking for, and asked at the bar, before being pointed in the right direction.

Squirrel wandered over to the reception hatch, and dinged on the service bell, the hatch and the bell seemed like they might have been here before the rest of the building, but it worked, and a friendly middle-aged woman appeared as if by magic in front of him.

Squirrel paid for three nights upfront, and came to an agreement with the woman that he could extend day by day if required after that. He was given a key with a fob attached to it that could be seen from space, bright yellow plastic, and chipped at the edges. He had been given room fifteen, and was pointed down a little corridor to the side of the reception hatch. The room was on the first floor, he could go across the car park, and up the stairs in the accommodation block, or up the stairs at the end of the corridor and across the covered footbridge.

Squirrel opted for the second, and made the way over to his room. The footbridge was no more than a prefab corridor suspended on stilts over the car park. The whole thing wobbled as he made his way over it and into the accommodation block. He might brave walking across the car park on the way back as he had visions of planting his foot down and it disappearing through the floor to dangle above the passing cars.

The room wasn't bad for the price, the furniture had probably seen better days, but there was a bed, chair, desk and wardrobe, and the bathroom had a shower over the bath, and it was clean. The bedding was fresh on, and there was a television in the corner of the room, which to his surprise had more than just the five terrestrial channels, and fed through some of the Sky channels from the pub. Unless breakfast was poisonous, this was going to be good value for money.

The next morning Squirrel was up, and after a nice, cooked breakfast out. There were lots of shops in Fallowfield, and he went in some of the bigger ones, asking if there were any jobs. He filled out application forms for Sainsbury's and Subway, but was going to struggle to hear back, living in a bed and breakfast and without a mobile phone.

In a newsagent's window he saw a couple of adverts for rooms in house shares, and took the numbers on the cards and went in search of a phone box. He went back to the Sainsbury's and bought himself an A-Z of Manchester. He'd need to be able to find these places he was ringing up about.

Of the three numbers he had written down, only one of them bothered answering the phone. They gave Squirrel an address in Longsight, and arranged to meet him the Friday morning. Squirrel worked out how he would get there by public transport and spent the rest of the afternoon and much of the following day wandering up Wilmslow Road looking for more job opportunities.

When he got back to the Drop Inn that evening, he only just managed to resist the temptation to go into the bar and have a couple of drinks, probably a wise decision whilst on a limited budget. Instead he spent the whole night writing out copies of his CV ready to hand over to any other unsuspecting establishments that were looking for employees.

Downtown Longsight was like a dingier version of Fallowfield, with more shops than bars, a market, and an Asda instead of Sainsbury's. He found the road the house he was going to see was on, and started the long trek up it. The Edwardian terrace building was spread over five floors, and the room available was up on the third floor, a little attic type space with a single bed, desk and chair and wardrobe, with a cubby hole space to the rear under the sloping roof, and a couple of shelves just about hanging onto the wall above the bed.

At twenty-five quid per week and a hundred quid deposit, it would do just fine. He handed the money over to the dodgy Manc who'd shown him around, got a set of keys and then headed back to check out of the Drop Inn.

155 Hamilton Road

With a ragtag collection of little bags, Squirrel let himself into the house and climbed up all the stairs. There were only two rooms on the third floor, and in the middle of the day the house was quiet. Most of the people occupying this house were working and not the students he had been expecting.

He had a look around the rest of the house. The first and second floors were laid out in the same way, three bedrooms and a bathroom on each. The ground floor had a large living room with multiple sofas, a couple of tables and a large TV, which was hooked up to Sky, with all the channels. There was one bedroom next to it, and then a large utility room with a couple of washer-dryers and hanging space. And next to a small yard was a long kitchen with multiple cookers, microwaves, and sinks. Then there was a basement, which was in the process of being done up. There would be another bathroom, another lounge, and a bedroom down there too.

There was the temptation to just crash on the sofa and watch TV, but instead he headed into the centre of Manchester and found a bank. He cancelled all existing direct debits and standing orders except one, and stopped any cheques that were out there but hadn't been cashed. He then found the Arndale shopping centre and had a mooch around. He picked up a cheap alarm clock / radio / CD player and picked up a single CD from HMV. When he needed an alarm for the next few weeks it would be the sounds of Duran Duran's Decade that would eventually bring him up into consciousness.

In the evening he made his way into the lounge and introduced himself. There was quite a mixed community in the house. The guy in the room opposite his was a proper cockney geezer. There were three Danes, two women and a bloke. A Turkish-Cypriot woman was sharing a room with a rude Austrian bloke. A small, quiet Chinese bloke had the room on the ground floor, and there was a solitary Manc living it the house. Apparently, there was a nice Iranian bloke that lived there as well, but in all the time he lived there he never saw him.

Squirrel spent Saturday looking around the market and the couple of charity shops in Longsight and picked up some additions for his wardrobe, and a pair of trainers that still had a reasonable amount of life left in them. He got some food essentials from Asda and got a better idea of the neighbourhood around the house before heading back. It had been mentioned that several of the housemates were going out that evening to watch the football, and he reckoned he had enough to be able to go with them.

England 5 – Germany 1

Squirrel's first weekend living in Manchester, and it was international break. World Cup qualifiers and England were away to Germany, needing a win to have any real chance of winning the group and getting qualification. But getting a win away in the Olympic Stadium in Munich was about as rare as rocking horse shit. There wasn't a lot of hope.

The other two English guys from the house, plus the three Danes were up for watching the football, and the suggestion was that they go to the Footage and Firkin, as they had the biggest screen in Manchester, and it was a good place to watch football. Half of Manchester had the same idea. The place was rammed, the queue for the bar was ridiculous, it was ten deep across the whole of the very wide bar. Despite getting to the Footage half an hour before kick-off, they were still queuing for drinks when the game kicked-off, and by the time Squirrel got served Germany had taken the lead, and England had had time to equalise. Squirrel couldn't be arsed with another wait like this, and ordered four pints and headed upstairs where the others had gone.

When Stevie G put England ahead just before half time, the pub erupted as if England had won the world cup. The loudest cheers were from the Danish contingent. If you ever thought that the English don't look upon the Germans with great fondness, then it's nothing compared with the ire the Danes hold for them. As the second half went on, and England fans went from happiness to dreamland as Michael Owen completed his hat trick, and even Emile Heskey managed to get a goal, the Danes went into a quite spectacular sweary overdrive. Basically telling the Germans to fuck off in three languages.

The others suggested heading into the centre of Manchester, and ended up on Peter Street. A quick drink in Square Bar was followed by a couple in Bar 38 before trying to get into a club. The first attempt was to get into Life or The Late Room. There were several bouncers, mainly checking out footwear. As Squirrel had had no idea where they'd be ending up, he was wearing the big chunky trainers he'd got from the charity shop earlier. They weren't letting trainers in, so he went for the socks only approach, and stuffed his trainers in his back pockets. The black socks worked in getting past the footwear police to an extent. One of the other bouncers noticed the trainers in Squirrel's back pocket and stopped him from entering. "Nice try mate."

A lot of the clubs on Peter Street were footwear Nazis, so more by accident than design they found themselves in Down Under, carrying on drinking until kicking out time. Expecting a long walk or a taxi to be required to get back, Squirrel was surprised to find that buses ran all night to a lot of the city, including one close to the house.

Get a Job

Sunday was a write off for doing anything productive, so Monday saw Squirrel job hunting again. He traipsed round lots of shops dropping off CV's or picking up application forms. He hadn't even thought about agencies until one of the guys mentioned it in the house on the Monday night. Tuesday was spent trying to find all the agencies to leave details with them, or arrange appointments. Being in the shared house also meant that he could add a contact number to the details he left with them.

One of the appointments was for the Wednesday morning with Adecco. Squirrel spent some time completing the online form for them, and then they set up a machine for him to do a speed and accuracy check. Having done lots of data entry before moving into IT management before Manchester, he was sure that any tests wouldn't pose a problem.

Yet when he had his sit down with an agent after the test, the agent had a look of consternation on her face when she looked at the output.

"Erm, there seems to be a problem with the test, the output number appears to be faulty, can you do it again please?"

Squirrel didn't mind, and he flew through the pages in front of him. When the output from the second test came through, the agent looked even more confused, and took the results from both tests to one of her colleagues to look at them. She came back a few minutes later, apologising as she did so. She hadn't seen any test scores come back with a score of over 10,000, so she thought his 12,400 was a mistake. When he posted 14,100 the second time around, she had to go and check whether it was possible. It appeared that he was natural for data entry, and they had a job he could start the next morning.

They gave him the name of a large well known outsourcing company and an address in Exchange Quays. After working out how to get there he realised that he didn't have any shirts, so it was Longsight market again, where he found two shirts. They would do for the last two days of the week.

17

Squirrel arrived at the office the next morning after a long search around the business park. The entrance was right at the end of a footpath at the very end of the park. The office was a hive of chaotic activity, and he was shown to a desk, and given a pile of timesheets, and shown how they were to be entered into SAP. After five minutes of intensive training he was left to get on with it.

The outsourcing company were doing the payroll for an energy company down south, and hadn't been working very long on that contract. Within a couple of hours Squirrel could see there was no rhyme or reason to what they were doing with the humungous piles of timesheets that seemed to be spewing forth from every cupboard. Those to be done were next to, or even in the same pile as those already done. There were lots of duplicate ones as well as when people hadn't been paid overtime, they'd sent another copy in. They were trying to catch up, so there was overtime available, something he was more than happy to do. It wasn't like he had anything else to do, and the money would come in useful. He worked both days over the weekend as well as doing extended hours on each of the normal days.

The following week started the same way, a few extra hours on the Monday, but Tuesday saw a change in the attitude in the office.

Boom!

Everything was normal until mid-afternoon on the Tuesday. Then suddenly, the phones went mad, nearly every phone in the office rang at the same time. There were shocked voices, and a fair bit of swearing, but Squirrel still had his head down bashing away at his keyboard. Then someone got up and put the TV on that hung on the wall behind the supervisor's desk, and whacked the volume right up.

All work in the office pretty much ground to a halt. Even Squirrel moved his head around to look what was happening. A special news bulletin was on. A plane had crashed into one of the twin towers of the World Trade Centre in New York. As the bulletin was running and reports were coming over, a second plane flew into the other tower.

No-one could believe what they were seeing. The first one was being viewed as a tragic accident, but no-one believed it was an accident after the second one hit. There was a stunned silence around the office, one that Squirrel broke by tapping away at the keyboard again. There wasn't a great deal of work done that afternoon as people watched countless re-runs and analysis of the crashes. More details came through of other crashes, one into the Pentagon building and one into a field outside Washington DC.

At five o'clock no-one was staying late, they were all off home. The tram and bus were full of chatter about it. Squirrel was glad he still had his Walkman, one of the few things he had brought from his old life. He could turn it up and block all of it out.

The police presence in the centre of Manchester was easily higher than normal, including a load carrying sub-machine guns. Once it had come out that it was a concerted terrorist attack, thoughts on security jumped through the roof. Squirrel was glad he wasn't going to be doing any travelling in the foreseeable future.

When he got back to the house the living room was full. All the housemates that were in were sat in the living room watching the pictures and listening to the news coming through. There was a lot of flicking through different channels, but the pictures were the same. The messages were the same. The only thing that changed was the accents.

19

It was a sombre household that evening, and there was a subdued atmosphere at work for the next couple of days.

In retrospect, it was probably a good thing that Squirrel hadn't started writing Surerandomality at that point. The fact that the only e-mail addresses he would know were those of the people in the office, and the fact he'd only been working there a week, and was a temp, meant they probably weren't ready for his sense of humour. Jokes about big apple crumbles and the like would have gone down like the proverbial lead balloon.

Additionally, pointing out to people that if you wrote 9/11 using wingdings font at the time it came out as ✈●❈▤▤ wasn't the way to win friends and influence people. There would be plenty of time to outrage public decency once he got to grips with knowing more people in Manchester, and once people had got used to him.

The Night Shift

The Friday of Squirrel's first full week at work came with a meeting around rearranging the work, especially around keying timesheets. They wanted to move the main batch of keying to overnight, having longer shifts and freeing up some space to get other stuff done during the day. Squirrel volunteered immediately, not caring about working nights, and with an eye on extra money.

The office manager was being removed from her role, and the supervisor was going to take over. When Squirrel had approached her about doing nights and being prepared to work longer hours to be a touch point between the day and night working, she was more than happy to let him. Not only that, but she gave Squirrel a set of keys to the building. Something Squirrel couldn't believe.

Seriously, who in their right minds would possibly give a temp, who hadn't been working there much over a week, the keys and alarm codes to the whole building? As it turns out, Squirrel didn't take the opportunity to use the keys to clear the whole building and sell it all on. And no one ever said the supervisor was in their right mind.

Night working was going to start from the following Tuesday, there would be three long night shifts on Tuesday, Wednesday & Thursday. With that and the frequent weekend overtime, plus the occasional daytime working on a Monday, Squirrel was going to regularly rack up seventy hours a week. On enhanced hourly rates for nights, and time and half or double time for anything over thirty-seven and a half hours a week. These were going to be the drinking years. Not only that, but there was no office dress code for working nights. He didn't need any more shirts.

It was the second week of working nights when the police knocked on the door. It was about three in the afternoon on the Thursday and Squirrel had only just got up. He was sat on the arm of a chair eating a bowl of cereals when he saw the police car pull up outside. He knew it was there to speak to him. He had been half expecting a visit ever since he'd given his address to the agency. Once they had done the wages for the first time it would have fed his address through to the DCI computer that the Government departments shared.

He watched the policeman get out of the car, still hoping that they would go to one of the neighbouring houses. It wasn't to be. The knock came on the door. Squirrel answered it, and the thought of lying ran through his head. Yet when the policeman asked if he knew if he lived there, he said who he was, and yes, he was living there. The ex he had run away from had filed a missing person's report, and since there was now a new address on the central computers, the local police had come to follow up.

They asked him if he was OK, and had he moved of his own free will. They asked him for a contact number, and he gave them the house phone number. Then they asked him if he wanted to let those people who had filed the missing person's report know where he was living. Squirrel firmly told the policeman no. He had left and had no intention of going back. The policeman told him they would pass the appropriate details over to the South Yorkshire force and left.

Squirrel had a sinking feeling in his stomach, and pulled his shit together to go to work. His mind certainly wasn't fully involved in timesheets that night, and for once he left pretty much on time on the Friday morning. He asked one of the others to drop his timesheet into the agency and he headed back to the shared house.

Even though the police had said they didn't have to report where he was living. Just that he had been found and was safe and well, he approached the house with the utmost caution. Instead of the usual long trek up Hamilton Road, he walked up the road parallel to it, and checked out the side street on either side of the block he was on. He crept down Hector Road until he got to the ginnel that went down the back of the houses on Hamilton Road. The back gate was closed and locked, and so he continued across to Mentor Street.

There was no sign of any car that he recognised from his ex's family, and so he crept up to the junction with Hamilton Road. He scanned all the cars he could see, looking if there were any people sat in the parked cars. If the police had his new address, then his ex could get it from the Benefit's Agency computers where she worked, as they were all linked.

When he was certain that the coast was clear he ran to the third house along, up the steps and after fumbling with his key, through the door. He ran up to his room and packed most of his stuff in a couple of bags and headed back down. He peered out of the living room window to check for any new vehicles or people in the vicinity before he was off out of the house, across the road and down Montgomery Road opposite the house.

Once out of sight of the house he slowed to a normal walking pace, got his bearings, and headed back to Fallowfield. He knew where there was a cheap bed and breakfast there.

The Drop Inn – Part Two

Half an hour later Squirrel was sitting in The Drop Inn again. It wasn't even eleven o'clock yet, and they hadn't started serving alcohol yet. Not that it would have been a good idea to go down that path yet. He needed a clear head for a couple of days to sort out what he was going to do next. The old woman in charge of the bed and breakfast part said he could check in about midday. So he sat there with a Pepsi reading the paper.

Ideally, he needed sleep, but that would have to wait as well, yet by the time he had got a room and dumped his stuff the bed looked too inviting to ignore and he was fast asleep.

When he woke it was early evening. He needed something to eat and so headed back out to the centre of Fallowfield and the glut of fast-food establishments there. He wanted to get some cash out as he was running low, but he was reluctant to draw cash out near to where he was, in effect, hiding out for the fear that he might be traced by that.

So after food he continued walking up the Wilmslow Road and into Rusholme. He realised he should have waited before getting food and got a curry. They called this the curry mile, and although it wasn't a mile long, nearly every other establishment on it was a curry house or take away. It was probably his idea of heaven.

One of the few shops that sat in the area was a newsagent, and as he'd done before he checked out the adverts in the window for potential places to rent. There were a couple at reasonable rates, so he took the numbers down. He still didn't have a mobile, something he'd sort out soon, but he could ring them up from work the following day.

The next morning he managed to persuade the Drop Inn to let him have an early breakfast and headed to work. He left it until most of the others went out to get lunch and made the phone calls. He made appointments for the Monday and continued.

The first of the two places Squirrel went to see was a box room in Withington. He had no idea of how anyone was supposed to live in that room, it was so small, the only way he'd have been able to sleep in there would be for him to lie diagonally corner to corner. The four foot long two-foot-wide camp bed wasn't going to cut it.

In comparison, the second room was a palace. A long room in a terraced house, with a normal sized single bed, and lots of wall space. The shared areas were functional, and it wasn't far from the main bus route into the city centre or Fallowfield. And even better it was only five minutes away from the curry mile. Squirrel just had to negotiate staying there. It was normally a student only house, and the landlady was worried on the effect having a non-student living there would have. Squirrel managed to talk her round, gave her a false name, and agreed to move in on the Friday morning.

The rest of the week saw Squirrel confusing the hell out of himself and the staff at the Drop Inn. Arriving home from work in the morning for breakfast, and sleeping during the day, he found himself being woken by the cleaning staff every day.

Friday morning he headed to the agency, arranged with them to have his payslips sent care of his work address and headed back to the Drop Inn, where he had breakfast, got his bags, and checked out before heading back up to another new address.

239 Heald Place

Squirrel had arranged to arrive at his new house share at eleven. He made it with a few minutes to spare. His new landlady wasn't as punctual. Three quarters of an hour he stood there waiting to get in and he only did so when one of the current occupants returned.

When he moved in, there were two other occupants, both of whom were Spanish. Diego let Squirrel in and left him in the lounge to await the landlady, who eventually turned up about half twelve. Squirrel paid her the deposit and a month's rent in cash, but even at £35 a week, it was still reasonable. Raul, the other occupant came back later, and Squirrel found that there may well be communication issues ahead. The two Spanish guys English was a bit patchy, and Squirrel's Spanish was non-existent.

After a couple of hours' kip, Squirrel went out for some food, and then once dark he headed back over to Hamilton Road. There was still some of his stuff left there, and he needed to leave his keys and a note for the landlord. He'd got the A-Z with him and found it wasn't that far across when walking, and realised that the bus into the city centre and back out would take a lot longer.

He employed the same level of care and attention when approaching the house on Hamilton Road as he had the morning after the police had turned up. He didn't want to be bumping into the ex or her family if they were there looking for him. With it being dark he found it harder to see into parked cars, but the lack of light would make it difficult for anyone to recognise him.

He got to the house without any difficulties and headed up to his room. He filled up the empty bags he had with him, and checked there was nothing else left in the room before closing the door behind him. He went down to the kitchen and got the few items of food that he had in the fridge and freezer, and put them in a bag too. He bumped into the little Chinese guy, just telling him to make sure that the landlord got the envelope he left on the hall table. In it were the keys and a note saying keep the deposit, he didn't want to leave a forwarding address or number. His payslip was on the table along with a couple of interview offers from CV's he'd left at places. He didn't take them up. He left Hamilton Road without saying goodbye to anyone else. It would be difficult to explain.

And then it was back to Heald Place. With payslips directed to work, he didn't bother to update his home address with Adecco, and he registered for council tax with a different surname. Good luck to anyone trying to find him now.

After working on the Saturday, Squirrel headed out to see what the pubs were like close by. He'd passed a couple when looking for the house on the Monday and thought he'd try them out. Osbourne House was less than two minutes away, and if he'd lived a couple of doors down Heald Place he would have been able to see it out of the back window. It was virtually empty, with not a lot to do, no quiz machine or pool table, so it was a quick drink there before moving on. Next up was the Gardeners Arms, it looked like a couple of terraced houses knocked through from the front, but there were a lot more people in there, a jukebox and a couple of pool tables. On to the Nelson, which just screamed aggravation from the moment he walked in. In the twenty minutes he was there he witnessed someone throw a brick in through the window, and the pub clear with most of the patrons carrying pool cues to use in the ensuing mass brawl outside. Swiftly moving on to The Albert for another drink, it was a decent possibility, as was the Clarence. Hardy's Well was huge and trendy before its time, but empty. How that would change when the students came back. The final one on Squirrel's route was The Huntsmen. The whole place stopped to stare when he walked in, it wasn't the most welcoming of places. He headed back to the Gardeners, and that would end up being his regular Saturday night haunt for the next couple of months.

Travel to work was easier from the new house, plus it had the bonus of there being a whole host of fast-food establishments from which to get breakfast in Squirrel time for his night shifts. He'd had kebab for breakfast quite a few times in his Leicester days, but it was always reheated. Rolling out of bed at half three in the afternoon meant he could have fresh kebab for breakfast. Not only that, but Manchester was more down the line of wrapping kebabs with naan breads not pittas.

The Friday pay packet that hit Squirrel's account that week was immense, over seventy hours worked and no bills, no bed and breakfast

27

costs, no deposits to pay meant he was, in relative terms a rich man. He expanded his wardrobe a bit, via a combination of the indoor market in the Arndale and High & Mighty. A couple of CD's were picked up; he needed some new alarm music as a change from Duran Duran. He also got himself a pay as you go mobile phone, a sturdy Eriksson number that would, over the years prove to be indestructible. Then it was home for a few hours' kip. He was going to go out tonight and have a few drinks.

The Drawing Of The Five

Squirrel headed into Fallowfield. Besides the Drop Inn he had seen there were quite a few bars there, so it looked like a good place to set out from. He started in the Drop Inn, but he'd drank there already. Hell he'd lived there twice since arriving in Manchester. So he moved on quickly. Next up was The Friendship Inn, a cross between a traditional old man's local's pub, and the buzz of a student bar.

He moved on, crossing the road heading for The Orange Grove, where he encountered the first problem. "Sorry mate, students only." He was stunned, he hadn't heard of anything so ridiculous, but he was to find out, it was standard in this part of the world. He bounced across the road to Revolution, but it was rammed and warm, and he was glad to get out.

He found a little bar on the corner of the crossroads. It was cocktails and shooters mainly, and over the next couple of months it would be a good place to neck a few cheap drinks before carrying on, but all these years later the name of it escapes him. The building housed many different bars over the years, but nothing stuck for long.

On the opposite corner was Glass, which was also rammed, spread over two floors it had a balcony overlooking the crossroads. How more drinks and glasses didn't rain down from there over the years was one of life's little mysteries. Just past Glass was Robinski's, a scream pub; and the second establishment of the evening that was students only. As was the next attempt, the Queen of Hearts, so he headed back to the bar he had missed on the way up, Bar XS.

He hadn't realised it had got that late, but they were now charging to get in, but on the plus side it was going to be open until two. There was a DJ playing and a bit of a space for a dance floor. As usual Squirrel gravitated towards the quiz machine. There were already a group of students playing on it, but Squirrel watched over their shoulders as they played on it, and shouted out answers. Which overall were correct answers.

There were a group of five of them, and Squirrel got chatting to them. Two of them, Hopalong and Radio lived in the same house,

29

another two The Chemist and The Quiet Man were in halls on the nearby campus, the final one – Ricky (as he was initially) Organ lived in halls at the other end of Rusholme.

Ricky Organ was keen for Squirrel to join them for a pub quiz on the Sunday night at RP's. Squirrel didn't have a clue where that was. When told it was on the campus it didn't help his understanding, not being from Manchester and not being a student meant his local knowledge was minimal. They agreed to meet back in XS on the Sunday evening before the quiz and they'd take Squirrel with them to RP's.

When Sunday came around Squirrel was early, he stopped at the cocktail bar first and got a few early drinks down his neck. He bumped into one of the Danish girls from Hamilton Road. Apparently, the house consensus was that he'd gone back to his ex. They didn't appear to have had any house visits from irate relatives.

Squirrel met Ricky Organ in XS, and they headed off to RP's Hopalong, The Chemist, Radio, and The Quiet Man were joined by Lamb, who had an on-off relationship with Hopalong, and Liver, who was seeing Ricky Organ.

The quiz was ridiculously hard, but the others found out that Squirrel could live with hard, they were the only team to get more than half the questions right and got more than double the number of points of any other team. They drank the prize before heading on to another of the bars on the student campus. The bar was called Squirrel's.

Now it needs to be pointed out that Squirrel did not get his nickname from this bar. Despite the vast amount of time and money he spent there over the next year. Not only that, but in these pre-Chez Didsbury chapters it opens the narrative to more confusion than normal, as it may well be difficult to tell where Squirrel the person ends, and where Squirrel's the bar starts.

Squirrel got some numbers put into his new phone, and arrangements were made to meet up in Squirrel's on the Friday.

A chance meeting over a quiz machine would lead to Squirrel being accepted into a student lifestyle. It would also lay the foundations for those twenty odd months in Chez Didsbury. Three of the other four permanent residents had already been met in Ricky Organ, Hopalong and The Chemist. The final one was still some way from joining them, but there were plenty of escapades to be had along the way.

Monday Night in Friday's

Squirrel had got into a routine of only sleeping six times a week due to the long night shifts he worked and then going out the nights he wasn't working. Home was only ranking number three on where he spent most time, after work and in pubs/clubs/curry houses. He met up with the others from the quiz machine meeting on Fridays, Sundays for the quiz and Mondays.

It was a Monday night a couple of weeks into the routine when there was karaoke in Squirrel's. Now Squirrel liked to have a go at karaoke. Not that he could sing very well mind you. He knew the words and timings, but there wasn't a lot of tuneage in the vocals. He'd been up a couple of times and done "Baggy Trousers" and "Going Underground," and met a reasonable response to doing so. Some of the others had tried "Come On Eileen," without realising that the verses before the foot stomping chorus are difficult.

At kicking out time there were a group looking at heading off elsewhere. Robinski's was the local option, but with Squirrel, Hopalong and Me Laird not being students they weren't having any of it. Squirrel had been chatting to one of the barmaids that the others knew, and despite both Hopalong and The Chemist advising him not to go near Gonfer; he was happily ignoring them as he held her hand whilst they decided where to go. Hopalong shouted Friday's and flagged a taxi down. Squirrel just looked confused, "but it's Monday?" Until someone else pointed out Fridays was a club on Palantine Road.

They arrived in two taxi loads and got in to find an almost empty club. They bought drinks and hit the dance floor. At some point during the evening in Friday's Squirrel ended up snogging Gonfer, and then when they headed back to Fallowfield, Squirrel paid for the taxi for those going to Owen's or Richmond Park and walked Gonfer back to her block before heading home.

When Squirrel arrived in Squirrel's on the Friday there was a somewhat glacial reception from Gonfer and her sidekick barmaid Frost. Squirrel shrugged it off; he'd seen similar reactions when daylight came on numerous occasions over the years. It wasn't until the following Monday that he found out the reason for the iciness.

Gonfer had told a couple of her friends that Squirrel had assaulted her. To say Squirrel was gobsmacked was an understatement. He was fuming and had to be talked out of going to the police himself. The Chemist and Hopalong told him that is exactly what they were trying to warn him about before they went to Friday's the week before. It turns out Gonfer was a little bit nuts. They just told him to ignore her, no one else believed a word she said. Squirrel let himself be guided by the others, but worried about the possibility of being reported to the police for something he didn't do for months.

He continued going into Squirrel's all the way through, getting served by other staff, much to the amusement of the others and Bern, the landlady of Squirrel's. It wasn't until the end of the summer term that Gonfer properly spoke to Squirrel again. She apologised and said she hadn't meant for things to get out of hand like that. Squirrel had shrugged it all off by then, and he accepted the apology with good grace.

But, But…You're Dead

Squirrel had the plan of getting settled in Manchester for a while before finding a flat for himself and getting all his stuff out of storage where it had been since selling his house over two years before. He had enough furniture to furnish a one-bedroom flat, plus he had all his books, videos, and music there as well; a couple of thousand records, hundreds of tapes, and CD's. He had been paying the storage company in Leicester by standing order.

One Friday he was checking his account when he saw that the standing order had been returned. He asked in the bank why it had been returned to be told it was at the storage company's end.

So Squirrel rang the storage company. He got through to the receptionist and asked the question.

"Hi, I was wondering if you could tell me why you have returned my standing order payment. I have a container in storage with you and obviously don't want it being sold on or anything."

"Yes, I can check that for you, can you give me your name and account number please?"

Squirrel gave her the details, and could hear tapping on a keyboard on the other end of the phone. A now nervous sounding receptionist spoke again.

"Erm, hi, can I confirm some additional details with you please."

Squirrel sighed, but said yes, and they checked details around date of birth, current address, address back in Leicester and some other ones. The voice on the other end of the phone sounded really worried now.

"Can you hold for a couple of minutes please; I just need to check something with the manager?"

"Yeah, that's fine."

A few minutes later there was a different voice on the phone. The worried tone remained the same though. Another round of validation questions came and went before the whole reason for the worry and nervousness became apparent.

"You see Mr. Squirrel; the issue is, according to our records. Well, I don't quite know how to put this, but, but... you're dead."

"Shit, you could have fooled me. I wish someone had told me, instead of letting me wander around in the land of the living."

"Erm......."

"And just how did you come to the conclusion that I was dead?"

"Your wife."

"Excuse me?"

"Your wife came to see us with a certification of registration of death certificate, and arrange for the container to be delivered to her address."

"When was this?"

"About a month ago, let me check. Yes, the 18th of October."

Squirrel groaned. He knew just what his ex had done; he was surprised at the speed it had happened though.

"So, this certificate, do you still have a copy in your files?"

"We do."

"Can you fax it to me?"

"We can, what for?"

"Well I need to make a couple of calls, to the police and the DSS."

"You do understand Mr Squirrel that we were following the correct procedure; this is an official document we have here."

"Yes, I do. I'm not blaming you, but I do need copies of any paperwork so I can try and sort this out."

Squirrel gave them the fax number at work and headed back there to pick them up. He was in a foul mood when he got there. He snatched the documents from the tray and stomped back out of the building and headed for the nearest DSS office. He took a ticket and sat there waiting. After what seemed like an eternity he was called to a booth.

"Can you explain how this document came to be printed please?" Squirrel started as he handed them the faxed copy of the Certification of registration of death.

"Yes, because the person named on it is dead."

"No, I'm not."

This caused the apathetic clerk to look up in surprise.

35

"Sorry, what was that?"

"I'm not dead; I'm sat here talking to you. So, I'll repeat my question. If I'm sat here talking to you, how the hell is there a document that requires a validated date of death to be on your computer systems before it can be printed in your hand."

"That's not possible."

"It is, that document, along with me sat here, and the passport I'm now showing you says it is."

"But if a date of death is on the system it can't be removed."

"Well, would you care to check then, as if I'm dead that I don't see any reason why I should be paying tax and NI on my wages?"

The clerk checked on the computer and then turned the screen towards Squirrel to show him there wasn't a date of death on the record.

"There's no date of death on there, so this document can't be real."

"Can I speak to your supervisor please?"

"Why?"

"Because I need someone with admin access to your DCI system so they can run an audit report."

"There isn't any such thing."

"Yes, there is. I spent five years working for the Benefit's Agency, three of those as the site dialogue expert. I know exactly how this can have been printed off and the system now shows me as alive, but I need someone with admin access to run it."

The clerk sullenly sloped off to find a supervisor. Fifteen minutes later he came back with another woman. She hadn't even got to the desk before she started with the defensiveness.

"There is no such thing as an audit log for DCI."

Squirrel shook his head, "There is, the fact that you may not know about it doesn't mean it doesn't exist."

"But I've been here years and never heard about it."

"How many times have you had reports of erroneous deaths here? Have you had many police investigations into misuse of systems?"

"No, we don't have that here."

"Well that may well be why you don't know about it. Have you got admin access?"

"Yes, of course I have, I'm the office manager."

"Good, have your colleague log off, and then log on yourself."

"I can't I'm logged on to another machine."

"Are you entering a JSA claim onto the system?"

"No."

"Then it doesn't matter, you're not doing anything that will mean a data loss. You can log on here and it will automatically end your other session."

"This is most irregular."

"Not half as irregular as having yourself declared dead, believe me."

"I'm not sure I can do this."

"I'm sure you can, but if there is any doubt, then I can always go to the police station, report everything so far to them, and then get them to come back and get you to do the search."

The supervisor eventually went to sit down, she barked at her colleague to get him to log off, and then went to log on herself. As she did Squirrel asked for a complaint form.

"You don't need one of those."

"Yes, I do, not for you – yet. But I do to log a complaint about being announced as dead."

The clerk shot off to get one before the supervisor could say anything to him.

"Have you logged on then?"

"Yes."

"Good."

Squirrel then proceeded to talk her through the screens to bring an audit report up, and to print it off. He suggested printing three copies off, he wanted a copy for himself, a copy to give to the police, and a copy for the supervisor to keep. The clerk came back with the complaint form and Squirrel filled it out as the supervisor went to get the prints. He gave it to them and asked for a copy of it. He took the prints, and the copy of the complaint form thanked them and left making a final suggestion as he did so to the supervisor. Get some training on her admin access.

Squirrel looked at the report; he recognised the ID numbers against the records on the audit report. There were three. His ex, her friend, and one of the supervisors in the office. The supervisor would have been required to lift the verified indicator on the date of death. The rest could be done by admin officers.

He took all the paperwork he had and went to the police station to present it all. Turns out his ex had taken the stuff out of storage and sold it all. She got the sack from the Benefit's Agency, and her friend got demoted. The removal firm pressed for charges against her, Squirrel didn't, and with all the stuff gone it was too late for that. The fraud still saw her do some jail time, but Squirrel refused to go and testify. He didn't want anything to do with it anymore.

The Benefit's Agency agreed compensation with Squirrel, and in a rare moment of lucidity decided not to take the cash, but to get them to add it to his pension pot. Jeez, Squirrel with £16k at that moment in time would have been a recipe for disaster. He was already a borderline alcoholic without adding a massive bank balance to the mix.

Plus with his record collection gone, he could funnel some of his spare cash each week away from drinking and back into collecting records. That would reduce his drinking as well – in theory anyway. He would now spend a lot of time when not working or drinking looking around the various record shops, charity shops and markets in Manchester and its suburbs.

Left To His Own Devices

Squirrel didn't always go down to Fallowfield to meet up with the others, occasionally he went out in Rusholme. There were seven pubs in quite a close concentration near Heald Place, Osborne House was the closest, but a bit quiet, and OK for a warmup drink. The Nelson was a lunatic asylum. Squirrel went there the once. He got a drink, and put a coin down to play pool and waited. There was a bad-tempered game going on, and the loser stormed out of the pub after the game.

Having been a bad loser in the past Squirrel paid no attention to it and put his money in and racked the balls up. He was just taking his first shot when a brick came flying through the window in the direction of the pool table. His opponent ran outside with his cue. Well, not ran, but jumped through the space where the window had been seconds before. And he set about the brick thrower with the cue. Most of the pub cleared out and a brawl ensued. Squirrel just sighed, looked at the ruin of the pool table, necked the rest of his drink and went out the back way.

The pub he did end up in that night, and most flying solo nights was the Gardener's Arms. It was pokier than the others, and had an Irish based clientele, and once he'd been in a couple of times, they were happy for him to stay when they had lock ins. Which was every night as far as he could tell. Having done a lot of childhood visits to Irish pubs, he was used to type of place it was. But their jukebox was the most ridiculously Irish collection of music he had ever seen.

It wasn't just the traditional fare of the Dubliners, Spinners, Foster & Allen, and Country & Western. Apart from the two most recent Now albums, every other of the ninety-six CD's was by Irish artists. U2, Van Morrison, Boyzone, Westlife, The Commitments, Samantha Mumba, B*Witched, The Nolans, Cranberries, Enya, Corrs, Pogues, Undertones, Johnny Logan, Thin Lizzy, and others he hadn't heard of, or hadn't realised were of Irish descent.

But the longer he knew the others, the more he went where they did, and the less Squirrel went back to the Gardener's Arms, until he never went.

Now, That's A Fire

Squirrel had noticed that as October came to an end there was a big bonfire being built in Platt Fields. By the time it had got to the Friday night the bonfire pile was over twenty feet high, ready for the bonfire and fireworks party on the Saturday night – 3rd November.

He asked the others if they had seen this previous years. They said there has been a bonfire at Platt Fields for all the years they had been studying in Manchester. So Squirrel asked if it had managed to survive to bonfire night every year, or had some scally managed to burn it down before the big event?

The others looked at Squirrel as if he were mad, why would anyone burn down the big display bonfire before bonfire night. Squirrel then recounted the tales of the big Leicester bonfire in Abbey Park being burnt down before bonfire night every year. Bigger fences, guards, police patrols had all been used and all failed. It always got burnt down before the event and then the organisers would have to run around like blue arsed flies on the day of the display to get enough material to make a replacement bonfire.

Squirrel thought it was usual behaviour, and had fully expected someone to burn the Platt Fields bonfire down before the big display. And after the conversation thought nothing else about it.

Squirrel wasn't sure what time he had got back home Friday night after another Queen of Hearts' night, but he'd got up and made it into work on the Saturday morning in time to open the building for others to work as well.

Then the messages started coming through on his phone.

"Did you do it?"

"Do what?"

"Burn down the Platt Fields bonfire."

"No."

Or at least he was sure he hadn't. Someone had though, and Squirrel hadn't even noticed the smoke or the smell when wandering off to work that morning.

The official display got cancelled, and Squirrel's friends jokingly blamed him and kept mentioning it for the next couple of weeks.

Squirrels' Christmas Party

Not Squirrel as in the person, but the student bar called Squirrel's (It was said this would get confusing at some point).

A couple of the girls from the OP student's union committee had arranged for the end of term party to be held in Squirrels. There was going to be a DJ, some food, and other things going on apart from the usual, drink as many cheap drinks as possible type things, that usually occurred on a Friday night. They were charging for pre-event tickets, and then going to charge two quid a ticket more to get in on the night. Somewhere along the way they decided they needed two more things. The first was to keep costs down to a minimum, and secondly that they would need a bouncer.

And so, they asked Squirrel to be the bouncer for Squirrels on the night. They were going to bung him fifty quid and he would break the habit of a Manchester lifetime and stay sober on a Friday night. And it happened.

Squirrel stood at the doors at the top of the stairs to the entrance to the bar and took people's tickets to get in if they had them, or took their money if they wanted to get in and didn't have tickets. And it went well. One of the usual crowd, Hopalong, or The Chemist would stick their head out of the door and pass Squirrel a lemonade or a coke, and he would stand there.

Now, no one would ever call Squirrel svelte. He was fat, and tall, but somewhere along the line of those first four months in Manchester he had bought himself a reversible padded jacket. It was far too warm for him, and it exaggerated his size enormously, and so he'd decided it was a great thing to wear when acting as a bouncer. Not knowing, or more likely not caring that it made him look even more like a fucking Weeble.

As the night drew on, those coming in and out past him to make their way down the stairs to the toilets became more inebriated. Some were more than willing to banter with Squirrel, a lot would have recognised him from propping the bar up for the last three months. It was all light-hearted stuff.

Of course, it wouldn't be a tale unless something happened that was out of the ordinary. And it would have to happen at the one moment Squirrel wasn't there. After consuming lots of fizzy drinks there came the inevitable time when he had to go to the toilet. He'd poked his head in the door and asked one of the usual cronies to take his place for a couple of minutes. But none of them could be bothered, so it ended up with the two girls who'd organised the evening on the door for a couple of minutes whilst Squirrel answered the call of nature.

When he got back to the door, one of the girls was crying and the other was screeching at him. Six non-students had turned up at the door, without tickets and brow beated the two young girls into letting them in without tickets and without paying, saying they were cleaning staff there and they didn't have to pay, and they'd forced their way in.

By the time Squirrel looked, they weren't at the bar and had disappeared down into the dance floor. Squirrel went back to the door. Only to have the girls come out crying again because there was a fight on the dancefloor.

When Squirrel got there, one of the guys who'd forced their way in had a nosebleed and their opposition was just standing there looking a bit spaced out. Nosebleed guy had his five friends giving it loads of verbals, Whereas spaced out guy just had his one annoying friend. Squirrel told spaced out guy and his friend to go back up to the bar and finish their drinks, and he shepherded out nosebleed guy and his five friends by the fire exit back to the toilet area.

The next ten to fifteen minutes were quite fraught. Nosebleed guy and his friends were kicking off wanting to get back in. Squirrel was telling them in no uncertain terms that they shouldn't have been in there in the first place, they hadn't paid and should have been ashamed of themselves, turning up pissed and bullying their way past young girls to get in, and then starting a fight. They were claiming they hadn't, but Squirrel had already had half a dozen people telling him nosebleed guy had started it and pushed spaced out guy, who had responded by smacking him in the face.

Now Squirrel had been bantering with spaced out guy all night, and he'd seemed in good humour every time. He was surprised he'd got involved in a fight. In fact, he would have laid good odds that his lanky

43

annoying twat of a mate with a dodgy scouse perm would have been the one fighting.

And so, it continued. Whilst Squirrel was trying to calm down nosebleed guy and his pissed mates and get them to leave; lanky twat kept coming out and taunting them and saying they see them outside. Squirrel told him to stop being a twat and stop interfering, to which lanky responding by showing him his doorman badge. Squirrel said thanks, but told him he couldn't be as he was pissed, but thanks for the warning that if he ever saw lanky on the door of a pub or club, he'd known to avoid it as it was likely to turn in to a war zone at any point.

One of the female friends of nosebleed guy had taken him to the toilets to get him cleaned up, and Squirrel took the opportunity, with a lull in proceedings to walk spaced out guy and lanky twat out through the fire escape and walk with them until they'd left Owen's Park. He went back into Squirrels and let it be known to nosebleed guy's mates that the others had left. That Squirrel had walked them out to Moseley Road. It took a couple of minutes for them to collect everyone, but the six of them left. Squirrel followed them out and smiled to himself as they all attempted to run, or stagger run, in the direction of Moseley Road. Knowing full well that spaced out guy and lanky twat had gone in the other direction.

The party passed without any more incident, and Squirrel had his first alcoholic drink at one in the morning as things were dying down. And no more was thought about it.

Until June. Squirrel got a call from the landlady of Squirrels. The police wanted to get a statement from 'the bouncer' on the night of the fight. Apparently, nosebleed guy was pressing charges for GBH against spaced out guy. So, Squirrel goes to the police station on Princess Road and gives a statement.

Only to get called to court in the September to give evidence at a magistrate's court trial. Now, Squirrel doesn't know if he was there as a witness for the defence or prosecution, but his evidence – as far as he was concerned – was purely in favour of spaced-out guy. So much so the prosecution barrister blanched when having asked 'did you consider that the nosebleed guy's uncoordinated behaviour could have been a direct result of spaced-out guy's punch' he got a response of, 'no, nosebleed guy seemed the same as every time Squirrel had seen him before and since the incident, pissed as a fart and overly aggressive.'

He would like to tell you the outcome of the trial, but Squirrel being Squirrel never bothered to find out.

Christmas and New Year

Squirrel found that once it got near Christmas, all his usual drinking buddies went home to their families. Something Squirrel couldn't do since his voluntary annexation. Not only that, but the student union bars closed at the end of term and some of the other bars in Fallowfield did likewise. He even missed out on the work Christmas party. As a temp who worked nights, they didn't invite him. It never seemed less like Christmas.

When he woke up Christmas morning after a particularly heavy night in the local Rusholme pubs where he vaguely remembered doing The Smiths' "Panic" on karaoke to the displeasure of the DJ, he even toyed with the idea of going to work. If there had been public transport running, he probably would have done. Instead he lay on his bed reading and playing random records.

Diego and Raul hadn't gone back to Spain for Christmas; they were flying back on New Year's Day. Raul stuck his head round the door to Squirrel's room to ask him if he was up for a Christmas Day curry.

Did the Pope shit in the woods? The mention of curry was enough to get Squirrel off his bed. After a shower and dressing he got down to the living room to find a room full of Spaniards, seven in total, all of whom spoke English better than Squirrel managed Spanish. They headed off into Rusholme for a curry. The curry mile was as alive on Christmas afternoon as it was any other day of the year, why wouldn't it be?

Squirrel then spent the next thirty minutes as the worst translator in the history of Christendom. The waiter's English wasn't great and there was a very heavy Pakistani accent. The Spaniards' English was better but with a heavy Spanish accent. Therefore the waiter didn't understand what the Spaniards were saying, and the Spaniards didn't have a clue what the waiter was saying. As Squirrel could just about make out what all of them were saying, all conversation around ordering went through him. It was probably one of the most ridiculous conversations of his life, and there were a lot of contenders for that title.

The food was good, and Christmas curry was something Squirrel would do a few times when he lived in Manchester. After food they went across the road to the Clarence for some drinks and some Spanglish chat, before weaving back to the house.

By New Year's Eve Hopalong had come back to Manchester, so they had gone out to Bar XS. It was local, didn't cost a lot to get into, and the drinks were reasonably priced, and the DJ was OK. It was also where they first met Sally. Hopalong had spotted her and moved in to chance his arm. Squirrel chipped into the conversation, especially when she mentioned she had lived in San Francisco, and had been out partying with the 49ers.

It turned out that Hopalong was barking up the wrong tree, as he was the wrong sex to attract Sally, plus she had a girlfriend already. Yet Squirrel ended up taking her home, mainly because she was struggling to remember where she lived. And so she crashed in Squirrel's bed, it being somewhat of a squeeze with Squirrel's bulk and a single bed. It would not be the last time they ended up sharing a bed over the next couple of years, but it was only ever to sleep, and not to "sleep together."

The early hours of that New Year's morning also saw Squirrel make a New Year's resolution, something he hadn't really done much of before. Yet in typical style, being at that stage of his life where he was trying hard to be different and awkward, living his second student lifestyle years, he took something up as a resolution. None of this giving something up to make your life better rubbish everyone else was doing. This was the opposite. When the words came out of his mouth, Hopalong just looked at him for a few seconds before saying.

"Squirrel, you're a fucking retard, you're supposed to give that sort of shit up for a New Year's resolution, not start doing it."

To be fair, he was right, but it was Hopalong's fault Squirrel decided to do it. For the previous three months solid, every time they were out, when Hopalong got himself a cigarette out, he would offer Squirrel one. And Squirrel would refuse.

But at two minutes past midnight on the first of January two thousand and two, he accepted the cigarette, got it lit and started smoking. Two minutes after a dozen or so countries had started using the Euro as their currency, he had started smoking. Five minutes later he was at the pub's vending machine buying his first pack of cigarettes.

Squirrel and Sally were woken early by the Spaniards leaving for the airport. The look of surprise on Raul's face was priceless when he popped his head round Squirrel's door and saw Sally lying there. The thought going through his mind was obvious, "how the hell had Squirrel managed to pull someone as fit as that." A fair question, as she was gorgeous, however he hadn't. Looks can be deceiving.

It was a bright crisp New Year's Day, and Squirrel and Sally eventually left the house. Squirrel needed to buy some cigarettes, as he was probably the first person in history to have taken up smoking as a New Year's resolution. Something he had agreed with Hopalong at some point during the night in XS.

The walk up to Wilmslow Road was enlivened by finding a shopping trolley, and so Sally got in it and Squirrel ran (well as much as Squirrel could ever run) pushing it up the road by the side of Kwik Save up to the dead end next to the pub, at which point the trolley hit the kerb and tipped forward, perfectly expelling Sally to a standing position.

They got cigarettes; Sally got a bottle of vodka, and headed home to Burnage. Squirrel didn't think there was anything wrong in buying spirits on New Year's Day; he bought beer and headed to Fallowfield and Hopalong's. Drinking continued as they watched football, and they headed out to the Orange Grove in the evening, nominally to get food, but also to meet up with Ed, who Hopalong knew from Uni, and was over from Ireland.

And with it being the 1$^{st\ of}$ January 2002, he came bearing Euros which had become the official currency of Ireland (and numerous other countries) that morning. There were quite a few more drinks consumed. Hopalong was bigging up Squirrel's quiz machine proficiency, and was getting Ed to ask Squirrel random questions. One about lettuce types that Squirrel managed to guess the answer to, and a second on the Irish constitution, where Ed didn't know Squirrel was of Irish descent and knew about these things.

It was a much later night than intended, especially as both Hopalong and Squirrel were working the next day.

A New Year

The New Year followed the pattern of the end of the previous one. Squirrel worked sixty-hour weeks, and drank for sixty hours a week and then slept for the remaining forty-eight hours.

He would only sleep six times a week. He worked long nights on Tuesdays, Wednesdays, and Thursday, and so would sleep during the day on Wednesday and Thursday. Then he would sleep Friday, Saturday, Sunday, and Monday nights (well it would be the early hours of the following morning before he'd get in from drinking). He would often work Saturday, Sunday and Monday during the day, so there weren't any lie ins.

Friday morning after work would be hand the timesheet in time, then some city centre shopping, clothes, records and CD's, a stop at Sainsbury's for some food to put in the fridge and then forget about, a change of clothes and then down to Fallowfield to start drinking mid-afternoon. On his own, if necessary, but there were often people out to start before the seven o'clock opening of Squirrels.

All night in there until kicking out time, then a late bar somewhere else in Fallowfield, back to Rusholme for a curry and then bed. Early start for work, then straight to the pub to do a repeat of Friday. Sunday would be work again, and then meeting up wherever people were watching the sport. And for a lot of weeks that would be Scubar. Set back from the Oxford Road near the universities and next to where they were building the aquatics centre for the Commonwealth Games, Scubar offered a wonderful array of drinks to kill yourself with, and Squirrel was quite happy going down that route and taking others with him.

They did eighteen different shooters, fishbowls, cocktails, and all at ridiculously cheap prices. Lots of large screen TV's and a gorgeous Irish barmaid. Squirrel loved it in there.

Sunday night would be the quiz at RP's. Where the object was for other teams to try and beat the team with Squirrel in. It did happen, just not very often. It was never as late a night on a Sunday with places closing earlier (unless it was back to Scubar as they opened until 1), but it was curry time again, or at the very least a kebab.

Mondays would try and mix it up a bit, and it was often into the city centre, some weeks with Me Laird, which would mean drinkers in Teasers and then dancing in Brannigans. Other weeks it would be Fifth Avenue and quadruple vodkas and red roosters.

Whatever it was it would get messy, and then back to work. And repeat.

Queen of Hearts

Friday nights after kicking out time at Squirrels. The Queen of Hearts was the regular late drinks and dancing venue of choice. It was one of two It's A Scream pubs in the downtown Fallowfield area, and as Squirrel and Hopalong were working squares without student ID, they couldn't get in the other one, Robinski's. It was also a wonderful use of an old building, as it had been a church, and the main nave area was now a large bar area with a dancefloor.

And there may have been pool tables, and fruit machines, and a quiz machine for breathers, but it was the dancefloor that was the attraction (besides the reasonably priced drinks that was). Despite the inherent laziness of Squirrel and Hopalong (and The Chemist for that matter), getting taxis everywhere to avoid walking, ringing the bar to order drinks from six foot away from the bar, etc. etc. Given a dancefloor after a lot of pints and shots, then it was hard to keep them still, they would dance all night, apart from trips to the bar to top up. Or if they'd pulled. Well, in Hopalong's case that was, Squirrel couldn't pull a Christmas cracker, let alone a cracker on the dancefloor.

Every week it would be the same tired banter with the door staff, arguing the toss about paying two quid to get in (but no qualms in paying twenty quid for rounds of shots, or sticking pound coins in the fruit machine). And every week they would dance like loons to nineties rave music. It wasn't just here, it was the whole of Fallowfield, it was the great 2002 rave revival. HMV had thirty different rave compilations on sale, with a core of thirty tracks the same, but then slight differences to fill it up. The DJ (using the term loosely) could stick any of them on and fuck off for an hour, and often did.

It had a smaller bar to the side in what must have been side chapels, with lower ceilings and many more original fittings and the stained-glass windows. It wasn't open for the late nights, and they rarely went in that side. Squirrel went in by himself one Sunday night and finished second in a team pub quiz and won a bottle of wine. Only to be given a bottle of Lambrini. Fucking trade descriptions act needs to be invoked there.

And then the music would stop, and the lights would come on. Drinks would be necked and then it would be out into the Fallowfield night to get food from the plethora of take aways. Or it would be a trip to the curry mile. Every sodding week.

Afternoon Delight

Squirrel would groggily get up in the afternoon and head to work whilst still not fully awake. His route to the bus stop would be through the alleys, ginnels, and footpaths to get to Wilmslow Road, avoiding most places with traffic until popping out on the main road right near where he needed to be.

It had felt a long week, one of the few where the week had outlasted his money, but he'd made sandwiches for work, and had a bus pass, so didn't need any money.

As he turned the corner from one alley to another he bumped into a woman. Literally. And he apologised, and she asked him if he had a spare five minutes. And after a "s 'pose so," she dragged him back around the corner and had his trousers down around his ankles in seconds and was giving him a blow job.

It had been a long barren spell, so he wasn't going to complain about it, even if it was out in the open in the middle of the day. Two minutes later the woman had a mouthful of cum, and Squirrel was a happy man. As he pulled his trousers back up, he noticed his wallet and pretty much everything from his pockets were on the floor.

Obviously whilst he was getting head, his head wasn't paying any attention to the woman rifling his pockets to try and steal any money he had. But as he didn't have any, she'd had a mouthful for nothing in return. And she wasn't very happy. So, he gave her his remaining few cigarettes, and carried on to work. And avoided dodgy looking women in the ginnels of Longsight when going to work.

5th Avenue

Not to be confused with 42nd Street (another club in Manchester), but often confused by Squirrel with Sector 5 (an old name of a club in Leicester).

A heaving mass of humanity. For nights when the Queen of Hearts just wasn't going to cut it. A taxi ride into the centre of Manchester and an inevitable queue to get into the club. It was supposed to be students only, but if you looked like a student and hung around with students, they would let you in anyway. Which was a good thing where Squirrel and Hopalong were concerned.

Down the stairs and straight to the bar. Where pretty much everything was a pound. Bottle of beer – one pound. Though what beer would change, and it wasn't always great, there was a spell where it was Castlemaine for fucks sake. Spirit and mixer – one pound. Which meant a vodka red bull was a pound. Only it wasn't red bull, it was a knock off called red rooster, and they would quite happily serve you doubles, trebles, and quadruples. Any hangover after vast amounts of vodka and red rooster would be called having your eyes pecked out by the red rooster.

So we would load up with drinks and head to the dancefloor for a few hours of indie classics (with an occasional classic from another genre thrown in for good measure). The only time the dancefloor was left was to get more drinks or to create some more room to put the drinks into. Dance and scream along to every song that came on with about two inches between you and the next person jumping around like a lunatic.

And with all drinks a pound and after a long evening of Fallowfield pre drinking before getting there, it would get messy. Squirrel would have sunglasses on without fail. And without fail people, mainly females would want to borrow the sunglasses and dance around in them for a few minutes. They would always get returned. Unless it was Ricky Organ taking them. He had a thing about Squirrel wearing sunglasses all the time and would take them and not give them back without a struggle. Until the time Squirrel pre-loaded with sunglasses.

54

When Ricky Organ took the wrap arounds Squirrel had on, there were knock off wayfarers underneath them. And when Ricky Organ took them as well there were John Lennon style-coloured glasses underneath them. At which point even Ricky Organ had to laugh and give up. It was amazing Squirrel could see anything at the time.

But 5th Avenue changed over time, they extended downstairs, and then had a balcony area above the dancefloor opened. Policy on sunglasses changed and the bouncers would stop Squirrel wearing them.

A night in 5th Avenue wouldn't be complete without the DJ playing the full version of the Stone Roses' "I Am The Resurrection", where the break in the instrumental bit towards the end would be filled by five hundred voices shouting as one. "Stone Fucking Roses."

Kicking out time was always fun and games. The stairs up and out into the night seemed much trickier to negotiate than they did coming in. And the side of the road would be littered with hundreds of people trying to flag a taxi down. Or it would be a case of wandering off to the army of kebab shops on Oxford Road to get a load of unhealthy food.

It would never be a quiet night out.

Evening Delight

Monday nights out consisted of a pattern that varied little from week to week. Squirrels (the bar not person) for a few drinks, then into town to Teasers, and potentially some dancing on the deserted bar – vastly different from trying to even get into the place on a Friday or Saturday night, and then on to Brannigan's just across the road for the end of the weekend blast.

There was one Monday night as they had come out of Brannigan's and had started making their way back up to Oxford Road to get buses back to Rusholme and Fallowfield. They had got as far as the corner with Whitfield Street near the Wetherspoons and Springbok when they were approached by what could be described as a more mature female. She wanted a cigarette and someone to light it.

Hopalong offered both, but she was telling him she wanted it off Squirrel instead, and Squirrel was going along with that, but then the woman was saying it was too windy to light the cigarette, and so they would need to go into the phone box to light it, which Squirrel did.

And as Hopalong might tell the story from this point Squirrel had sex with a grubby looking female tramp in a phone box on the way back from Brannigan's on one of those Monday nights. Squirrel meanwhile claims not to remember it quite that way. Well you wouldn't be able to remember such things now, would you?

There were quite a few references to tramps and phone boxes made over the next few weeks.

Scubar

Another random bar found during the early months of the year, and adopted quickly due to shooters and goldfish bowls.

Situated next to the newly erected aquatics centre (built for the forthcoming Commonwealth Games), and near the main campus for the universities, this turned out to be another regular haunt over the next couple of years.

What wasn't there to like. Saturdays and Sundays it would be open in time for the sport to be on, with multiple big screens and comfy chairs, and the drinks menu.

Now the drinks menu was a thing of beauty. There were eighteen shooters, shot glass size mini cocktails. Eight full sized cocktails on there as well, and three types of goldfish bowl. The goldfish bowls were exactly what you might imagine them to be, but filled with ice, and pretty much a jug full of cocktail, and in the top half a dozen two-foot-long straws for people to share it with. That's before you start on the array of draught and bottled beers and the spirit choice, which included all three colours of Absinthe.

And there were lots of drinks promotions. Such as the bottle of beer (usually Becks unfortunately) and a shooter for one pound fifty. No one can remember who found the place the first time, or how, but they need to be congratulated.

Especially as it was open until 1am on Sunday nights if you were in there by 11pm. Or later if you became regulars, and so weekend drinking could be extended.

As if anyone really needed that.

St. Patrick's Day

And speaking of Scubar, one of the wildest drinking sessions took place there.

Squirrel wasn't working on a Sunday for a change, and the Sunday was St Patrick's Day. Back in Leicester Squirrel would have spent the day bouncing around various Irish pubs (not the fake plastic shit ones like O'Neill's), the authentic, run by the Irish, drunk in by the Irish pubs. Whilst out with friends he would always bump into his dad in various pubs during the day.

But there wasn't really the same array of Irish pubs in Manchester, or if there was Squirrel didn't know them. And so with sport on all day he headed to Scubar at midday. And started on the drinks offers. A bottle of Becks and a shooter. And as there was football and rugby watched during the day, others dipped in and out of the place, and Squirrel worked his way through the entire shooters' menu. All eighteen of them. Each with a bottle of Becks.

With Ireland playing Wales in the six nations there was somewhat of a St Patrick's Day party vibe happening around him, which was probably sweeping the drinking along. Once the shooter menu had been exhausted, Squirrel moved onto he cocktail menu and demolished all eight of them as well.

The three types of goldfish bowl followed, during which Dylan stumbled in the prop the bar up with Squirrel. He had been out with his new girlfriend watching the rugby and was even worse for wear than Squirrel. And as they stood at the bar, they were downing pints of Stella and Guinness and whatever else was on tap, and helping the pints along by doing shots of tequila, before moving on to shots of Absinthe, the blue, green, and turquoise versions.

Squirrel blinked and Dylan had gone. Assumedly home, but who knows?

Well, it got to quarter past one and Squirrel was persuaded it might be a good idea for him to go home. So he walked the thirty yards or so to Oxford Road and went to get a bus.

Seeing a Fingland's one coming, he stepped into the road to stop it. The door opened, he got on, put a pound down and said 'Rusholme please mate,' and sat down. The bus had been moving a while before Squirrel took any notice of his surroundings. There were no lights on. There was no one else on the bus. It wasn't in service. He supposed that if he'd have given a destination after Rusholme he wouldn't have been let on, but as it was a stop before the bus depot the driver probably thought, fuck it, let the pisshead on.

Once at the other end, Squirrel went for a wrap from the Lebanese place and whilst waiting checked for keys to prepare for arrival home at Heald Place. And in doing so he put them in a convenient, easy to get to, pocket.

Only to forget he had done that and not be able to find his keys ten minutes later when he arrived back at the house. He had to bang on the door until eventually Warm got up and let him in the front door. Squirrel had to then break into his own room to get to bed.

In the morning he fixed his room door and went to work with the spare set of keys he had had cut for just this kind of emergency.

It got to Friday after a full week at work and he was sorting his washing out, Squirrel found the original set of keys there in the wash basket.

He had put them in his shirt pocket for easy access when he got back to the house, only to forget his shirt even had a pocket in the ten-minute walk from the Lebanese place back to the house. Easily done.

At least they hadn't been through a week in the fridge unlike Squirrel's phone had done previously.

Easter Weekend

Squirrel had the whole weekend off, and so drinking started early on the Thursday and ended late on the Monday.

Good Friday morning saw the normal kind of finish time and some shopping on the way home to Chez Rusholme. A couple of hours sleep was interrupted by Hopalong, who was coming to meet the landlady with a view to moving in. Mid-afternoon saw Mate ringing up, to get their attendance at XS to watch Southampton take on Everton, never two to refuse an excuse for beers, Squirrel and Hopalong were there and an early start on the Stella followed. After the match they moved onto the Friendship, where they sat outside sorting out arrangements to go over to Blackburn on the Monday to see Southampton play Blackburn, and meet up with Radio for an all-day session.

Dylan, his current missis, and Pod arrived, and soon they moved inside as it got colder. Once in there, Squirrel saw a couple of women from his agency and stood at the bar talking to them. Hopalong came over, but was soon distracted by the start of the Sheffield Wednesday game. Squirrel went and sat down with the two women from the agency, but the lack of sleep and food, mixed with the double figures amount of Stella, meant he found himself desperately needing fresh air. Twenty minutes later he found himself awake on the table outside, he rushed back in to find the women, and all his possessions missing, however Hopalong had them (the belongings, not the women unfortunately) at the other side of the pub.

They watched the end of the football, before Hopalong managed to upset Dylan's missis, and Dylan managed to have an argument with one of his housemates. Hopalong and Squirrel then moved on to Jabez (Squirrel's first ever visit), before leaving and going for a curry.

Saturday saw an early start with the Liverpool Vs Man Unt game having a 12.30 kick-off. Hopalong and Squirrel watched the first half in the Friendship, before being summoned to the Drop Inn by Mate for the second half. More football and many more beers followed, and a meeting with Cabbage and his mates. After reaching double figures, Squirrel, Hopalong and Mate got a taxi to Scubar, where shooters, goldfish bowls, cocktails and pints ended up with Mate having to take a pit stop to puke. Then they crashed an 18th birthday party downstairs before departing to make their way to Jabez, where even more alcohol was consumed before miraculously arriving at their respective houses.

Midday Sunday saw Squirrel knocking on Hopalong's door armed with a crate of Becks to go with the Crate brought the previous day. He then forced Hopalong to drink for the remainder of the day and into the early hours of Monday morning, whilst watching DVD's and being introduced to the delights of Snatch, before getting a taxi home at 3 in the morning.

Sunday didn't smile so well on Mate who had a lunch meeting with his missis and her parents in a posh Chinese restaurant. He only just managed to make it to the toilet before puking, obviously suffering from his heroic efforts to keep up with Squirrel and Hopalong (heroic considering he's half the size of them) drink for drink (and managing it) the previous day.

Monday morning saw Squirrel in the bar at Victoria waiting for Mate to turn up so that they could get the train to Blackburn, when he eventually arrived, they'd missed the planned train and were late meeting Radio in Blackburn. Straight to the pub for the Tottenham Vs Leeds game, and then a pub crawl up to Ewood Park for the Evening's game.

Radio had told them they would be fine in the Blackburn pubs, just don't wear colours, which was directed more at Mate as a Saints fan, than at Squirrel. And he also told them not to make a show of their cigarette packets. Apparently smoking Marlboro Lights wasn't manly enough for the folks of Blackburn.

Half a dozen pubs later they were at the ground. Up on the second tier of the away stand. There weren't lots of Southampton fans who had made the journey up to Blackburn on a Monday night.

There was however a row of about a dozen Blackpool fans dressed in bright orange replica shirts. As if they had got lost or were confused and have arrived in Blackburn instead of Blackpool. Mate went and spoke to them at half time. Turns out they were all there to see

Brett Ormerod who had recently transferred from Blackpool to Southampton. Different.

After a piss poor Saints performance it was back to Blackburn station for a beer, and they were pretty much the only people in the pub, and the train back to Manchester was empty too. And Manchester seemed shut when getting back into Victoria Station, and the famous rain was coming down washing away the remnants of a tip top weekend of carnage.

Hopalong Moves In

With the Spanish guys having moved out and only one of the three other rooms filled by Warm, there was scope for Hopalong to move in from his current place on the floor in his shared house with Lamb and Radio.

When the Spanish guys moved out it had become a fully working household rather than the student one the landlady originally wanted it to be. Warm wasn't a student and therefore the fact Hopalong was no longer a student meant there wasn't much problem getting the landlady to agree to him moving in.

Of course, it filled a vacant room and brought money in, so it was never going to be much of an issue. Hopalong had two choices to a room, both upstairs and he went for the one at the back which had been painted bright orange by one of the Spanish guys (as had the room Warm had taken downstairs).

It was a surprise that he didn't take the other one at the front of the house next to Squirrel's room. It was slightly smaller, but had the bonus of not searing your retinas every time you opened your eyes there. There was no accounting for taste.

There had always been a TV in the shared living room of the house, but Squirrel had never seen it on. With Hopalong moving in it meant there was more than just a TV. He brought his PS2 and DVD collection with him, and so the TV was turned on, and it worked.

Which would mean late night, post pub / club watching. Without any real thought to how sound carried in the house. Something that will be returned to later.

What's My Name?

How can you tell a hangover and a half? When you go to the barbers, and they ask you your name and you have to turn to your mate and ask them to answer on your behalf.

Not long after Hopalong moved in there was another standard Friday night out. An early start, lots of cheap drinks in Squirrels, and then onwards, whether that was to the Queen of Hearts or 5th Avenue, who can remember now?

But it had been very messy.

It was also a rare Saturday on which Squirrel wasn't working, and so Hopalong and Squirrel headed out. The pubs would be open in a bit and there would be the chance for all day breakfast to be shovelled in.

First though, Hopalong was insisting that he needed a haircut and when they passed a barbers on Wilmslow Road, Hopalong said 'this will do.' He had already been moaning about how far he'd had to walk (not far), but most of what came out of his mouth was utter gibberish.

Which was entertaining when he flapped down in the chair and the barber started to try and have a conversation

"How are you doing?"

"eh what?"

"Are you alright sir?"

"Yeah."

"What's your name."

"It's… erm. I'm not sure, Squirrel what's my name."

Laughter all round.

"Hopalong."

"Do you live close by?"

"Yes, no, not sure, it felt a long way."

Squirrel "No, only on Heald Place."

"Good night last night then?"

"No idea."

"What are you doing today?"

"Getting some food, and probably drinking. I need to get a haircut as well."

"What do you think you're doing now?"

"No idea."

It didn't get much better, even after breakfast at the World's End.

Going into the Huntsman was probably a mistake. They don't really like students in there, and despite the fact neither Hopalong nor Squirrel were students, they had the look of them. (Squirrel's green hair wasn't helping), and it was a quick drink in there.

All the other pubs local to Heald Place, both on the curry mile and the backstreets between it and the house were visited. For most of them it was a case of one and out as far as Hopalong was concerned. Squirrel doesn't think he went in any of them again after that day.

Cent

<Deep sigh>

A month or so after Hopalong moved in, Warm moved out. A job elsewhere apparently, and nothing to do with the constant stream of late night pissed DVD watching.

It couldn't have been more than five minutes after Warm left the building before Hopalong grabbed his old room, the biggest in the house, the front room downstairs. Replacing one bright orange paint job for another.

Then a new housemate turned up. Cent. Looking and sounding like he was a missing link between the Gallagher brothers and Escape From Planet of the Apes. He said he was a student, but fuck knows what he could have been studying.

To be fair he seemed OK at first. He had a chat with Hopalong and Squirrel in the living room, appeared normal, went to the Queen of Hearts with them, but said he was waiting for his next payment. (Not sure what of.) They let him have some of their beers. Said he would replace them. But it went on for a while. Lots of drinking beers, but no buying of beers. Both Hopalong and Squirrel were getting pissed off with it. When eventually Cent bought a case of lager, Squirrel and Hopalong stayed up most of the night and finished the lot and built an empty can pyramid on top of the chest freezer.

Cent wasn't impressed. Either by the drinking of all the beers, or the fact the beer can pyramid made it impossible to get into the chest freezer.

Ah yes, Cent's diet. Apart from everyone else's beer, it would seem the only things Cent consumed were fish fingers and mint Viennettas. The chest freezer was full of them. And every plate in the house had traces of mint Viennetta or breadcrumbs on it as Cent was allergic to washing up. Or moving plates. Just leaving them where he had finished eating. Hopalong would regularly collect them up and leave them outside the door to Cent's room. (He'd taken the non-orange room at the front of the house upstairs, next to Squirrel's.)

Alongside the allergy to washing up, there was an allergy to washing his clothes. At least in the washing machine. He did stink most of the time. And you could tell the odd occasions when he used the shower. It was easy to tell. Fuck knows how he had a shower, but every surface in the bathroom, the ceiling, the walls, the window, the floor, the door, the toilet, the bath, the sink, the mirror. It would all be covered in water. As if there had been a fireman's hose let loose in there for twenty seconds.

The longer he lived there the stranger it became. He said he was in a brass band. And he had a fuck off massive brass instrument, like a tuba, only bigger. And it had one of those things you put in the end so that only the person playing the instrument can hear it. There were occasions when he didn't plug it in. Shit the bed. He reckoned he was one of the best in his brass band. Dread to think what the rest sounded like. He was fucking abysmal.

When he wasn't murdering a poor brass instrument, there was the Charlotte Church obsession. Posters, all the CD's (pre pop career), high volume, and the attempt to sing along. Perhaps he wasn't that bad on the brass instrument after all.

There was an increasing catalogue of bizarre behaviour. One afternoon Squirrel and Hopalong had to go and drag him back in to the house as he was laying in the middle of the road in Heald Place in just his underpants.

Another day Squirrel got home to find the living room completely full of wheelie bins. Cent had been out and got them from all down the street. It took a while to put them all back.

He was frightening the new neighbours on an almost daily basis. (Four young female students had moved in next door.) And his room was beginning to smell like a tramp had died in it.

When G Man (yes, we haven't got to the point where he joins us yet) asked him what the tablets were he was taking, Cent replied by saying "Well, I say that they are for stress, but the doctor says they are for schizophrenia."

Which probably explained a great deal. When Baby G was over for the weekend, he made the mistake of leaving his weed out in the living room and everyone got up to find Cent passed out on the living room floor in the living room and no weed left.

The catalogue of lunacy was carefully noted, and Squirrel persuaded the landlady to evict Cent. And he was, not long before everyone else decided they would be moving out anyway.

Sleep Is For Wimps

June saw glorious weather, the start of the World Cup, and a ridiculous lack of sleep from Squirrel.

The World Cup was being held in Japan and South Korea and so the games were kicking off at 7.30am, 10.30am, and 1.30pm UK time. And Squirrel didn't want to miss a minute of it all. And he didn't apart from the second half of the Germany vs Saudi Arabia game when Germany were already 6-0 up at half time. Hopalong and Squirrel couldn't watch anymore of that, thought fuck this, and headed out instead.

Squirrel worked nights on Tuesdays, Wednesdays, and Thursdays. He would start at about 5pm and work through to 8am, and then sleep through the day. But the World Cup was on during the day. And so he would finish at 7am, which gave him just about enough time to get home for the 7.30am kick off, which he would watch, then have an hour's kip, get up and watch the 10.30am kick off. After which there would be another hour's sleep and it would be up again to watch the 1.30pm kick off. Another hour of sleep and then out to work, still starting at 5pm.

By the end of the quarter final stage, on the first day there were no fixtures, there was the opportunity for a longer unbroken period of sleep. Probably well needed (if not deserved).

Hopalong did ask the question.

"How the fuck are you still alive?"

To be fair that was a question a lot of people would ask a lot of times over the coming years.

There's doubt anyone who knew Squirrel when he lived in Manchester who gave a hope in hell of Squirrel still being alive by the time he was forty, let alone to be well into his fifties and still alive.

Twenty-Four Hour Drinking Person

It's a Sunday, there is football on, it's a special Bank Holiday weekend due to the Queen's Golden Jubilee, so what better excuse could there be for being up at half six in the morning doing shots of Baileys?

There were no street parties involved. Nobody even knows if there were any held near where they lived at the time, but if there was, they weren't the kind of person you'd have wanted to invite to them, especially not if you had polite company there already.

There may have been various proper celebrations in the city, but there was too much of an alcoholic haze to follow much of what was going on.

Apart from the football.

The Sunday of the Jubilee weekend saw England play their first game of the 2002 World Cup finals. It was a 10:30 am kick off against Sweden. There was a 7:30 am game on before that, so like any sane person, Squirrel was up cooking double bacon cheeseburgers and drinking shots of Baileys for breakfast with Hopalong. Undoubtedly the breakfast of champions.

After the first game had finished the pair of them headed off to Squirrels (the bar not the person, they were already where Squirrel lived) to watch the England game, and par for the course they had a couple of bottles of beer to accompany them on the walk down there.

It was a Sunday morning, and although the bar was open, they weren't serving alcohol until midday. But being of the alcoholic bent, Squirrel had planned to cover this dry hour and a half. The night before, at last orders, he had bought six orange reefs and poured them into a large jug and placed the jug in the fridge behind the bar, as they pretty much did what they wanted in there most of the time. And when he got in, as the hordes ordered their soft drinks, Squirrel just asked for his pre-pared jug out of the fridge and continued drinking whilst everyone else was on soft drinks. And no, the greedy bastard didn't share any of it with anyone else.

The game was tense, and not high quality, with the biggest cheer coming when the bar opened at midday. After the game, the bar

70

emptied out, leaving the regulars lounging in their usual booths. They all stayed to watch the two remaining games on that day. They ordered pizzas to be delivered to Squirrels from the Dominos they could see out of the window opposite Owens Park. And they kept phoning the bar to order drinks instead of walking the three yards to it. Stockpiling drinks to keep them going for that 3 to 6 pm window when the bar would be shut for alcoholic drinks again. Occasionally wandering off to play pool downstairs.

Word had reached their muddled brains that some of the clubs in the city centre were going to be open until two, and not just midnight as was usual at the time on a Sunday night. And so, still wearing England flags as capes they headed off to the city centre. They bounced around a few pubs, and then ended up in Satan's Hollow. There was more drinks and dancing involved, and people had started to disappear off home.

By kicking out time there was only Squirrel (of the original group out), and Cinderella's stepsisters (Gonfer and Frost) left out. It seemed a good idea to walk back to Rusholme. Made even better by the fact that half a dozen places on the curry mile still being open.

Curry was the order of the morning. Squirrel managed to pad that meal out to two hours to keep the drinking going, and it was 5 am when they got out and headed back. The stepsisters lived in one of the streets near to Heald Place, but they had no alcohol, whereas Squirrel knew there were lots of beers in the fridge in the house, plus he had bottles of spirits squirreled away in his room.

Once in, and with drinks, Gonfer was complaining of feeling tired, and so Squirrel, pulled the sofa out to have it as the sofa bed it made. She went to sleep and Squirrel and Frost continued drinking and talking. Squirrel took to laying down next to Gonfer, which considering what had gone on previously was either very brave or remarkably stupid. And in reaching over himself to pick a bottle of beer up from the floor he caught one of his rings on his earing and ripped it out. He never did put one back in.

In no time at all it seemed, it was 7:30 am and the next day's fixtures were starting. Brazil vs Turkey. Just before it kicked off Hopalong stumbled into the living room. He looked at the beer in one of Squirrel's hands, and the glass of Baileys in the other, then at Frost sat on the other sofa, and then at Gonfer asleep with her arm over him and asked what the actual fuck is going on, and then at Squirrel and said, 'you didn't did you?' Squirrel laughed and shook his head. Hopalong asked if he was still drinking from yesterday.

Squirred nodded and told Hopalong it was his turn to cook breakfast in between games. The day didn't improve much from there and by the time they got a cab home from town that night it was already 2 am Tuesday morning, and the last day of the extended Jubilee weekend saw inert figures lying on sofas just about watching the football.

The four-day weekend was the (equal) longest period Squirrel didn't work for in the first eighteen months or so of living in Manchester.

G Man

Hopalong's best mate from back in Harrogate had been travelling for a year since finishing university. Now he was back, and he moved in with Hopalong and Squirrel at Heald Place. Unofficially at first, kipping in the spare bright orange room which Hopalong used to inhabit.

Whilst G Man was taking his year out travelling (meeting lots of people who will pop up later), he had left Hopalong in charge of / being his agent, in dealing with the student loan company. With instructions for Hopalong to defer as G Man was out of the country. However, Hopalong forgot / couldn't be arsed, and so the student loan company had written to G Man's home address and so his parents found out that he had taken out student loans and he had got a right dressing down about it.

G Man was named because of his surname which began with a G. He hit it off with Squirrel almost straight away and they would be out drinking together most of the time.

Because of this it meant this was the time Squirrel picked up his monicker as well. Not as many might have thought, from the inordinate amount of time and money spent in Squirrels bar on Owens Park, but because with there being a G Man, it meant there was a full-on Happy Mondays, Madchester thing happening.

And their album title of Squirrel and G Man, Twenty-Four Hour Party People, Plastic Face, Carnt Smile (White Out) was now officially in full effect.

All five future residents of Chez Didsbury were now in Manchester. If they hadn't been before, things were really going to get messy now.

Commonwealth Games

They'd put all the athletes in the student accommodation in Owen's Park and Richmond Park. To do this they had made the end of term earlier for the students and moved them out before they usually would. And then they'd put more fences and more security in at all entrances to the campus. Which in turn meant that Squirrel's was now off limits until all Commonwealth Games athletes had fucked off back to their own countries. but friends and relatives needed somewhere to stay, so our landlady had rented the spare (but used most of the time by G Man) room out for eight days at a ridiculous price.

It had been taken on by a Canadian woman, whose name escapes everyone. Her boyfriend was a Canadian at the time, but having been born in Bermuda he was competing for Bermuda in the men's cycling road race. Having looked up the competitors twenty years later we believe it to have been Christopher Hedges.

For the eight days the woman was in Heald Place, Hopalong had gone down to Swindon to see Lamb and so G Man had taken his room which left the upstairs orange room free for a temporary resident. At no point would any of the usual residents of the house (which still included Cent at that time unfortunately) have said the shared house was anything other than a complete shit hole.

Despite this, the athlete had visited the house, seen it, spoken to the almost permanently drunk or deranged residents and decided it was a better alternative to living in the athlete's accommodation on Owen's Park, and he stayed most nights at Heald Place.

There will have been training involved, but the Bermudan team didn't go and use the local motorways to ride on, unlike the Kenyan team did. What we are sure wouldn't have been in the training plan was to be staying in a house on a Friday night before the big road race on the Saturday where two of its residents (Squirrel and G Man) would go out on the Friday night into Fallowfield, get completely ratted, come back to the house, and have a mini disco in the living room until 4am. And then to be woken up at 7.30am by Squirrel's alarm going off.

Which was more than could be said for Squirrel. He wasn't only supposed to be working on the Saturday, but had the keys to the office building to let others in. He woke confused at about eleven to find his alarm unplugged and assumed he must have done it during the night. He checked his phone and found no messages and no missed calls asking where the hell he was. He rang round the other three people who were supposed to be going into work only to find none of them were bothering. So the lack of alarm didn't matter.

The cyclist had been carrying an injury and was taking cortisone injections or the like even to start the race. He wasn't expecting to finish but had promised to put on a good show for Bermuda, and apparently kept to his word, leading the race on laps two and three of the seven circuits around the city they were doing. Before he withdrew from the race.

Not that Squirrel or G Man saw any of this first hand. Despite the games being on their doorstep they didn't go to a single session of any event, and didn't even put the TV on.

They did go out for a curry with the Canadians on the Sunday night. At which point Squirrel found out his alarm had gone off on the Saturday morning as the Canadians had heard a few songs at the start of the Now 53 album before it had gone off. They had also heard Cent crashing about. Turns out Cent had been woken by the alarm, gone into Squirrel's room and unplugged it, without bothering to wake Squirrel.

When Cent surfaced on the Monday evening Squirrel read him the riot act. The only time anyone else saw him lose his shit at anyone whilst they knew him in Manchester.

Tuesday was the last day the Canadian woman was supposed to be staying. And it led to the landlady losing her mind. It wasn't even 10am and the landlady was in and forcibly trying to eject the woman, throwing her stuff out into the street, and screaming at her to get out. Squirrel intervened as it had woken him up and it was way out of order and disproportionate. It wasn't as if there was anyone else moving in that day.

But from the following weekend, G Man became an official resident of Heald Place.

First Day of the Season

Yes, they'd been out the night before. But they were trying not to show the effects. G Man's parents were in town. Mummy and Daddy G had come over to Manchester and were taking G Man, Hopalong, and Squirrel out for lunch in Didsbury. When they turned up at Heald Place they couldn't wait to get out. The residents all knew it was a shithole, but it would seem the level hadn't quite been expressed to Mummy and Daddy G. This disdain was probably one of the drivers for the hunt for a new shared house which led them to Scarisbrick Avenue.

Lunch was at Cote, the first time Squirrel had been in one, and far posher than he was used to. After some polite, if awkward conversation, the lunch was over, Mummy and Daddy G were heading off, and the terrible trio were unleashed on the rest of the day.

The day was the first day of the Football League season, and with the new season starting, it was the first opportunity for them to head to the bookies and make ridiculous bets on the fixed odds sheets. A weekly tradition that lasted well past the end of this book.

With the bets on they settled down to drinking in the Clocktower with a view to a big screen and Soccer Saturday so they could watch their betted money disappear. There is always one major surprise result on the first day of the season, and Hopalong had chosen Millwall to beat Rotherham (some Sheffield Wednesday supporting biases in play there no doubt). Only for Rotherham to romp home 5-1 winners.

There were no winners in the pub, the betting slips were discarded, and serious drinking started. The three of them did a couple more pubs in Didsbury before getting a bus back to the usual Fallowfield stomping grounds. Grand Central, Orange Grove, Vodka Revolution were all visited before they ended up in Bar XS. They bumped into Dylan in there, and he was lagging behind them in the consumption stakes.

It wasn't long before midnight before G Man gave up and headed for home as totally ratted. Hopalong lasted until about 1am, leaving Squirrel and Dylan on the dancefloor and carrying on drinking.

When it came to chucking out time, they did the only sensible thing possible, and headed to Rusholme for a curry.

Nearing the end of having the curry, Squirrel, who along with Dylan was going to head back to Heald Place to continue drinking, got a text message from Hopalong asking,

"Can you get me tabs please?"

It was a reasonable request and Squirrel responded

"Yeah, no worries, I'll be back home in about ten minutes."

At which point the text exchange took an unexpected turn.

"I'm not at home."

"Where are you then?"

"I'm in A&E at the infirmary."

"What the fuck are you doing there?"

"Well, G Man and me got into a fight."

"How the fuck did you manage that when G Man left an hour before you did?"

"Just bring the tabs and I'll tell you when you get here."

And so Squirrel and Dylan didn't head back to Heald Place and continue drinking. Instead there was a stop at the twenty-four-hour garage to buy cigarettes, and a bus down to the infirmary. Where they found Hopalong in a wheelchair and G Man lying across a fixed bench of four seats, dead to the world with his trainers off and underneath the chairs. Dylan took a seat for a bit before deciding he didn't need to be there and heading for home.

Meanwhile, Squirrel was on wheelchair pushing duties, which he enjoyed far more than poor old Hopalong did sat in said wheelchair. Outside for a cigarette, around the hospital for x-rays, consultations, and to get a temporary cast on. All the time Hopalong was worried that Squirrel would hit his already broken ankle on a wall or a door as he careered around like a demented F1 driver.

So, how did Hopalong end up with a broken ankle? And how the hell was he with G Man anyway? Well, when Hopalong left Bar XS he hadn't gotten far when he saw G Man sat on the kerb outside one of the takeaways on Wilmslow Road. It was as far as he had managed to get in his pissed state. The pair of them continued to walk back towards home, only for them to get into a verbal spat with a couple of lads who were intent on taking the piss out of Hopalong. One of the randoms make a crack about betting Hopalong's missis was fat. Hopalong was about to say something along the lines of 'Yes, but…' when G Man decided to defend Hopalong's girlfriend's honour by swinging a punch. And the verbal altercation turned physical. During the altercation Hopalong attempted some kind of a jumping action towards the tormenters as if he were Jackie Chan, but got it all wrong, landed awkwardly and broke his ankle. He was then lying on the ground in pain and calling for an ambulance. The others just disappeared.

And in that one action, we have the reason for Hopalong's monicker.

They didn't get an ambulance, instead they flagged a taxi down and went to A&E.

Whilst waiting for the various stages of Hopalong's treatment, Squirrel was amusing himself by trying to wake G Man up. The chosen method being employed by Squirrel was to drop G Man's own trainers onto his bollocks. There may have been an occasional flinch, but G Man stayed soundly asleep.

Once Hopalong's treatment was complete, and armed with crutches, G Man was tipped off the chairs to wake him and they headed back to Heald Place in a taxi in the morning light of the Sunday morning.

When G Man got up later that day and was asked how he was feeling his response was, not bad, the only thing that really aches are my bollocks, but I don't know why. Hopalong and Squirrel burst out laughing before Squirrel owned up to say

"Yeah, the reason for that would be me. I was trying to wake you up in A&E by dropping your trainers on them, nothing to do with the fight."

Hopalong meanwhile spent the first day of six weeks confined to quarters.

Boing Boing Baggies

G Man was a season ticket holder at Old Trafford. No it hadn't been mentioned before. No we wouldn't mind going to the first game of the season. Daddy G, Baby G, and G Man had season tickets and had had for several years.

The first game of the new season was against West Bromwich Albion, and Daddy G couldn't make the game and so Baby G had been entrusted with the spare season ticket to bring it over to Manchester so that on of G Man's housemates could go. Under normal circumstances it would have been Hopalong going, but as he was incapacitated with his broken ankle, Squirrel was to be going instead. And once he knew this, he adopted the saying Boing Boing Baggies in the lead up to the game.

Baby G arrived in Manchester on the Friday night and there was drinking and smoking, seeing as he had arrived with a stash of weed. But they didn't leave the house until it was time to head to Old Trafford on the Saturday. It was Squirrel's first visit. Once at the ground G Man commented on the Boing Boing Baggies not being so freely mentioned by Squirrel when there were so many United fans around.

United won, but it wasn't as comfortable as many of the fans around them would have liked. After the game, the three of them headed back and ended up in Fallowfield before heading back to the house for some more smoking.

As previously mentioned, Baby G made a schoolboy error and left the tin with the weed and Rizla's out in the living room before heading to bed. And when they all got up the next morning, Cent was passed out on the living room floor, and all the weed was gone.

Hopalong was also moaning at Squirrel and G Man for having Baby G in Manchester for two nights but then staying in the first night and going to fucking Bar XS again on the second night instead of taking him out into town. But Baby G didn't seem to mind.

There were other spare ticket opportunities over the next couple of years. Squirrel went to another game, but he decided not to take up the spare ticket offer for the game against Tottenham as he couldn't trust himself not to get up and get involved in cheering for his own team, even when surrounded by thousands of United fans. It was the correct decision, as that was the game with the Pedro Mendes 'goal.' The one that was two foot over the line before Roy Carroll scooped it back, and which none of the officials saw or gave. It came up as a goal on the Vidi printer on Sky Sports before being corrected, but even G Man said it was over the line and he was sat in line with the goal at the other end of the pitch. There was no way Squirrel wouldn't have reacted to that if he were in the ground.

Believe

With Squirrel's (the bar not the person) still shut for the summer and Fallowfield being a bit dead, it was a Friday night and G Man, Ricky Organ and Squirrel were off out for a drink, leaving Hopalong at home. They weren't going far, they had found the Albert Inn and settled in to play some pool and have some beers. Oh and put some tunes on the jukebox. Which is part of where all the fun started.

It was, as they all were at the time, a CD jukebox, but it was a bit old, and probably in need of some maintenance if not replacing. It had a bit of an issue with what it played. It couldn't find all the CDs or tracks on some CDs, and when it couldn't find what was requested it would default to playing the same track time after time – Cher's "Believe."

So, people would be putting a quid in the jukebox and selecting five tracks, and there would be a high likelihood that at least one of the tracks chosen wouldn't play and the dulcet tones of Cher would come floating out of the speakers.

However, this was making one local very unhappy. And the more it happened, the more animated this bloke was getting about it, shouting, and swearing at the staff. Moaning about the fucking jukebox playing the same fucking shit song, and he was sick of putting money in the jukebox only for in to not play his chosen songs, and playing fucking Cher again.

This would have been funny enough by itself. But then Ricky Organ got involved to 'help' the situation along. He went to the jukebox, put a quid in and selected "Believe" five times and then came and sat back down to enjoy the view as we watched what happened.

If the bloke had been a volcano, the top of his head would have blown off. By play three on the trot of Cher, he had lost the plot entirely and had gone full Pet Shop Boys "West End Girls," as he was kicking in chairs and knocking down tables in a dive bar. And throwing glasses. The full meltdown before he was ejected. And Squirrel, G Man and Ricky Organ sat around the pool table pissing themselves laughing.

Cheap entertainment for a quid.

Chubb Christmas Party

Yes, it was a little late, and it wasn't an early one despite being closer to next Christmas than the last one. It must be said that no one had heard of a company having a Christmas party in July. But Chubb were, which kind of played into G Man's hands as it meant he could go despite not having been working there back at Christmas. The only thing was it was in Preston, so a bit of a trek on the train, and the last train back was at eleven. And for some reason G Man thought it would be a good idea to bring Squirrel along with him. After all, what could go wrong?

It started off sedately enough. Drinks in a bar by the train station before moving on. There were obviously some of the people there who G Man got on well with already despite not having been at Chubb very long. It did take until bar three before it looked like it was going to start to get messy. Shots were ordered. And there was a pint downing race between G Man and Squirrel, which G Man won.

At some point over the next couple of bars, time went out of the window and suddenly the last train back to transcentral, sorry Manchester had gone. But G Man had managed to blag crash space on the floor of the hotel room a couple of the women were sharing, despite the remarks on the facial hair of one of them.

By the time they got to a club it was the opposite of sedate. Drinks had been going down at record rates. Squirrel fell over on the dancefloor and refused offers of help to get back up and instead proceeded to push himself around on his back whilst cackling with laughter. Only getting up when it was time for another drink.

And then it was chucking out time. People fragmented. Squirrel had lost G Man (and probably the plot as well). He had been ringing G Man but wasn't getting any response, and when he saw someone he recognised from the party he asked if they had seen G Man. There was a curt reply. "Chippy." Before they stomped off. Squirrel asked around where the chippy was and was pointed in the right direction. G Man stood outside with a bag of chips. And delivered the news that the offer of crash space on the hotel room floor had been rescinded due to the fact

G Man had declared his undying love to the bearded lady, and so they were stuck in Preston.

A taxi would be needed. They made their way along the taxi rank, where drivers looked at the pair of them, heard where they were going and said no, or maybe fuck off. But it certainly wasn't a yes. It got to taxi number six or seven before the driver thought he would put the pair of them off by quoting forty quid for the journey. But he hadn't reckoned with Squirrel and his emergency cash stash. The one he kept in the random little extra pocket at the front of jeans. Squirrel took the forty quid out, gave it to the driver and jumped in, told the driver St Peter's Square please and dragged G Man in behind him.

The taxi driver wasn't as cocky now, slammed his little window and put the meter on and turned the music up to ear splitting volumes. Not that it kept G Man awake. Once in Manchester the meter only said thirty-five quid, but Squirrel couldn't persuade the driver to take them on towards the curry mile instead, so they got out.

On the way over to Oxford Road to get a bus, G Man decided he needed to take a piss, and he chose the War Memorial as the place to do it. Once finished he decided to try some chat to a passing female with the introductory line of "hello sweet cheeks," oblivious to the fact that she was arm in arm with her boyfriend, and whilst he was still putting himself away. Squirrel intervened to prevent a kicking.

Back in Rusholme they were walking down Heald Place when they bumped into one of their newish neighbours, Sallytoo, who was coming back from a club with two of her friends from home. All of them ended up going back into Squirrel and G Man's shared house as Squirrel was promising alcohol. Drinks had been served and Snatch had been put on the DVD, only for G Man to take one swig of his bottle of beer, recall a memory and say to Sallytoo,

"You're the lesbian, aren't you?"

Then looking at her two friends said,

"Suppose you're both lesbians as well."

And with that he put the beer down, got up and went to bed. Squirrel and the girls continued drinking and watching Snatch. The girls left at some point and Squirrel woke on the sofa with Klint's "Diamond" playing on loop from the DVD's main menu.

Again.

Snatch

Now it's been mentioned that Hopalong had introduced Squirrel to Snatch over the New Year period. Little did he know what a monster this would introduce.

Once Hopalong had broken his ankle he wasn't able to go out drinking with Squirrel and G Man. But he did find out how paper thin the walls were when they got home from a night out. (And he also realised his comments months before about how he'd like to shag Warm's girlfriend would easily have been heard by them in the room he now occupied.)

Every time they went out at night, they got back and put Snatch on. And then they would promptly fall asleep. Hopalong found this waring very quickly and so when they were out one night he hobbled from his room and removed the Snatch DVD from the PS2 and hid it in another random DVD case in his room.

It worked that night, but Squirrel just went out the next day and bought his own copy (well two copies, just in case), and so when Squirrel and G Man returned pissed the following night on went Snatch again. At high volume.

When they got up the next morning, they found that Hopalong had been in and reclaimed the PS2 from the living room to prevent any further episodes. But Squirrel wasn't taking that, he went out and bought a cheap DVD player and connected it up. And yes, Squirrel and G Man went out that night, came home and put Snatch on.

This prompted Hopalong to get up, hobble out of his room and poke his head into the living room, look at Squirrel and say,

"You're a cunt."

Before shuffling back off to bed.

Which amused Squirrel and G Man even more.

Giving Up Smoking

Whilst Hopalong was confined to the house with his broken ankle, everyone refused to go out and buy him any cigarettes. And this went on for weeks.

So much so he had resorted to standing in the front door and desperately begging passersby to go and buy him some cigarettes from the shop on the corner of the next street. Only to give up on that when people stopped and agreed, took his money, and fucked off never to be seen again.

But he must have found some poor sucker to take pity on him because he was sat in the living room smoking when Squirrel came back from whatever drinking session it was that day.

Squirrel said to Hopalong that it had been four weeks, and it should have been enough to break the nicotine cycle by now, and he should have been able to give up. Hopalong countered that it wasn't that easy.

Squirrel looked at his own packet of cigarettes (oh, sorry, it wasn't mentioned that whilst they wouldn't buy any cigarettes for Hopalong, they were quite happy to buy and smoke their own in the house), and there was one left. So he told Hopalong,

"This is my last one in this packet, and I haven't got any more packets in the house, so I'll have this one and then give up."

Hopalong scoffed at the idea, saying Squirrel would never manage it.

But Squirrel did. Gave up. Just like that.

Which a week or so later brought another outburst of Hopalong poking his head into the living room, looking at Squirrel saying,

"You're a cunt."

That's Just Taking The Piss

Ricky Organ was in the process of moving out of his posh halls of residence, he was going to be moving in briefly to Heald Place as a holding location. The new shared house at Scarisbrick Avenue had been checked out and the tenancy agreements had been signed. So he was kipping on the floor at Heald Place, or at other houses before the move happened.

And whilst he did this, he had some of his belongings sat in his car.

Now, Heald Place may have been in Rusholme, but it was only just the case. About two hundred yards away was the border with the notorious Moss Side. And so having anything lying in a car parked in the area was always going to be a bit of a risk.

And sure enough Ricky Organ returned to his car one day to find a window smashed in and the belongings gone. Which isn't what anyone wants or needs.

But there was a tinge of humour to the situation, as you see the erstwhile thieves didn't take all the belongings. In the car was a box of videos. The thieves took the box, but in the box, there were some Arsenal videos. Which the thieves took out of the box and left them behind on the back seat of the car.

It would appear that everyone is a critic, and not even Manc scallys want anything to do with Arsenal videos.

How To Freshen The Place Up

By now they all knew they were moving out. The landlady only had one person moving in. So, the four of them were having a house leaving party in effect.

It's early on the Friday evening. Hopalong is in his normal position in the lounge of Chez Rusholme, with his plaster clad leg up on a chair. Ricky Organ is a temporary resident for the week prior to the big move to Chez Didsbury, and after a trip with Squirrel to get more Stella, they are sat watching the TV (in fact a Snatch viewing may well have been taking place). G Man, meanwhile, is round at the neighbours, and trying desperately to stay out of drinking mode. Meanwhile the Stellas are flowing well, and G Man joins in on his return from the neighbours. Pretty soon it's two in the morning and all the Stella's have gone, which leaves the only alcohol in the house as a bottle of Vodka and a bottle of Irish Cream. G Man Suggests making white Russians, only use the Irish Cream instead of Kahlua. Squirrel gets a couple of pint glasses and makes pints of what have gone down in history as dirty white Russians, vodka, Irish cream, and full fat milk. Hopalong, on his first day drinking in about 6 weeks, accepts the challenge, and Squirrel was never going to say no, but Ricky Organ and G Man give the concoction a wide birth. Fast forward to five in the morning, and all the vodka, Irish cream, and four pints of full fat milk have gone, G Man and Ricky Organ have gone to bed, and Squirrel is asleep on the sofa (for a change). Hopalong is feeling somewhat worse for wear, and due to his leg injury is none too mobile. He needs to be sick, and needs help, and prods Squirrel with his walking stick, but Squirrel is dead to the world, so he tries to make a move, and starts to be sick, and boy, was he sick. The splatter area included the sofa, the bin, the phone, and the floor, before he picked up a plate and puked the last onto that. He then shuffled into the kitchen with the plate, which he proceeded to drop on the floor, and therefore got puke in the kitchen as well. He hobbled back to his room and asked Ricky Organ (who was kipping on his floor) to help him clean up as he'd been sick, to which the obvious response was "fuck off". Hopalong then rang Lamb for help, though just what she was going to do at five in the morning when she was in Swindon is anybody's guess, and what the reaction was is a mystery, but would surely have been down the lines of Ricky Organ's response.

Saturday arrived with G Man the first to venture into the lounge, to find the puke wilderness it had become. He went back upstairs and asked Squirrel who puked, Squirrel who had little recollection of making it to bed had no idea, so G Man hammered on the bathroom door to wake up Hopalong, who had fell asleep on the toilet, to ask who had puked. The faint answer was Squirrel, which brought about a shout from Squirrel's room of "No it wasn't". Just then Ricky Organ stuck his head out of Hopalong's door and said that it was Hopalong that puked. When Hopalong finally emerged from the bathroom, he slid down the stairs and went back to bed telling everyone they could clear up. G Man, Ricky Organ and Squirrel then went about the unpleasant task of cleaning up the puke, and had to bin the duvet that was doubling as a throw. Once completed they settled down to watch a game, before heading into Didsbury to give in all the details required for their move to Chez Didsbury, it was then on to pick up some boxes for packing stuff before back home for soccer Saturday. It was at this point that the new tenant of Chez Rusholme was arriving. Ricky Organ headed out to stop at a mate's in Salford, so Squirrel and G Man took pity on the newcomer and took Gates to Squirrel's, seeing as it was fresher's week, so they could check out the new talent (OK talent in Squirrel's is stretching it a bit). Well after a few drinks it could be seen that Gates didn't have the required drinking temperament, and was as boring as fuck, and at the first opportunity G Man sloped off. Squirrel then upped the pace drinking, only to find that Gates couldn't cope and was going as well. Therefore Squirrel stayed at the bar drinking until wandering off for food and home.

Sunday saw little activity during the day, with football to watch, Ricky Organ popped in to say that during his stay in Salford his car had been nicked, but it had been recovered not far away with minimal damage. Squirrel and G Man had another viewing of Snatch. Gates meanwhile said he'd left the previous night as Squirrel was chatting up some fit blonde bird at the bar. It later turned out that Gates' eyesight was not to be trusted, as it was Frost he was talking to.

Monday saw Squirrel nip to Squirrel's for a quick drink only to get drawn into staying, as there was a comedy night featuring someone from Phoenix Nights on as part of fresher's week. After running out of money he was then fed drinks by the gruesome twosome, until leaving just after one, at which stage he wandered home and cooked chilli for himself and Hopalong.

This is after Hopalong had threw his toys out of the pram over the Snatch DVD and his pillow that had gotten into the bin, though he wasn't doing so until after G Man had cooked him dinner, this problem was relieved somewhat when Hopalong went to stay at Lamb's for a couple of days in the middle of the week, leaving G Man to enjoy the delights of Gates' company.

8 Scarisbrook Road

When it came to moving day, there was a host of help on hand. Cars, vans, family, friends, hangers-on, liquorice all sorts and more. They were all there to see the new shared house in all its glory. Or as is more likely, they were there to make sure that they left Heald Place.

Squirrel had traded with the other three moving in on that first day, that he was happy to have the box room as his bedroom, but that he would have the one double bed in the house in there (leaving no real room for anything apart from the wardrobe that was in there as well). Additionally he was going to use one of the three large rooms on the ground floor to store all his stuff. The books, records, CDs, DVDs etc, and it was Squirrel who had the most stuff to move. He was doing a lot of lifting and shifting. You always underestimate just how heavy books and records are, and he had collected a lot of them in the year he had been in Manchester.

Once everything had been moved in it was going to be time to head out. There was drinking in the city centre planned, and showers were needed. There were two showers in the house, one above the bath in the bathroom upstairs, and a second one downstairs in the wet room to the side of the conservatory behind the living room. Squirrel had gone down there. It was supposed to be instant hot water. Three minutes later he got out of the cold shower and with just a towel wrapped around him, he stomped out to go back to his room, channelling Eddie Murphy from "Delirious" shouting, "That ain't no instamatic muthafucker."

Only to find the main living room, which had been empty on his way to the shower, was now full. Housemates, friends, and Hopalong's dad and partner, now all being met by a fat, half naked, wet bloke, swearing like a trooper.

Once everyone was ready, Squirrel, G Man, Ricky Organ, Mate, Dickie Boy, Tyka, and others made their way into Manchester. Various bars were visited until they got to Deansgate Locks. A venue upgrade to match their living accommodation upgrade. They ended up in Vodka Revolution. Now, Deansgate Locks was a bit strange. There were multiple bars, and to get to them you had to cross over one of three footbridges to the road level entrances of what looked to be single storey buildings. Yet they all had a downstairs and balconies out onto the side of the canal. And they were all mainly just bars upstairs, and dancefloors down below.

And it was to the dancefloor area everyone had gone. It was a long day of drinking and so it got unsurprisingly messy, and time rushed by. Whilst queuing to get a drink G Man saw an opportunity to get freebies. The side of the bar was open and there were bottles just behind it, so he reached round the side of the bar, grabbed a bottle, and took a long swig. However he hadn't looked at the bottle, and therefore took a long swig of orange cordial, which made him gag more than tequila might have done. Not only that, but he got spotted doing so and was chased away be the staff. He ran upstairs, but was found and ejected from the premises.

When it got to closing time Squirrel jumped into a taxi with Mate, Dickie Boy, Tyka, and someone else to head back towards Didsbury. The others were in a house on Austin Drive, just off Fog Lane. So Squirrel got out of the taxi there, rather than trying to remember the name of the road he'd moved into that day. He knew where it was, but couldn't remember the name.

And once on Fog Lane he didn't know which direction he was facing, and so didn't know which direction to head in to get to the house. His first thought was he knew he was between Wilmslow Road and Parrs Wood Road, and that the new house was on the other side of Parrs Wood Road, and therefore to the east. He thought he would wait to see from which direction the sun came up and head in that direction. After five minutes he realised he was better off just walking, even if he went the wrong way it would still only be a ten-minute detour, rather than the couple of hours wait for the sun to come up, and it might be cloudy anyway.

By jumping in that taxi it meant Ricky Organ was travelling back solo as well, and therefore should have probably gotten back before Squirrel, but even he had difficulties and took a couple of attempts to find his way back. G Man was even worse, and didn't get back until it was becoming light. Despite having left first, he had spent much of the night since being ejected travelling up and down Kingsway trying to direct various taxi drivers down the correct turn off towards the house.

The residents' sense of direction did improve, and finding the place became easier. Apart from the one time Squirrel was on automatic pilot coming home from work one day and ended up back at Heald Place instead.

Housewarming

Of course, it wasn't possible to move into a new gaff without having a housewarming party, was it? The weekend started as it meant to go on.

The planned Squirrel Friday afternoon sleep never happened, as Sally turned up mid-afternoon, and drinking started. Not long after Cabbage turned up, and that really was the end of any plans to take things easy. Hopalong was still in his cast and so wasn't coming out, but as soon as Ricky Organ and G Man had got back from work and had a bite to eat, the rest were out to go to Squirrels. They met up with some of Cabbage's mates and Dylan. Next stop was 5th Avenue, where things began to get messy. First to leave just after midnight was Ricky Organ who got a cab back to Chez Didsbury, and on its arrival, he decided it was the perfect time for projectile vomiting. This led to Hopalong having to give the driver a £50 cheque, and get buckets of water to slop the cab out. Meanwhile the thirty plus hours without sleep and the stupid number of vodkas meant that Squirrel was asleep stood up on the dance floor, being kept upright by Sally who was just nudging him if he went to lean over too far. This came to a stop when she went to the toilet, and Cabbage, G Man and Dylan carried him up the stairs and into a cab. Dylan went back in and left at closing time with Sally.

Saturday saw a lot of people who weren't very with it, even after a fry up. Ricky Organ's sister and mate arrived just after midday and along with G Man headed to town, where they spent the afternoon in Waxy O'Connor's in the extremely comfortable armchairs. Meanwhile Hopalong was tidying the house and Squirrel was preparing food for the housewarming party that evening. Radio arrived just after six, and the others got back from town, just in time to settle down for the Slovakia Vs England qualifier. After the game, some people started turning up, with several people from Ricky Organ's work, Sally, Sallytoo (yes different people), and two of the new next-door neighbours, Asset, and Button. Food was thrown, drink was drunk and from about one people started heading home. Then the spirit drinking started in force, Button and Asset went home about three, only for Button to reappear an hour later. Sensible people started going to bed, which left Radio (cos he had no choice as he was sleeping on the sofa), Squirrel, Sally, G Man and Button up drinking. Radio attempted to go to sleep at five, and G Man went to bed, Button went home, but Squirrel and Sally continued drinking til six before going and crashing out.

Sunday saw slow movement, from everyone. Squirrel and Sally found and finished all the dregs from the punch, and then Squirrel, G Man and Ricky Organ went into town for the first ever instalment of pissed shopping. Squirrel was somewhat confused by a text message from H (no not the one from steps) saying that he'd just seen Morrissey, and was in a club dancing to The Jam. It took some considerable time for him to remember that H was in Australia at the time. The evening saw Radio, G Man, Hopalong and Ricky Organ having a FIFA tournament. Squirrel went to see how the neighbours were and found that Button had been puking all day, and couldn't face food, and that Asset had only just surfaced, and was coming round for food.

Monday saw the madness continuing, with a couple of people that G Man had met travelling, Shine and his mate, coming over to Manchester. A couple of beers at home, then to the Dog and Partridge, then another Squirrel's visit, before a journey into town, which gave Squirrel a chance to give Frost abuse when she tried to say hello on the bus. Brannigan's was the first destination in town, before crossing the road to Infinity, where there was a foam party. Kicking out time saw a taxi back to Chez Didsbury where Hopalong was still up, and willing to join in the drinking that continued until the following morning. G Man, showing courage above the call of duty went into work after an hour's sleep, and while still pissed. Squirrel went to bed just after nine for a few hours' sleep before the start of his working week.

One of the longest, messiest, but altogether tip top weekends.

Part 2 – The Surerandomality Notes

Squirrel got it into his head to send out a surreal and random e-mail on a Thursday night whilst at work. Little did anyone else know what this would lead to.

It was a short story called Walter's Story, and after a mixed reaction, Squirrel went the whole hog the following week and started an e-zine, e-mailed out at five AM every Friday morning. No one knew how it would grow arms and legs and get out of control and take over Squirrel's life for the next two years, or how it would document all the idiocy of Chez Didsbury and beyond for that period for posterity. Those sleep deprived e-mails every week at first, and then moving to every fortnight after a year now forms the bulk of the remains of this book, as without much (or any really) editing they will follow.

Unlike part one, this has a lot of notes, lots of documentation, and even lots of photos. None of which are useable, especially if we are to protect those who took part in all of this.

Each of the chapters in this part will have the name / number of the issue of Squirrel's e-zine – Surerandomality. The first issue went out at the end of October 2022.

Issue 1

Not actually a run down, there was no write up of events in the first issue, but there is one incident that was worth recalling.

Squirrel and Ricky Organ had finished drinking in the early hours of the morning somewhere in Fallowfield, they had gotten food and were walking along Wilmslow Road in the general direction of Withington and home beyond. As they did so, Ricky Organ pointed out his ex's (Liver), lived in the block of flats they were passing. And that he thought it was a good idea to ring her up as they were passing. Squirrel couldn't dissuade him from this course of action and soon he could hear the phone ringing at the other end.

It rang and rang and Ricky Organ refused to hang up. After a couple of minutes there was an answer and a very sleepy and confused sounding woman answered. Only it wasn't Liver answering the phone. He had picked the wrong number from his contacts and had rung the home of Liver's parents and had gotten her mum out of bed at three in the morning.

You would have thought that after that comedy misdial, he would have given up for the night, but no, he then rang Liver's actual mobile. It didn't take as long to get an answer, but it wasn't anywhere near as polite as the one Ricky Organ had got from her mum.

Issue 2

The plan had been to have a nice easy going Friday night as there was a late night planned for the Saturday. Of course, Squirrel's definition of an easy going Friday night isn't just not in the same postcode as anyone else's, but it would be hard going to say it was even in the same country. A little doze on the sofa whilst waiting for others to get back from work meant a fully refreshed lunatic with a bottle of beer in his hand as the workers returned. And by eight PM a few beers in the living room whilst endlessly flicking through the music channels on Sky had only made them want to go out.

It went as it usually did, a drink in Didsbury, and then to Fallowfield, and Squirrel subverting the evening by dragging them all into Bar XS. A kebab and a taxi home and Squirrel was still up to go to work at stupid o'clock in the morning.

But that was nothing compared to the Saturday. It was Sallytoo's birthday, and the safety net of Didsbury and Fallowfield were going out of the window. Instead it was off to Canal Street with the old neighbours, some of their friends and Sally. After a few drinks in a few different bars alongside the canal it was off to Essential who didn't even open until eleven. Squirrel, G Man, Ricky Organ, and Hopalong, were split up to go in with various females out, as it was unlikely that they would have gotten into Essential as a group of four pissed, straight, males.

Essential was open until six in the morning, but stopped serving alcohol at three, so there was a large drinks order at ten to three and they were stashed along the back wall of one of the dancefloors. Some of those who had gone out left after a polite period. Others left as the alcohol stopped being served. The birthday girl left about four, and even Sally left before closing. The only one left, still drinking the stash and dancing was Squirrel, who left at closing time, found a kebab shop, and then went to wait for a tram to work in St Peter's Square.

Issue Gamma

It was another of those weeks, Squirrel went out on the Friday night, again without sleep during the day and in a surprise to no one ever managed to get blasted at Bar XS again, when he got back to Chez Didsbury, the stairs looked too problematic for him and so he crashed out on the sofa. (An ongoing theme.)

As he did, his side splittingly funny housemates thought it would be a good idea to try and shave one of his eyebrows off, but because they're incompetent fucks they managed a botched job on it, so much so that Squirrel didn't even notice until he was on his way home from work Saturday afternoon. He had looked in the mirror several times during the day and not noticed. He only noticed it as he went to rub his forehead and felt stubble on his eye.

His first words when back at Chez Didsbury were "which one of you incompetent fucks was it that tried to shave my eyebrow off? You made a complete of hash of it as well." There is no honour amongst halfwits, and G Man squealed about it being Hopalong within about twenty seconds. Squirrel pointed out that they had to sleep at some point, and that he had clippers. *(Note 1)

People went out on Saturday evening, but at some point, they all got separated and once again Squirrel managed not to make it home again until Sunday afternoon. There is no written evidence of where he ended up. Under a bush somewhere is more likely than in anyone's bed though.

Squirrel was then running a music quiz at Squirrel's on the Sunday night and no one else went, but Squirrel eventually got into his bed for the first time since getting up to go to work Thursday afternoon, at quarter to two Monday morning. Only to be up to go to work Monday morning before rolling into his usual midweek night shifts.

Note 1. It was a couple of weeks before the camera in circulation at the time got the pictures developed. Not content with trying and failing to shave Squirrel's eyebrow off, they were also playing a game of Squirrel buckaroo, as there are pictures of Squirrel fast asleep on the sofa with lots of empty cans piled up all over his body.

Issue IV

Only brief highlights of what happened this week can be offered. There was no sleep again on Friday, the time being spent drinking and playing poker instead, there was lots of alcohol involved, plus there were visitors turning up for G Man's birthday weekend, people he had met in Australia whilst travelling. And once again they had all somehow ended up dancing in Bar XS, with that somehow pretty much guaranteed to have been Squirrel subverting the original plans.

When people woke up Saturday morning it was a bombsite, empty bottles, glasses with rum and baileys, poker chips in every room in the house, CD's all over the place and what seemed like loads of dead bodies on most of the floors, in addition to which in the room where there was only Sargin asleep were three opened johnnies, none appeared to have been used, though the wearer may have been wankrupt, and there was one still hiding under the stereo.

Squirrel started on doing cooked breakfast for those who were able to move. Although not quick enough for some, as Gopher led a delegation to find a greasy spoon café not far from Chez Didsbury. And despite being a first-time visitor he was ahead of the housemates who hadn't found the place themselves.

Everyone was back in the pub by two. Local at first, and then into central Manchester and to rarely used pubs along Peter Street. Well, why not, everyone was smartly dressed so that they could go to the Casino (Viva Las Vegas). There was some window-shopping Amsterdam style as Squirrel, Ricky Organ & Me Laird schlepped around the seedier parts of the Northern Quarter. Then back to Chez Didsbury and more drink.

Which meant more dead bodies Sunday morning. Breakfast was foregone and it was pub lunch, back to Chez Didsbury to continue drinking, watch football, before going back out. Getting in a taxi they met a dope dealing taxi driver who took them to Rusholme and a curry. Sane people would have retired, but no, more pubs, and back to the casino (Viva Las Vegas), and then back to Chez Didsbury to continue drinking - finishing the rum and Baileys, foregoing sleep to stay up and watch DVDs, as no one appeared to be working on Monday.

They still didn't manage to make Scubar. Respect to the birthday boy G Man for managing to lose his passport and cash card in the women's toilets in Bar 38 on the Saturday night. He got a phone call the Sunday night from his dad asking had he lost anything while he was out last night. Well at least he got his passport and card back (after he'd already reported it lost).

Lots of problems with trains on the Monday meant extra-long stays for some people, including Gromit who spent an hour waiting for a train, during which time he was chatting up a schoolgirl, before he got cold and came back to Chez Didsbury and trying again on the Tuesday. Hopalong finally made it back to work after a long time off since his broken ankle debacle back in August.

Issue E

After a slow start on the Friday with Squirrel and G Man not going out until after eight (the time and not the mints), things managed to heat up quite nicely, after a quick one at Oak House, and a posh one at Something Blu (not named after Hopalong's favourite boy band), they raided Bar XS where they tried the "we're not from Manchester can you tell us where's good to go?" approach that had worked so well for them in Preston, but it wasn't such a success in Bar XS, well trying it on first year students wasn't the best move, especially when the same students came back an hour later and accused the pair of them of nicking their phone.

Somewhat put out by this the pair of them moved on to 5th Avenue, where the "I'm the drummer from Supergrass and this is my minder" approach was more successful, as was the buy the barmaid drinks approach. G Man had to leave early as Daddy and Mummy G were coming to town the next day, but he did manage to try to persuade two young Greek girls to return to Chez Didsbury, without any success.

Squirrel meanwhile, made it to Jewel in the Crown with the barmaid from 5th Avenue, but fell asleep during the curry, and he was (deservedly) deserted. In the meantime, elsewhere, Ricky Organ's Darth Maul pulling pants were successful for the second Friday on the trot.

Saturday was spent lounging about the house, and it brought about a new addition to the Chez Didsbury household; the baby beer fridge is doing well and is greatly appreciated. They now don't have to leave the comfy seats in the living room to carry on drinking.

Saturday night meant next door's house party, and another long night, though G Man, Ricky Organ, and Hopalong wandered off to Friday's as it wasn't the most exciting party. But Squirrel preferred to stay and look longingly at Asset.

There was more lounging on Sunday, mainly just watching the football again.

But Monday night turned out to be a mad one again with the destination being 5th Avenue for the second time over the extended weekend, with Squirrel, G Man, Hopalong and Ricky Organ, all making it there. Later in the evening Ricky Organ tried getting in a fight, and the four of them all had to be escorted from the premises into a waiting taxi to end the proceedings early. On the way home they also managed to abuse nearly everyone they encountered that night. And G Man was in such a bad way the following morning that he had to shell out twenty-five quid to get a taxi to work the next morning (at eleven). The main surprise there was that he bothered at all, and didn't pull a standard sickie.

As a side note for the week, an extra special round of applause for Squirrel, who managed to send out the most ill-advised, dumbass, completely fucking stupid e-mail in the history of electronic communication this week.

EDITOR'S NOTE. There is no evidence remaining as to what this e-mail contained, but the suspicion is that Squirrel was declaring undying love to inappropriate people.

Issue Six

What a week - again. Squirrel headed out by himself early on Friday at five and as the night went on, he got to Bar XS where he met up with Scottie who he hadn't seen for months, and she was just as crazy as she had always been. Then Dylan arrived, and not long after that G Man turned up, then Sally, and then finally Ricky Organ and his mate Ory turned up. Squirrel was pried out of his spiritual home and over the road to the Orange Grove. Where they left Sally and Scottie behind to head on to Jabez.

G Man wandered off early, leaving his famous "this has been around the world with me" jumper behind, never to be seen again (and boy have we heard about it - talk about whine), Ricky Organ managed to get another female's number, he's obviously a Friday night man. Squirrel and Dylan stopped off for curry in Rusholme on the way back. Dylan suddenly lost the plot, got up, threw his curry at the wall, and abused the staff. It ended up with a scuffle outside with the bouncer from the next-door curry house getting involved, punching Squirrel as well who was trying to break it up. It was not a tip top ending to the evening, and it turns out Dylan has a perforated ear drum for his troubles.

Saturday involved wandering round town pretending to shop, only to find the comfy chairs in Waxy O'Connor's again, and Squirrel going to work, before going out and doing a quarter of the Didsbury dozen with G Man, Ricky Organ and Ory. In the meantime Hopalong was being a cultured man and was at the opera (we think he got lost and then couldn't talk his way out). Ricky Organ and Ory went home, and Squirrel and G Man went on to XS where they met Sally, and G Man got Minda's number (yes that is the correct spelling, the D shouldn't be a G), then on to the casino (Viva Las Vegas) where they found no alcohol on sale, and blew a tenner each before going for curry, they got in, woke Ricky Organ up to play cards, then thinking he was out, woke Hopalong up as well.

Hopalong extracted revenge the following morning by waking G Man at 10 am telling him he was missing the Man U game as it was

104

half time. G man shot up and was dressed and in front of the telly in a matter of seconds, only to be sat there for quarter of an hour before realising he'd been duped.

Squirrel ran a quiz in the evening, and got home to find everyone had gone to bed. Monday, Tuesday & Wednesday found both G Man and Hopalong off sick, though the feeling remains that one of these illnesses was Mickey Mouse, spurious, not genuine, and left the chances of G Man doing two full weeks on the trot at fuck all, in fact after Hopalong went back to work on Thursday, G Man was still off, despite going out with Sallytoo on the Wednesday night.

Thursday night saw Hopalong and G Man out again, this time with the destination being Jabez, and on exit they were having a wrestling match, whilst speaking to Squirrel on the phone, somehow there's little chance of either of them being at work this morning.

This week also saw the introduction of Electric Six into the Chez Didsbury's residents' lives. They all saw the "Danger! High Voltage" video for the first time, and certainly not the last time either.

Seventh Issue Of

As expected, G Man never made it to work on Friday morning, however somewhat surprisingly Hopalong did. Squirrel spent a couple of hours dozing on the sofa before G Man surfaced. Big Olas turned up at around half three. G Man went home to Harrogate for the weekend, leaving Squirrel, Ricky Organ, Hopalong and Big Olas to go out on Friday night.

Squirrel met up with Sally, Dylan, and his workmates for Dylan 's birthday in Bar XS. The other three went to Squirrels and met up with Lamb and Sallytoo, and arranged to meet up with everyone else later. The group from Bar XS moved on and met up with Pod and Dylan's brother in Paramount and headed to Walkabout via Teasers. In fine tradition Dylan got himself thrown out of Walkabout (cause unknown), and Squirrel, Sally, Pod, and Dylan 's brother wandered off to Chinatown, therefore just missing the others who had just arrived at Walkabout.

Dylan managed to get thrown out of the Chinese for arguing with a waiter, and Squirrel went after him, but couldn't find him, and when he went back everyone else had gone, and he'd left his phone behind, he later found out Sally had it.

Saturday meant work for Squirrel, and he met up with Sally and her mum in town, and got his phone back and then headed straight to XS. Ricky Organ, Hopalong and Big Olas turned up later, then Lamb and her housemates and then a somewhat sheepish and worse for wear Dylan. They all tried to go and get in the Queen of Hearts, but there was a queue!!! And it wasn't moving so they went back to XS and got blasted.

They did absolutely nothing on Sunday, except order curry, and listen to Ricky Organ arguing with a neighbour over where he'd parked his car. Parking on a cul-de-sac without drives was a contentious issue. There was one neighbour (Wayout), who had seemed friendly at first and had invited the housemates over for a drink. Mainly to show off the board game he had invented. But it went downhill rapidly after that.

Monday, did nothing again except relax and recharge, whereas everyone else was at work (Including surprisingly enough G Man). Overall, it was another tip top weekend.

Ricky and Hopalong both had their Office Christmas parties last night, both managed to meet up later and there was a stop press message at ten past four this morning from them saying that they'd just won £140 at the casino (Viva Las Vegas), Obviously this again casts doubt on their ability to make it to work this morning.

A brief announcement from Squirrel – "I'm not a fucking Brummie!!!!" (Being from Leicester it was decided he was therefore nearly from Birmingham and therefore sounded like a Brummie – i.e. thick as pig shit.)

Congratulations to G Man for managing to do a full week for only the second time since before publication started.

Issue Christmas Edition

Early hours on Friday afternoon, and The Quiet Man makes it over from Liverpool, Ricky Organ gets home, picks up The Quiet Man and Squirrel, then off to Middleton to pick G Man up from work and then it was road trip to Newcastle time to meet up with The Chemist. Mate didn't manage to make it as he forgot that Southampton vs. Newcastle was being played in Southampton and so would be at the other end of the country.

Once in Newcastle it was straight to Ba Ja where large amounts of alcohol were consumed, and G Man mistook a glass of salt for his glass of Tequila with the obvious hilarious consequences, making up random lines to use, and then watching each other spectacularly crash and burn from the balcony. In fact they all used the same line. There was a group of women dancing together, one in a Santa outfit, several dressed as fairies, and one dressed in green. So, the line was 'if your mate there is Santa, and those are all fairies, does that mean you are a gobbling?' The look of bemusement on her face as seemingly random blokes came up and asked her the same thing was a picture from where the others stood on the balcony. Ricky Organ pulled again, and rumours have it so did G Man.

It took two hours and a torturous route to get back to The Chemist's, which include various wrestling moves, and the hammer style throwing of a sandbag in the middle of the Motorway which runs through the centre of Newcastle. There were many questions to The Chemist along the lines of 'was he sure he knew where he lived?'

They all woke up too late to see the start of the Man Unt game on Saturday, but were in the Cornerhouse before the end of the first half then on to the Punch Bowl to watch Chelsea on German TV. G Man needed to pick up some winnings from the bookies, and it was all kicking off in there. Some Scandinavian bloke was going mental because all his picks had come in, but he'd marked them all with an X instead of a one and therefore had picked them all as draws instead of the intended home wins, he wasn't happy.

Then it was back to The Chemist's, for a quick change and out to Osborne's so that G Man could meet up with Kaz. Then on to the Pitcher & Piano where they met up with Jumbo, one of The Chemist's mates and then onto The Boat, complete with its ten dance floors (including the infamous revolving one). Ricky Organ, who is in a rich vein of form, pulled again. Which is more than could be said for the Rod Stewart impersonator in the eighties disco dancing away to "Baby Jane" as if it was his actual song.

They managed to get back a lot quicker with Jumbo leading the way home, even if it was done at a route marching pace. But once back at The Chemist's they continued drinking til well after four.

The next morning Squirrel was paying for the route marching the previous evening with leaden legs. They were back in the Cornerhouse for the Tottenham game, and then it was the reverse road trip. There was much taking the piss out of Squirrel around his easting of the roast dinner is alphabetical order. And Squirrel started off a new often used phrase. Hope...Hell where he used his left hand for the first and right hand for the second word, whilst putting them as far apart as possible. They got back to Chez Didsbury to find that Hopalong had had an early Christmas with Lamb, and one of the presents was a dart board. It only needs an optic run and a pool table and there will be no leaving the house ever.

Monday night saw Squirrel meet up with Me Laird at Squirrels, then onto Teasers, and Brannigans, then more Amsterdam style window shopping at Pandora's.

Tuesday saw Hopalong, Ricky Organ and G Man out and about in town, and after Brannigans they made a trip to the casino (Viva Las Vegas), but at this point things turn sour, first G Man kicks a door of another club as he walks past, at which stage the bouncer comes out and smacks him, then once in the casino (Viva Las Vegas) Hopalong starts losing and Ricky Organ and G Man can't get him to leave, they give up with him £150 down and go for a curry, where Ricky Organ, trying to keep his run going tries it on with a couple of lesbians and fails as his infamous "I'm not gay you know" line doesn't quite hit the spot, though they do manage to bag themselves a very fetching helmet style felt hat as a beer trophy. Hopalong eventually crawls in at 6.30, £75 up, and manages to make it to work, which is more than G Man could manage, as he had a spurious not genuine ankle injury.

There was also the additional information offered up by Me Laird in one of his infrequent additions to the regular publishing.

Hello to those that know me, and errrm, I suppose I should be nice, hello to those that don't also. Following on from my evening with Squirrel last Monday I have proceeded to move back to the family home for Christmas and the New Year with little, or no idea, what I am doing when it arrives. Imagine my shock/horror/disbelief to find, upon pulling up the drive (a little under 1/4 of a mile long for those statto's out there) that the entire house now very closely resembles Santa's Grotto, and my old room has been shang-highed as a "Nursery" for my recently arrived Niece (She was actually born years ago, but my sister was 'with the Prince' (Valium, NOT Charles) for so long that she has only recently been rediscovered beneath an old Fortnum and Mason hamper, snuggly covered by copies of Forbes and Burkes Peerage. Anyway, due to the 'strategic domestic realignment' or nicking my old room, I have now been forced to move into the outbuildings, which means I don't have to have any daily contact with my beloved family!!

This is where the problem comes, I had been in Manchester for 2 years, and was very used to the frequent visits to Abdul's, Teasers, Casino (Viva Las Vegas), the, errrm 'shopping district' (I saw a mouse, where, there on the stair, where on the stair, right there) [ask Squirrel to explain that one Hopalong] and now I find myself in a village with ONE public house (and it's a Mansfield house at that) and errrm, no, that's it, no chippy, no Chinese (and when I say no Chinese, I mean no Chinese food, or people of ethnic origin, they just aren't PLU enough) it is 4 miles to the nearest chip-shop, 7 miles to a Pizza joint and forget getting a decent curry this side of Selby, in fact Hull is about 22 miles away and the only thing it has going for it is a fantastic Napoleons (Viva Las Vegas), a docks museum and a bigger 'shopping district'(I saw a mouse, where, there on the stair, where on the stair, right there)than Manchester; so please, when you are out this Christmas, and trying a DDT in the middle of the M6, or indulging in a spot of hit n run (Dylan style, as in, getting twatted because you forgot to run) spare me a thought.

111

Anyway, I am reliably informed that the 11:24 bus from the bottom of our drive actually gets into Hull before midnight tonight, if I am lucky there may even be another bus back before Tuesday!!! Take it steady folks, and apologies to those who have not enjoyed the ramblings of a sad old man hankering for the good life he has left behind, better go, and make sure the hired hands aren't stealing the silver. Merry Christmas, Happy New Year and don't do anything I wouldn't, which leaves u lots of scope, in fact, it leaves you with every option known to man other than a small Inn somewhere in Devon / The West Country and a certain young 'lady/man' (god that would be a 50/50 on Millionaire) who was the recipient of Squirrels infamous "When is it due" line.

Issue Neuf

Another bumper week of chaos and mayhem, some good and some that was not quite so tip top.

Friday saw Squirrel out on his work do and at the same time trying the dusk till dawn effort on the longest night of the year. Starting early at home, he made a quick stop (finally) at Scubar, before meeting up with a couple of work colleagues in Fat Cat on Deansgate locks, a few there, then stops at Rain Bar, Paramount and the New Union before arriving at the meal. After the meal with quite a few others it was on to Jumping Jaks, Jar Bar, and finally Infinity, before getting home just after the trio of G Man, Hopalong, and Ricky Organ, who had been out to the Slug and Lettuce on Stella and Tequila before heading into town and on to the Champagne in Bar 38, on exit Ricky Organ managed to puke twice, before getting home. The dusk till dawn effort failed by some three hours.

Saturday brought an early afternoon start for Squirrel while the other three housemates were shopping, on the way out from town he got dropped off in Fallowfield where he was going to meet up with Dylan, but Dylan had already moved on so Squirrel had himself a mini pub crawl before hitting the off license and getting spirits to drink at home. Dylan in the meantime managed to get involved in a little scuffle in Jabez and got thrown out and got a beating from the bouncers as well.

Sunday was Chez Didsbury's Christmas party, which started with watching the football and beers, but after the opening of presents, a drinking shots game was started using two of Squirrels presents, porno playing cards and a spin the wheel shots board. It got messy from there, just before 11 it was out to Fallowfield to the Orange Grove, and then into town to Jumping Jaks, then to the casino (Viva Las Vegas), where Hopalong managed to blow £190 in two hours, before wandering off to Chez Didsbury at 3. On returning to Chez Didsbury, Ricky Organ and Squirrel had quite the discussion on whether it was better to be an alcoholic (a la Squirrel) or a gambling addict (a la Hopalong), and which was best for long term health and stability. It wasn't pretty.

G Man and Ricky Organ went home to their families on Monday and somewhat surprisingly Squirrel went to Bar XS where he met up with Sally and Dylan for a few beers.

Hopalong and Dylan both went home to families on Christmas Eve, only leaving Squirrel floating about in Manchester. Into the Friendship at 6 where Sally and all the Bar XS regulars were, out at closing time then home where Squirrel and Sally continued drinking.

Christmas day dawned and the spirits started well before ten, with Sally bringing the shot roulette up to bed to wake Squirrel up. Then the shot roulette took a trip to the neighbour's house and poor Button didn't know what the hell was hitting him and his dreads at that early time on Christmas morning. And then all the spirits had gone by two. Comi came round and cooked the Christmas dinner (lamb) he and Sally would have had at theirs. Plus he brought the industrial sized bottle of Smirnoff round. He read one of Squirrel's Agatha Christie books as Squirrel and Sally demolished the vodka before Comi and Sally went home in the early hours. Boxing day brought lounging at home watching football and crap films, and saw the return of G Man.

And congratulations to G Man who it has emerged this week is an Uncle.

2002 SPECIAL AWARD ZONE

The "Stella Live" event of the year – G Man's birthday weekend
The "Tone Deaf" Karaoke anthem of the year – Spandau Ballet – Gold
The "Dancing Bear" dance anthem of the year – Alcazar – Crying at the Discotec
The "Sunken Battleship" award for most alcohol (total volume) consumed – Squirrel
The "Pavement Pizza" puking champion of the year – Hopalong
The "Lawrence Llewelyn-Bowen" award for interior taxi design – Ricky Organ
The "Bryan Adams" Waking up the neighbours' award (1) Door Knocking – Hopalong
The "Bryan Adams" Waking up the neighbours' award (2) Singing / Music – Squirrel
The "Anne Widdecombe" award for biggest minger pulled – Squirrel

114

The "It's good to talk" best comedy misdial at 3am award – Ricky Organ

The "Fuck off Santa" award for most embarrassing moment at a work do – G Man (Closely followed by two of his housemates)

The "ZZ Top" worst shaver award – Hopalong, disablely helped by G Man for their piss poor attempt to shave Squirrel's eyebrow

The "Eminem Guilty Conscience" award for minimal contact – Big Olas in Walkabout

The "I know a shortcut" most torturous route home award – The Chemist

The "David Bailey" where's my camera missed photo opportunity award – Hopalong, the morning after the England – Sweden world cup game

The "Kronk's Gym" best punchbag award – Dylan

The "Walkabout" best use of a table – Sally on Squirrel's birthday in the Footage and Firkin

The "Keith Gillespie" gambler of the year award – Hopalong

The "Darren 'sicknote' Anderton" award for outstanding attendance at work – G Man

The "Young Ones" dedicated student award – Radio

The "Jamie Theakston" most frequent window shopper (Amsterdam style) award – Me Laird

The "Oxfam Special Appeal" buy a longer, baggier top award – Shared, Gonfer & Frost

Issue New Year Edition

Well, it's been one hell of a rollercoaster week. Friday started in traditional fashion with Squirrel and G Man on a pub crawl, this time down Deansgate, before hitting Walkabout and Teasers and on for a curry, whilst Hopalong stayed at home, which of course led to the early hours of the morning "let's ring Hopalong up phone call", and a great comedy voice mail, due to the fact that G Man couldn't remember anything after the first tequila in Walkabout, and Squirrel thinking that G Man was actually talking to Hopalong and not leaving a message on his answer phone. When they eventually got home, they put the stereo on full blast and proceeded to cause untold damage to G Man's room, with a smashed lamp, and broken CD's being a couple of the casualties.

Saturday saw Squirrel working, and Hopalong getting revenge for being woken the previous evening by deciding to record himself a minidisc by playing CDs at the maximum possible volume, and it also saw the return of Ricky Organ. In the evening Squirrel went out to meet up with Dylan, Sally, and Geezer, but found out that Sally had been rushed into hospital. He still met up with Dylan, Pod, and Jobs. Dylan and Pod went into town, and Jobs went home after an epic pool session, which left Squirrel to his own devices in the Orange Grove, he quickly moved on to XS seeing as how the Orange Grove was scally central, little did he know that it was going to be the Manchester reunion of www.fatminger.com there. He pulled two that were friends, and then went to retreat home quickly upon last orders, this was somewhat slowed by the entire Greater Manchester Constabulary being parked outside and all around XS and through most of Fallowfield after some kind of serious scally gang fight.

Dylan, somewhat amazingly, and in stark contrast to both his previous form and local events managed to make it through the evening without fighting. Sunday saw Squirrel visiting Sally in hospital, along with Geezer, and the quote from Sally "I've not been sick for ages," just prior to puking within moments of being given her first dose of Morphine. That was when she was eventually given some painkillers. They had tried to give her paracetamol, only for Squirrel to point out she was yellow already from some kind of liver damage, and that perhaps paracetamol wasn't the best thing to be giving to her. They really can't get the staff.

As an aside, how bad must Squirrel's drinking be to manage to hospitalise an alcoholic with liver failure whilst not even getting a hangover.

When Squirrel got home G Man and Ricky Organ were in full flight of what turned out to be a three-day marathon to complete The Getaway, as they played Monday, Squirrel was visiting the hospital again, and then out for a few swift drinks in Revolution with Geezer.

It was this obsession with playing The Getaway that led to the extended nickname of Ricky Organ coming about. The main character in the game is called Hammond. And the artist formerly known as Ricky was going about telling everyone to call him Hammond. So Squirrel added Organ to his name as that was the closest he was going to get to being Hammond.

New Year's Eve started with Hopalong off for a meal with Lamb before going to The Old House At Home, The Chemist made the trip down from Newcastle, and went out with Ricky Organ and G Man, Squirrel met up with them later in Hogshead after another hospital visiting session, they went on to Jabez, where all four of them managed to pull, their arrival back at Chez Didsbury was accompanied by the now familiar tones of Gold being sung at the top of their voices (well Squirrel's anyway).

Dylan ended up in XS for a not so tip top evening, and Me Laird had a mad one that finished at 3pm New Year's Day. New Year's day was lounging, mixed with watching sport and hospital visits, and saw some New Year resolutions, the most outrageous being that Squirrel is giving up drinking, which has led to a book being formed on the length of time he is going to manage to keep to this. And so, one year draws to a close and another one starts,

Issue Ocean's

Never in the history of tattoo sporting pikeys, has so little been stretched into so much.

Friday was the first of a long test on Squirrel's resolve to stick to his new year's resolution. After visiting Sally he met up with G Man and Ricky Organ in Kro Bar, and then on to the extremely successful New Year's Eve stomping ground of Jabez. The only thing being that most of Manchester is still recovering, as it wasn't anywhere near being full, and lacked the atmosphere and range of talent from the previous outing, in fact it was somewhat less than the previous tip top outing there.

Despite this G Man still managed to pull, but when he let his guard down and turned round, she ran off, as fast as her little legs would carry her never to be seen again, in fact it was so quick that the British Olympic Selection team are out scouring the streets of Manchester for her now.

Ricky Organ had a nightmare evening of knock backs and blankings, which after his lengthy run of pulling managed to change his tune, about Jabez as a pulling venue. After leaving Jabez and a spot of wrestling they moved on to Shere Khan for a curry, where G Man managed to leave another item of clothing (but he managed to get this one back), but another celebrity curry house plate for the collection was obtained.

Then onto home where after a game of darts they all went to bed, but G Man had to blast Hopalong (and Lamb) out of bed with loud music. Hopalong got his revenge in the morning by setting his stereo to go off at 7 at full blast, safe in the knowledge that he was downstairs watching telly having been driven there by G Man's music at 5.

It has to be said that since then it has been one of the quietest weeks in living memory, with the return to work of everyone, where everyone apart from G Man seem to be busy little bastards, the normal party mentality seems to have deserted Chez Didsbury, except for an excursion into Manchester for G Man and Hopalong on Wednesday night, which started straight from work, and involved Paramount,

Square Bar, Springbok and Mutz Nutz where G Man got into an altercation over dancing with someone else's girlfriend, which led to them being thrown out and G Man getting kicked in the head by the bouncer.

They then tried (unsuccessfully) to get into 5th Avenue, Fab Café, and the casino (Viva Las Vegas). Thursday morning led to the pair of them ringing in sick, both with very dodgy excuses. Apart from that all that seems to have been done is copious amounts of PS2 game time (Hawk and FIFA, thankfully no Getaway this week), long spells of sport watching and long stints at work. It also must be said that Squirrel is keeping to his new year's resolution and hasn't had a drink yet. At the same time Hopalong's resolution of giving up smoking went out of the window on Wednesday's little excursion.

Tribes of Israel Issue

Due to feeling like absolute shit this week, this probably isn't going to be the most coherent edition ever written.

Friday saw G Man and Hopalong going for the two days off work look more convincing than one excuse, which led to lots of chess, darts, and Hawk playing. Squirrel went to visit Sally in hospital, and when he got back everyone was just lounging, and watching Scarface, when at 12.30 Squirrel got a phone call from Morning asking, "Why aren't you in XS?", within 15 minutes, Squirrel, G Man and Ricky Organ were in XS, where they bumped into Dylan , who was sporting a nice bandage around his right wrist, an injury he'd picked up fighting the previous Saturday. Morning was in a very agitated state (something to do with Barbie's other half) by the end of the evening, and had tried completely reshaping Squirrel's shirt. Her mates had all buggered off, so she got the bus back to Chez Didsbury and got a taxi from there (after bitching about having to walk down Fog Lane).

Saturday saw no inclination from G Man or Hopalong to do anything, but Ricky Organ was up for going out, and so when Squirrel got in, off they went. Wanting to do something slightly different they started in Edwards, and then did AM:PM, Wave and Yates,' all of which had a clientele made up of 18-year-old scallys or forty somethings. They then headed on to the casino (Viva Las Vegas), where Ricky Organ used the chips he'd had since his last visit, and he came out even.

Sunday saw a mega lounging day, with the only person to leave the house being Ricky Organ who went and bought a blender and shitloads of fruit and then proceeded to make smoothies. Monday saw Squirrel taking a rare day off work, and meeting up with Sally (who'd got leave from hospital for the day since it was her birthday), and Geezer who was up for the day, Then on to Kosmos for a meal which due to various afflictions was only thoroughly enjoyed by Comi. For the first time in ages there weren't any mid-week excursions, and it looks like a full week at work by everyone.

Baker's Dozen Issue

Another tip top weekend, with a level of carnage to outdo anything achieved so far this year. Friday saw the release of Sally from hospital in the early afternoon, and another step on the road to full recovery. Meanwhile the evening saw Squirrel, G Man, Ricky Organ and Hopalong sat around watching the Sheffield derby, before breaking the habits of a lifetime by going somewhere different and ending up in Po Na Na for a soul and funk night. Hopalong left early, as it wasn't really his scene, and he seemed to have had the jam taken out of his doughnut by being there.

The remaining three remained til kicking out time, but G Man seems to have found his vocation in life. He stepped up to the plate to talk to a girl, and it was another attempt at the land speed record, as she (along with her friend) rushed from the dance floor. After the Jabez incident a couple of weeks before, there is a real job opportunity for the G Man as a trainer for the women's Olympic Athletics squad. Place him behind the start line and watch them run to get away quickly. It could also be adapted to the throwing events as well. He could stand just beyond the line marking the world record, and watch the records tumble as they try to hit him.

On the way home Ricky Organ managed to scare a 19-year-old girl on the bus, with his normal line of drivel, to the extent that she went and stood with the driver for the rest of the journey.

Saturday involved lots of lounging and a trip to the fancy dress shop for costumes for the evening's party. Hopalong and Lamb went out for a meal, and Squirrel, G Man, and Ricky Organ got ready. Squirrel dressed as a schoolmaster, Ricky went as a policeman, and G Man went as a convict. On arrival it was obvious that the main uniform for females was school uniform (Gromit would have been in his element), and it must be said there were some seriously sexy looking schoolgirls.

Ricky Organ was a bit apprehensive about introducing the Squirrel and G Man random factor to his work colleagues. This caused him to get lured into and locked in the garage with an Essex girl (and this after submitting the Essex girl jokes that appeared last week). Despite being locked in the garage with her for 2 hours, and then in a bedroom for 7 hours, he claims that he failed to get his spunk passport stamped.

Meanwhile G Man was engaging in his best training schedule. After talking to Kimber for a couple of hours he went to get a drink and she disappeared (went to bed – but he didn't know that) he was later spotted all over some woman in scrubs, though when he was momentarily distracted by Squirrel, she made good her escape into the kitchen. As a final attempt, he tried following Raquel and Liann to their room when they said they were going to bed, just to be told; "Just go away!"

Unsurprisingly the last two up and about were Squirrel and G Man, who finished the night off by having a 15-minute cushion and truncheon fight, before collapsing to go to sleep, which was repeatedly distracted by further outbreaks, and finished completely at ten by some of the early to bed early to rise party goers. When Ricky Organ eventually surfaced (it must be said that Ricky Organ felt like a twat because he might have ruined things with the foxy young thing from his office) they went to Pizza hut, and then spent the rest of the day watching football, dodgy movies, and American Football.

Monday evening saw more movies being watched and Squirrel using some of his more autistic abilities to do a jigsaw. The week amazingly enough saw no further midweek outings, and it also saw the second complete week on the trot at work by G Man, which is something of a record since he was taken on a permanent contract. Furthermore Squirrel still hasn't had a drink!

122

Bert Meriwether's rebuttal.

The accusation about G Man's role as a trainer for the women's Olympic running squad in Poo Na Na's is a completely unfounded spurious rumour. I myself was in the same said establishment and saw events in quite a different light. The way I remember it the G Man was fighting off the attentions of numerous women on the upstairs dance floor before being dragged out to a taxi, bound for a kebab shop in Didsbury. Any sprinting that was done, incidentally, was by Ricky Organ, away from Winston the 7-foot black fella whose drink he spilled!

Issue Vierzehn

Squirrel thought that a couple of weeks ago was a quiet week, well it had nothing on the past week. Friday afternoon saw Squirrel and Sally going to see Good Girl at the cinema, which by all accounts shouldn't be seen by those of you who are depressed, or may be feeling borderline depressed. Even those that are happy should beware, as it is quite possible to come out depressed after watching it.

After getting back to Chez Didsbury, absolutely nothing was done, except mong in front of the TV before an early night. Saturday saw Squirrel drag G Man and Ricky Organ to a record fair, just so that they could see there are people more seriously autistic than Squirrel, and then on to Argos so that G Man and Ricky Organ could get a weights bench. Again the evening saw them monging in front of the TV, with talk of going to Wilmslow squashed by the obvious high price of taxis there and back, the only time Ricky Organ sparked into life was when he got a text message from one of his work colleagues.

Sunday saw lots of football watching, with a brief break for a Subway stop, and then the night finished off by watching the Superbowl.

Monday saw Squirrel with another day off, which was spent traipsing round second hand shops for music and books. Another evening in was only disrupted by a brief visit to XS by Squirrel to meet up with Sally and Comi. Meanwhile back at Chez Didsbury Ricky Organ and G Man were continuing this weekend's fad by spending their time doing weights and seeing who could have the ab toner on at the highest voltage, for the longest time.

The week saw no breakout from the confines of Chez Didsbury, and even saw the G Man rack up his third consecutive full week at work, a new record.

Me Laird's Addition to Surerandomality Issue Vierzehn

Greetings one and all from the Northeastern correspondent, may I start by offering my commiserations to anyone reading this update via WAP in some snowdrift just off the M11 or M25, funnier pictures of southern softies with 4x4's not going far have yet to pass my eyes.

Not a great deal of goings on for the past few weeks, but unfortunately Monday sees me return to paid employment. I am hopeful, however, that this will be the usual experience of driving/flying to various different cities for meeting which I know nothing about, flirting with young admin pool girls (and failing remarkably) and flashing around my poncy business card and reminding people that I am a SENIOR manager so they should pay due deference. More than likely I will be exposed for a fraud by some young minor manager who thinks that, just because he went to university, had bad acne, got syphilis and is a demon pool player, he is also qualified to pontificate as much as my good self.

My main reason for writing is to raise a note of concern, I feel that Surerandomality Issue Vierzehn is the latest issue of Surerandomality to demonstrate the leanings of the administration to a more moderate line, especially when it comes to drinking and GOING TO THE CINEMA TO SEE GIRLY FILMS, WITH A GIRL!

I have long suspected that Squirrel's extended stay in Manchester has somehow led to the pollution of his mind, I seriously fear that he may be off to join some secular pact intent on bringing down the values of the west (Viva Las Vegas, Window Shopping Amsterdam Style, Herbal Remedies and Worshipping of Mild, Stout, Lager, Bitter etc.) I would not be surprised if the next Surerandomality was entitled Surerandomality Death to the Infidel and sponsored by member countries of OPEC, perhaps Squirrel plans to join the People's Front of Judea, not the Judean People's Front mind, who are a much more vitriolic bunch all together. So, it is with a heavy heart, that I have to demand that those domiciled with Squirrel do everything in their combined (and recently honed/electrocuted) powers to get some alcohol down the man and get him back to his usual self, I feel he is turning to the dark side and some form of subliminal campaign is imminent to turn the readership of Surerandomality into clean living, non-polluted conscientious worker types, I for one am not up for that, I was not born into the aristocracy to stand idly by and watch my fellow man make something of themselves! People fought WARS to prevent us from becoming an efficient, moderate, progressive, and enlightened race (German).

(To the tune of If your happy and you know it)
If your public ratings slipping
BOMB IRAQ
If your forces are sat waiting
BOMB IRAQ
If the Oil is getting pricey, the economy is dicey, Saddam's started playing nicey
BOMB IRAQ

I leave you with a wise word......
Confucius say, married woman only last half as long as husbands shift

Minutes of Fame Issue

Thanks once again to the Northeast of England correspondent for his inane ramblings last week. It is often wondered just what he's being paid for. Bloody reporters have no concept of how to use spell check before sending their correspondence, just making it look unprofessional, in fact There is some gladness he's back in Manchester where he can be kept a watch on, rather than letting him loose in the wilds of Yorkshire.

You will notice that there is a new later issue time for Surerandomality, this is because Squirrel has finished working nights, and has joined the ranks of normal day working people! Loads to catch up on after a tip top week. G Man didn't make it three weeks on the trot, due to going to Scotland Thursday night to meet up with C-Bitt and Gopher, to spend the weekend with nine in a six-bed apartment.

He rang in sick on Friday with a spurious crick in the neck, having spent the evening getting blasted in a Glasgow pub, before having to get up early on Friday to go to Aviemore to cause serious damage snowboarding, fully believing that he could transfer all his hours of playing Hawk into competent snowboarding, while at the same time use his training capabilities on female snowboarders.

Squirrel met Scottie at lunchtime, and then Sally joined them later, before they went off to various places. Squirrel went on to Squirrels, before going back to an empty Chez Didsbury, because Hopalong was at Lamb's and Ricky Organ had gone to Brussels with work. Saturday saw an early start for Squirrel, who met up with Sally and went to Troff, and then onto Bruins to meet up with Comi and his cycling cronies. Dylan joined them later, before most of them went home, leaving just Dylan and Squirrel to head on to XS, where Dylan was frightened by the female equivalent of G Man in Olympic training standards.

In the meantime G Man was having difficulties reconciling the amount of alcohol drunk the previous evening with his downhill activities, and proceeded to puke up in at the bottom of the slope in front of an unsuspecting line of queuing families. He managed to make it home via a tortured route on Sunday, which wasn't helped by the snowy conditions, an hour searching for lost car keys, and piss poor rail services.

Sunday evening saw some strangely cerebral activities in Chez Didsbury with Squirrel and Hopalong playing chess and scrabble. Ricky Organ in the meantime must have been having a whale of a time in Brussels, as over the week he rang up to do his transfer in the fantasy league, then to ask how his players had done on Saturday and who he had playing on Sunday, then to ask if Sarah Jessica Parker had ever been in Baywatch, plus texting to ask which U2 songs goes "in the name of love", obviously a man living a full and wholesome life while in Belgium.

Tuesday saw G Man extend his training activities to swimming where he startled one poor unsuspecting female into doing 50m in 27 seconds just outside the world record.

Wednesday saw Hopalong and G Man out in Rain Bar from work, with Squirrel joining them later. Upon leaving Hopalong insisted he was going to the casino (Viva Las Vegas), and Squirrel went home, and was surprised when G Man and Hopalong arrived home only three quarters of an hour after him, and even more surprised to learn that Hopalong was £135 up.

Thursday saw Squirrel meeting Sally in XS and then meeting up with G Man and his cousins in Font, before they all got home in the early hours.

Valentine's Issue

And that's just because it happens to be Valentine's Day today, not because of any love thing going on. Yes, Squirrel knows that this edition is hitting your mailboxes quite a bit later this week than normal, this is because he has been a busy little bastard this week, and he's had to sort out his cessation of temping with Adecco, this morning before getting into work. Hopefully, normal service will be resumed next week.

Overall the weekend didn't see much action, with Hopalong being out with Lamb both Friday and Saturday, and G Man not going out Friday night as he was off snowboarding with his family on Saturday and had to be up at 4.30. Squirrel went out straight from work, meeting up with Dylan in Squirrels, and proceeded to take a bit of a hammering at pool. Ricky Organ decided not to come out due to a distinct possibility of there being a clash of personalities.

Squirrel and Dylan met up with Sally and Geezer in Scubar, which has had a major refit and now has a swish upstairs bar. Sally and Geezer went home early, and Squirrel and Dylan went on to Jabez, where Dylan made an early claim to have pulled the biggest minger of the year. Meanwhile Squirrel bumped into Mate, who seemed horrified and disappointed at Squirrel's reformed behaviour, and the fact that he had given up drinking (and smoking), at the same time he seemed out of sorts with what was going on with his life in general. Squirrel and Dylan then headed off to Lal Qila for curry, before wandering home.

Saturday saw Ricky Organ go on a date (after getting his SP stamped in Brussels), and then come home early for a cosy little chat in his room. Sunday was the normal, watch sport, drink smoothies, and play board games type of day that has come to be somewhat of a tradition in Chez Didsbury. Monday saw Nessy (EDITOR'S NOTE, absolutely no idea who this person is or who they came around to see) come round to Chez Didsbury to watch a film and chat.

Tuesday morning saw Hopalong manage to lock himself in the bathroom after the lock stopped working properly, and Ricky Organ had to break in to rescue him (although the image of Hopalong having to escape via the bathroom window would be funny enough). Hopalong started his CIMA course in the evening, but returned in time to get a completed drubbing at darts from Squirrel, with Ricky Organ being out on another date.

Wednesday saw the inmates of Chez Didsbury watching the excuse of an England team getting ritually humiliated by the fucking Aussies at yet another sport, followed by more dart action.

Manchester's Burning Issue

What a slow week it's been, so slow that it would make Koalas look like busy little bastards. Added to this it has also been a piss poor week for offerings, and it leads to the conclusion that you're lucky there's an issue at all.

Friday saw Hopalong out and about with Lamb, Squirrel doing nothing but playing music at home, but he found himself moving to the TV lounge when Ricky Organ arrived back after his Valentine's meal with his date, as the creaking between songs was a bit off putting. Sally's planned evening with Geezer was scuppered by Geezer having to spend all day in London, and Sally being on weed all day.

Saturday saw the return of G Man from his week's family vacation snowboarding, from which the highlight seemed to be his ability to land face first. On one such occasion he did this and managed to break the pair of Oakley's he was wearing, his family were suitably concerned, and spent five minutes trying to see if the broken sunglasses could be mended.

Squirrel met Scottie in town and spent the day bumming round Affleck's Palace buying more music. The evening saw very little being done, except for watching DVD's and playing darts, the planned excursion to the beach party was cancelled due to a general apathy from the house, they couldn't even be arsed to go for a curry, and ordered in instead.

Sunday was much the same, with watching football, and a shopping trip thrown in, after which the kitchen of Chez Didsbury began to resemble a Caribbean fruit stall.

Monday saw more lounging, football watching and dart playing, but there was a comedy phone moment from the G Man, but more of that in story time.

Tuesday saw more football, and Hopalong out with Lamb.

Wednesday saw Ricky Organ out for a meal again, but only after G Man had suggested that he was being a cheapskate by staying in and ordering Dominos, when he came back, he disappeared to his room.

Hopalong meanwhile had gone straight out from work and had difficulties getting back in when he arrived home at half past one. This was because he had forgotten his keys and didn't have his phone, and the doorbell seemed to have stopped working. He eventually managed to get back in after hammering at the door for some considerable time, very lucky that Ricky Organ was still up watching Snatch.

Squirrel managed to fix the doorbell before going to work on Thursday, who would have thought that it would work better if the batteries were in it. Anyway, back to that phone call.

The Boy Who Cried Fire (with apologies to Aesop)

There was once a young man called G Man. G Man lived with three of his friends in a big house in what the letting agents called East Didsbury, but was nearer to Burnage.

One Monday G Man rang his friends in state of great excitement. He virtually shouted "Lads, there's a massive fire in Burnage, near to the railway station, a whole block of flats is on fire, they've blocked the roads off, the flames are massive, you can see them and the smoke from miles away. I've never seen a fire so big, in fact I'm just going back out now so I can stand with all the old dears and watch it. If I'm lucky then I might even see the fire engine with its siren on and lights flashing. I'll have to be careful though as there are massive flaming embers floating down out of the sky into our street, and I wouldn't want to get burnt. If you hurry home, you might see all the action"

One by one, his three housemates returned home, they all looked out for the fire expecting to see flames, smoke, burnt out buildings, and the fire brigade, but what did they see? Nothing, there was no sign of there being a fire, no smoke, no flames, no fire brigade, no burnt-out buildings, and no pools of water.

They ridiculed him, saying he had imagined it all, and that there had never been a fire, and because there was no damage, any flame he had seen couldn't have been very big, and he must have been leading a very sheltered upbringing. Someone lit a match to taunt him, saying that "Here's a bigger flame."

G Man was upset, and vowed to get the Manchester Evening News the next day, so that he could prove there was a fire. "It will be front page news," he declared, "A fire that big, that stopped the traffic will be the main story." Tuesday evening came, and so did the edition of the Manchester Evening News, and though he searched and searched he couldn't find any mention of the fire. His housemates ridiculed him more, "Why do you make up these stories?" "Couldn't you have been more original and thought of somewhere better to have an imaginary fire than BURN-age?"

G Man felt devastated, and went away saying, "I'll show you; I don't make up stories."

Weeks passed, and the ridiculing had stopped, when one night G Man woke and smelt something burning, he jumped out of bed (OK, I know that's pushing the bounds of reality a little too far) and went to investigate and found flames coming from the sofa downstairs. He rushed upstairs and woke his housemates. "FIRE, there's a fire downstairs, we all need to get out otherwise we'll be burnt alive." They all laughed at him, they told him there was no fire and to go back to bed. They also told him not to wake them again as there would be a fire, as they would burn him.

Reluctantly he went back to bed, wondering in his own mind had he really imagined it, and thinking he was going crazy, sobbed himself to sleep. G Man didn't wake in the morning, in fact none of the housemates did, they had all burnt to death in their sleep, because they didn't believe that G Man was telling the truth (this time).

Issue Wheeler

A week that has seen the return of the tip top kind of weekend that chez Didsbury was once renowned for.

Friday started somewhat tentatively with a few hours sat round at home before Squirrel, G Man and Ricky Organ departed to head into town, leaving Hopalong in sole control of the baby. First stop was Font, for some hip hop, before heading on to the Attic, where it appeared that a few scallies had put on a night at the equivalent of the local youth club. It was quickly decided that this wasn't to be the destination for the evening, and so the move was made to go to Subspace for Northern Funk, stopping on the way to pick up (in true cheapskate style) some discarded flyers off the street to enable half price entry.

It didn't take long to hit the dance floor, where once again G Man was up to his normal training techniques, as he singled out his latest victim, a split second intervention from Ricky Organ saw the prey escape as if by teleporter, but G Man was not to be denied this time, and by sheer persistence, and the nightclub equivalent of Chinese water torture, did manage to get off with her by the end of the night, despite the fact she was a lesbian doctor with the highly unlikely name of Nada. After closing time it was off to the casino (Viva Las Vegas) where both Ricky Organ and G Man came away up on the evening, before heading to McDonalds for food.

Saturday morning saw Squirrel off to the record fair, and a hefty dent to his bank account, meanwhile Mummy and Daddy G took G Man out for lunch. Ricky Organ was picked up by the current love of his life and spent the day with her. After an afternoon of lounging watching football, Squirrel, G Man and Hopalong went out in search of somewhere to play pool, and after taking Hopalong on what he claimed was his longest walk of 2003 they arrived at Ye Olde Cock Inn, only to find that their pool table was out of order. After a few quite rapid drinks it was decided that a move to a venue with pool tables might be in order, and so another journey was started, but this time the use of a bus or taxi was required, as they made their way to the Golden Lion, where they did indeed find pool tables, and proceeded to play pool for the remainder of the evening, before leaving the venue and getting food from next door.

Despite the fact that it was only a reasonably short walk home, Hopalong insisted on getting a taxi, and therefore an hour later they eventually got home via the cash point and garage where Hopalong had to get tabs, after abusing and harassing every one he came in contact with trying to get cigarettes, including one bloke in the take away who had a top with loads of what looked like scout badges on, and one of which G Man insisted was a tab smoking badge.

Sunday saw very little motion, apart from some darts, and goggle box watching, with the only real motion of the day being Dylan moving into a new flat, twenty seconds from the Friendship, and sharing with one other bloke and six women, and Ricky Organ springing into action when Chez Didsbury extensive grounds got invaded by four young scallies, and shouting at them, and scaring them so much that one fell over. Whether he would have been the same if it were older scallies is debateable.

Monday was much the same, as was Tuesday, with only Ricky Organ breaking the trend by going out with his beloved again, and when he got back going for a cosy chat, which prevented any of the other residents of Chez Didsbury having an early night, as they didn't want to overhear his cosy chat. Yet again more of the same on Wednesday and Thursday

Squirrel managed to find his lost phone after a few days. It wasn't in the fridge for a change, but in another jacket on silent – Tit!

And an announcement.

To all the females who seem to have lost their minds this week, just two minor things that need pointing out. 1. Justin Timberlake has not rung you, doesn't have your number, and will never ever ring you. 2. Justin Timberlake is not your boyfriend, does not know who you are, and will never be your boyfriend. So get a grip, and stop talking utter shite in pubs, as that is the role of the residents of Chez Didsbury.

And from the letters page.

Several readers wrote with connection to the "Boy who cried fire" story last week. First it must be said that most of the story was factual, with only the last couple of paragraphs made up, and that the man in question G Man, also managed to have an imaginary bomb scare at the Aquatics Centre on Thursday evening. Secondly, it was mentioned that the story seemed a bit morose with the deaths at the end. Squirrel would like to say that fire is an extremely serious subject kiddiewinks and should not be treated lightly. Fire kills, normally by burning, so watching out for fire is important, however making up instances of fire is not good form, and should be frowned upon and ridiculed.

Paul Hardcastle Issue

The first thing to do is to update the end of last week, as Thursday saw the majority of Chez Didsbury being busy little bastards. Squirrel finished work late and wandered home to relax and watch football, to find the house deserted. He had been offered the chance to meet up with Hopalong in Squirrels at 5, but had declined, however G Man didn't and met up with Hopalong at 6. After many games of pool, quite a few beers and several tequilas, they wandered out into Wilmslow Road to get a kebab and start the long journey home, however, they got distracted and were enticed into going to Robinski's, where more alcohol was consumed, and then another kebab before venturing home. Ricky Organ in the meantime had gone out with his work colleagues and ended up going to the Raymond Blanc restaurant and blowing £45 on a meal, before wandering home in the early hours of the morning.

G Man miraculously managed to make it in to work on the Friday, as did Ricky Organ, but Hopalong took full advantage of the day he'd booked off, by not getting up until mid-afternoon. Friday evening saw Hopalong and G Man taking it easy by not leaving the house, Ricky Organ spent the evening with his other half. Squirrel however was out straight from work, with Destroy, and they went to the Garrett to meet up with H (not the one from steps, as the Garrett would have been too far away from the village), who was having a leaving do. Various other people were out, and they were joined later by Sally. As the night went on, people left, leaving only Squirrel, Sally, Destroy, H and his other half to go to 5th Avenue. Destroy was hoping to meet some of the other Surerandomality celebrities, and was looking around for Hopalong and G Man, even though he didn't know what they looked like.

By two everyone had left 5th Avenue, Squirrel and Sally got a taxi back, and left Destroy waiting for his outside, it eventually turned up at half two, and he got home only to find that he hadn't got his flat keys, and he couldn't wake his flat mate. The tit then tried unsuccessfully to construct some form of makeshift tent in the back

137

yard, before giving up and walking to his dad's, where he arrived cold and tired at half four in the morning.

Saturday saw G Man up at the unearthly hour of half eight in the morning making smoothies, everyone else got up through the day, and went to the bookies, and then started watching the football. There was a brief excursion into town to buy a sit up bench, and then an evening doing very little.

Sunday saw more football watching, with Squirrel meeting Scottie in the Friendship to watch the games. Ricky Organ left Chez Didsbury in the afternoon for a few days, as he's off on another course. The usual disturbing Sunday night viewing was partaken in.

Monday evening was more football, and early nights all round, and Tuesday saw the same, though Hopalong and G Man did manage to have a couple of pints and a kebab on the way home.

Wednesday would have been the same except for the fact that Squirrel, G Man and Hopalong were at Old Trafford to watch the somewhat uninspiring war of the roses game, instead of being cocooned in front of the TV as normal.

Thursday saw Hopalong's last day in his current employment, and he celebrated the fact by going to the pub straight from work, and then by meeting up with Lamb later. Ricky Organ returned, after what he claimed felt like months, and G Man spent the entire evening sprucing up Chez Didsbury in time for the impending arrival of his fabled Swiss maid.

The Score

It's been another of those weeks, where it seems that lots has happened, yet at the same time it seems as if it's been quiet. After a week away Ricky Organ was back on Friday, but after a hectic week had to have the afternoon off so that he could get some sleep. The Quiet Man and The Chemist arrived in time to go out Friday evening, and whilst sitting around before going out, Ricky Organ started complaining about a painful wrist, cause unknown, though it is believed that rumours, saying that this, attached to his tiredness could be attributed to his participation in the national wanking championships, are in fact spurious, not genuine, and worth second prize.

Anyway digression is in play, Ricky Organ, The Quiet Man and The Chemist, along with Squirrel and G Man headed into town, and were planning to go straight to the (not so) Fab Café, however when they arrived, they found that they couldn't get in because there was a power problem. Somewhat strange, considering that the music was still blasting out, however it was clarified that the problem was behind the bar, so the five of them wandered off to see if they could find G Man's origins, and went in the Old Monkey, where the "Diamond" lager tasted more like coal rejected from a slag heap. After one, they went back to the not so Fab Café, where despite probably the worst cravings since giving up drinking, Squirrel managed (just) to stay on the soft drinks. After a few in there, next destination was called, and as they poured out into the street, only to be poured on by the weather, the nearby bright lights of the casino (Viva Las Vegas) served like a homing beacon. Twenty short minutes later they were on their way to Rusholme after Ricky Organ blew £190 on roulette and G Man had come out £30 up. Shezan for a curry, and then another taxi back to Chez Didsbury.

Saturday saw Squirrel up early to go out round second-hand shops. Meanwhile G Man was off to the airport to pick up his Swiss Miss, who he then took to Urbis. The evening saw Squirrel, Ricky Organ, The Quiet Man and The Chemist undecided what to do, so they went to Pizza Hut to feed and pass time, and where the ordering was reminiscent of a Two Ronnies sketch (the one with John Cleese). After this they came, and dismantled the bed and the tidying that G Man had spent so long sorting prior to his visitor's arrival. Then it was on to Fallowfield, with a brief stop in Squirrel's, before due to a process of elimination, a visit to XS, where they met Sally. A taxi back to Chez Didsbury followed, with loud music being on the agenda on arrival, waking the confused looking G Man, from his reconstructed bed. The Swiss Miss thought it strange that G Man didn't have an assembled bed when they got back. And he had to explain that his housemates though they were being funny in having dismantled the bed. Which she found funny. Meanwhile in Oldham, Blondie was starting off the violent women weekend, by punching some random bloke outside Liquid.

Sunday saw The Chemist and The Quiet Man returning home, and saw Hopalong making his first appearance back at Chez Didsbury since his last day at work on the Thursday. In the evening Ricky Organ had a visit from a workmate and her sister, and along with Squirrel decided it was a good idea to play darts. However his suspect throwing action, ("You throw like a faggot") suggested that it wasn't just his left wrist that was injured. Furthermore it was suggested that his moniker would be suited to a hairdresser. Later that night the violent women weekend continued with Garden breaking her fiancée's nose with a well-aimed head butt.

Monday and Tuesday saw the normal kind of inactivity weekdays bring.

Wednesday would have done, except the G Man and his Swiss miss went to Old Trafford to see the bore draw. Meanwhile Hopalong and Ricky Organ were on a mission to empty the baby of all its beers, and joined by the still teetotal Squirrel, went on a darts and poker playing marathon, which ended after a curry in the early hours of the morning.

G Man took his Swiss miss to Harrogate on the Thursday to meet the parents, Ricky Organ spent the evening with Plane, Hopalong went to college, and Squirrel went to visit his neighbours.

Just a brief note from Squirrel.

"I do not need to go to the fucking doctors! If I cough it is NOT a problem, and it is in fact perfectly normal, and the day I don't cough, you can rest assured that I will be at the doctor's asking why not."

The Key To The Door

Friday started early and ended late, seeing a well overdue return to the kind of carnage that legend had bestowed on the residents of Chez Didsbury. G Man returned mid-afternoon, after seeing off his Swiss miss at the airport. From a residency in Piccadilly Gardens with the illegal immigrants and cider drinkers, he contacted the other residents of Chez Didsbury, inviting them to an early start. Hopalong was the first to pick up the gauntlet thrown down, and a 5pm start in the Friendship got things underway.

By the time Squirrel got there at 7, they had already been joined by Lamb and Pecs (G Man's ex), plus the twat in the hat (nothing to do with Jamiroquai). It was obvious from early on that it was going to get messy. It was also obvious that Lamb didn't want to be there, and would have preferred to be at home watching comic relief. Ricky Organ and Plane joined the throng at about half nine, and shortly afterwards Hopalong and Lamb went for food. Whilst they were gone Sally and Geezer turned up. Geezer had been drinking since midday, as even a half-drunk midget monkey could have told, and G Man did notice. Hopalong returned to the fray alone after a slight domestic, with the intention of going home, something he was talked out of by G Man and Pecs.

Geezer went home before time with the somewhat lame excuse of study the next day (and she's not a student), and after an hour of musical chairs and wandering aimlessly around, a move was made to go to the next pub. On the way the crowd lost the twat in the hat (and his mate baldy, who had turned up at some stage), and Hopalong had gone to try and resolve his differences with Lamb.

This left Squirrel, G Man, Ricky Organ, Plane, Sally, and Pecs going into XS. Hopalong arrived not long after negotiations for peace had been unsuccessful. Squirrel, Sally, and Plane danced, G Man and Pecs got reacquainted with tonsil hockey, and Ricky Organ and Hopalong reacquainted themselves with the quiz machine. Sally left just before last orders, and the remaining six were finishing off, when all hell broke loose, with a shower of glasses and bottles in the bar, and a stabbing. Upon their hasty departure, Squirrel went to get food, and the other five got a taxi back to Chez Didsbury.

Squirrel after wandering home, and sending random text messages, got in just after 3 and settled down to watch MTV, assuming everyone was in bed. He was therefore amazed when the door went at just after 4 and G Man and Hopalong came in. Pecs had gone home after the Olympic training had suddenly kicked in again for G Man. Hopalong had suggested going for a curry and off they went. Pecs meanwhile had had a somewhat disturbing journey home, after flagging down what turned out was a private car, the driver wasn't quite sane, and took her phone off her and drove her to a random location, saying he was teaching her a lesson. He let her get out of the car, gave her phone back and drove off.

Saturday saw Ricky Organ off home for a family party, and Hopalong eventually sober enough to go round to Lamb's at 5. Meanwhile Squirrel just stayed in bed until twenty to seven. Squirrel and G Man had every intention of staying in, and doing nothing, but as happens so often, someone mentions the word out, and off they go, this time it was their neighbours Asset and new resident Ginger Ninja, who managed to get his monicker changed in less than one paragraph to become Mogodon Man. A few quiet drinks in Didsbury was the plan, but, due to repeated anecdotes from Mogodon Man, a louder destination was needed, and despite the previous night's violence they ended up in XS, where they met with Sally and Geezer. G Man added another string to his bow of impressive accomplishments, by managing to bore Asset into falling asleep, by talking non-stop for over an hour, a feat made even more impressive by the fact that Ginger Ninja wasn't speaking, just wandering aimlessly around XS so that everyone could laugh at the ginger hair / Hawaiian shirt combination. On leaving it was Abdul's for food and a taxi back, where Asset just managed to negotiate the short walk to her front door.

Sunday saw lounging, football, both playing and watching, pizza and films. Monday had more fun and games. Hopalong had a G Man-esque imaginary vision, where whilst at Lamb's he saw a fight outside the window, and rang the police, of course when the police turned up, there was no sign of any one or any trouble in the street. This is however thought to be more plausible than the great fire of Burnage story. Squirrel went out walking, and returned to a locked house, fortunately the remaining residents had failed to bolt both the back doors and he found his way in, however whilst out they had taken control of his phone and sent out random text messages. Ricky Organ got his air pistol out and was going to go in the back garden when Squirrel's phone beeped, he read the message and then went to the source, who happened to be Asset from next door. It was while there, he found out that his phone had been used to send out random messages, He returned to find the doors locked again, and couldn't be arsed to piss about and proceeded to shoulder barge the door, which prompted the rapid unlocking of it. Squirrel went off on one as he felt that his phone being in his pockets, meant it was out of bounds, as it wasn't that he'd left it lying around in the open.

Tuesday saw moping about the house and an attempt to watch the football, and Garden had a mega domestic.

Wednesday saw Hopalong off to Oakham and Rockingham with Lamb for the weekend, allegedly to do with motor racing, but with the box having a Blue week, we know that he's really gone away so that he can watch the Blue week in peace. Garden became a one-night temporary resident of Chez Didsbury, and Squirrel did one of his patented can't be arsed to moved so sleep on the sofa with the tv on (oh and by the way Arsenal lost, ha ha ha! Ricky Organ is gutted).

Thursday saw more football watching, and Ricky Organ having Plane in his room. Squirrel has got to the end of the week, but still hasn't done anything, fucking sissy. EDITOR'S NOTE: Not quite sure what Squirrel was supposed to be doing, but it is likely to have been asking Asset out on a date – something he never actually got around to.

The Two Little Ducks

It's been a return to the old school this week, with the near on three months teetotalism by Squirrel had a weekend's break of tip top drunkenness. After a bombardment to drink on Saturday on work's night out for Blondie's birthday, he finally cracked at 8.45 Friday evening, and had the first taste of that sweet Stella he had been missing all year. What was going to be a quiet night in soon descended into carnage. After a couple of cans with G Man, they got Asset to come out, and managed to tempt Ricky Organ and Plane to come out, instead of the quiet night in they had planned.

A swift walk into Didsbury for one in The Dog and Partridge, was followed by a taxi to Big Hands (Small inside). Several rapid beers suddenly had the night at after 1pm. Ricky Organ and Plane left not long afterwards. At about the same time Squirrel and G Man's memory of night's events went as well. Only reports from Asset can indicate what happened after that (and she's well pleased to say that she was the most sober after going drinking with Squirrel and G Man).

Squirrel was bored to sleep by G Man (second week on the trot as mogodon man, he's certainly after Mogodon Man's title). They were the last to leave Big Hands, after some not so gentle persuasion by the door staff. Next door into Abduls, where a spot of late-night WWE Pissed as fuck took place, before a taxi home, with Squirrel singing G Man's theme tune (I wish I was a little bit taller) all the way home. Squirrel fell asleep, and G Man disappeared, leaving Asset to her own devices, which involved surrounding Squirrel with every sauce bottle in Chez Didsbury, before getting bored and going home.

Saturday saw Mummy and Daddy G arriving to pick up G Man to go to football, and dropping a TV off, neither of which he was really prepared for. In the afternoon Gopher and Gory arrived for a visit before their morning flight off to Andorra, and along with Squirrel and G Man were in the Clock Tower at 5. Me Laird travelled over from his country estate to join them. Squirrel and Me Laird then went to The Moon Under Water to meet up With Garden and Blondie, and her mate also called Blondie. G Man, Gopher and Gory (The three G's) arrived too late to share the champagne. On to the Hogshead for a swift drink, before heading for Teasers. Lots more drinking, a little dancing, some armpit licking, was followed by some puking by Garden which led to her ejection.

At the same time Blondie (number 2) was puking in the toilets. Everyone left in separate parties, though Squirrel, Garden, Me Laird and the 3 G's all met up on the way to the bus stop for the journey back to Chez Didsbury. G Man managed one of the longest and loudest Bgerks in history on to Ricky Organ's answer phone. It was so good that people were coming downstairs to see what was happening. A Kebab, and a taxi journey followed before a rendition of that all-time favourite Gold. Snatch was the nights recommended movie. Gopher and Gory managed to get out of the house at 6.30 to go to the airport, only to find their flight delayed and an extended stay at the airport. Me Laird and Garden left before 11, and to finish the weekend off, there was a dirty fry up.

The afternoon saw Frisbee, football, and throwing the pan up the tree, which managed to get a reasonable sized audience from the surrounding properties. Whilst playing football they had managed to get the ball stuck up the top of a bushy spruce tree in the garden. To try and get it down they tried various ways. What stuck was putting the end of the washing line through the end of the frying pan handle and then using that to spin around to get momentum before launching it up the tree. This continued for a considerable amount of time with no success before G Man dressed up in Squirrel's puffer jacket, ski gloves and ski goggles, a scarf around the rest of his face and a hat on to climb the tree to get the ball down and end the general entertainment for the rest of the neighbours. Hopalong came back from his Rutland experience, to find out he'd missed a Squirrel on the piss weekend. After the usual nasty Sunday night DVD, it was back to work. Well for most people it was, but G Man was feeling the aftereffects of the weekend and had to have two Hawk days. The rest of the week was comprised of watching football, films, and early nights.

The Tropics

As if Squirrel was going to let everyone get away with last weekend's shenanigans. He just like to make them sweat, but he made a small concession, in that the names were changed to protect the innocent (or the not so innocent in some cases), that and just to confuse the fuck out of everybody, but for this version they've all been converted back.

Friday arrived with Squirrel meeting up with Sally in XS, and within half an hour the no drinking resolution had flown the coup, not much after that they met up with G Man, Ricky Organ, Asset and Plane in Karma. Hopalong couldn't be tempted into coming out, and was spending a quiet night in with Lamb. The party posse moved on to Something Blu, and sat somewhat sedately having respectable conversation, this ended with the return to XS.

After a couple of drinks, Ricky Organ, much to the general distain of Plane, insisted it was time to go, and things started taking off from there. Asset kicked things off by getting a round of Tequilas in, which was quickly followed by G Man suggesting to Squirrel that they get a dirty round in, Tequila, Reef and Stella fitted the bill, and the down in one phase of the evening started. More of everything continued, until the phase, just before kicking out time when G Man and Asset were spotted on the dance floor playing tonsil hockey, the journey home was by the mystical beer scooter taxi, and once back at Chez Didsbury Squirrel fell asleep, G Man and Asset went to his room, but Asset had the first puking session of the night. Sally joined them and was sat on the bed with Asset, while G Man did his best impression of a worm and crawled to the bathroom to commence his puking. When he crawled back Sally and Asset were kissing on his bed (which by some accounts may have been a one-way thing due to Asset's coma), and there was an indication that a threesome could be in order, but the G Man couldn't drag himself off the floor and lay on a pile of Sally's clothes moaning.

During one of his regular crawls to the bathroom, Plane came out of Ricky Organ's room in a distressed state bemoaning the fact that Ricky Organ had dozed off whilst on the receiving end of fellacio.

AGAIN. Sally helped G Man to the bathroom again, where he sat on the toilet, head over sink not knowing whether he wanted to shit or puke. They helped him back to his room where they put him on his bed next to Asset, but he promptly proceeded to fall off, and when asked was he OK, replied with the words, "Yes, I'm just not sure about the colour". While he crawled round his room, Sally crashed out on Squirrel's bed. G Man woke from his daze briefly at some stage, went to get in his bed only to find Asset already in it, so he went and slept on the couch.

Asset woke at 6.30 wondering where she was, and made the long journey home to next door. Saturday saw shopping in town, before Ricky Organ made a move to have a Cheshire set weekend. After Squirrel and Hopalong had drank through the piss poor football, they finally got G Man drinking again in the Golden Lion, where after a few games of pool and pints, they moved into town, and met up with Asset and the rest of the neighbours in Font. After getting bored of waiting to get into Friends and Family, (and after Hopalong had ripped shit out of the Ginger Ninja world champion and his shirt) and they headed to 5th Avenue.

By some miraculous chance they had managed to avoid going into the casino (Viva Las Vegas) despite walking straight past it. After a large amount of alcohol in a not very long period, things started to get hazy. Squirrel, G Man, and Hopalong all managed to leave at different times, but then got the same taxi to Fallowfield, where they all split up again, with Hopalong going round to Lamb's, G Man going straight back to Chez Didsbury, where he arrived not long after Ricky Organ and Plane who had spent the evening with the Cheshire set in Jabez. Squirrel managed to make a diversion via West Didsbury and a Kebab shop before arriving back at Chez Didsbury just after 5, after dozing he eventually made it to bed at 10am.

Sunday saw Ricky Organ out with the Cheshire set again, and G Man and Squirrel started on a mammoth disturbing DVD watch, Asset came round for an hour still trying to piece together Friday's events. The week saw everyone doing the normal lounging, watching sport and films, playing poker, making smoothies, pretending to exercise, and generally talking shit. Some things never change. Including Ricky Organ's shopping habits, as he was spotted coming back from the Trafford centre on Thursday evening with a tight-fitting beige cardigan.

The Hours

The events

No. Honestly, that's it, it really has been that quiet, some people didn't even leave Chez Didsbury, although there was a text message suggesting a trip to the casino (Viva Las Vegas) but that was it.

Me Laird's Addition to Surerandomality The Hours

Good morning/afternoon/evening folks; I appreciate it has been quite some time since this particular correspondent has been in touch, forgive me for the lack of effort but, in truth, I couldn't be arsed!

Anyway, seen as though last week was such a sham misery for the occupants of Chez Didsbury, I thought I might try and recount my past couple of weeks since the random evening arranged at short notice with Squirrel (+ vomiting others).

Well, fair to say I have been keeping some of the fine old Surren' traditions going, some clever soul has opened a new 'gentleman's' club near to my favourite Casino (Viva Las Vegas!), suffice to say that a quiet meal in Napoleons (Viva Las Vegas) is now considerably more expensive especially seen as though my recently acquired significant other (amazing what you can get on the internet nowadays) also seems to enjoy going in if only because people seem to keep buying her drinks and attempting to outbid each other for a private dance with her! [To the best of my knowledge her new car was purchased from her legitimate living as a Meteorologist **if you ever meet her, please do not make my life impossible by referring to her as a weather girl, she IS meteorologist (or whatever the word is), although girl is more in keeping with her penchant for Prada handbags!**]

Other than trips into town, the local watering hole had, up until last night, become a fairly safe refuge. Unfortunately, last night saw some underhand shenanigans from yours truly to beat the sad old bastards that always win the music quiz, many thanks to Squirrel for his

149

help via text, and I would also like to pass on my thanks to www.ask.co.uk for the couple of answers I got via WAP!!! Anyway, the £90 was returned under the threat of a lifetime ban and having to cook meals for myself in future!

I think that's enough from me, apart from a complaint regarding the joke in The Hours regarding the lady who had her vanetians refurbished, this is one of my ALL-TIME jokes and the woman concerned is actually Joan Collins, makes the punch line a little funnier.

Anyway, week ahead holds, unfortunately, 2 days in Ardrossan for me, if you don't know where Ardrossan is then look up "Armpit of Scotland" in a dictionary, you will see that Ardrossan is referred to as a "puss ridden boil, just below the Armpit of Scotland".

Oh yea, for the of you attending the Surren' night out on the 25th, please bear in mind that I have RESERVED the sofa at Chez Didsbury, I am not too sure about 5th Avenue unless Hopalong plans on making an appearance, although given the wholehearted attempt at a pincer vomiting movement in Teasers the other week it may be wise for me to avoid the place for a while.

Remember, you don't need a smoking gun to justify decisions, just guns and smoke is fine, if they are within a few miles of each other then all the better.

there now follows two random text messages received in the last 24 hours....

I was nervous at first.... It was big and long and went straight up!..... I had to try it.... I eased myself onto it.... I LIKED it!!...I went up and down on it until my back and legs ached.... I LOVE ESCALATORS!!!!!

Two blokes stood at the urinals in New Union, one looks down and sees the other has a nicorette patch on his cock..."Does that work" he enquires "Sure does" the gentleman replies "I'm down to TWO BUTTS a day"

.... goodnight....

150

The Easter EggStravaganza

It's been another weekend of carnage, without any time available to save your breath to cool your pies. It has been tip top, and unplanned and unscripted. Friday saw Ricky Organ off to China for some time, only no one can remember how long for after this weekend. Squirrel had the intention of doing nothing, BUT with G Man and Hopalong playing Hawk, it drove him to raid the baby and get a beer. This led to several more beers, before a mini road trip, through 3 Didsbury pubs, and a torturous bus journey into town.

The dirty, cheap, and cheerful venue of 5th Avenue called, and as expected things got messy early on. Twenty vodka and red roosters each, along with numerous bottles, meant that the time space continuum failed and before they knew it, it was after 3, and they were outside arguing the toss over whether to go to the casino (Viva Las Vegas) or not. Squirrel opted for the taxi journey home, leaving G Man and Hopalong to raid the casino (Viva Las Vegas) and for once in his life Hopalong came home with over £300, and no it wasn't straight out of the cash machine.

After a short sleeping spell, fried breakfast was conjured up, and the football was put on. With absolutely no need whatsoever Squirrel started the half bottle of Bacardi, and within an hour the beers were flowing, however this did lead to the unfortunate affliction of Squirrel spending the rest of the day speaking in Pikey, much to the annoyment of G Man and Hopalong. After two proper and one Portuguese shower, they went out, with a brief stop at the co-op to totally embarrass Hopalong, they went to check out their local, the somewhat strangely named (for the time of year) The Sun in September.

After persuading the G Man that continued drinking was a good idea, they got a taxi to Scubar, where they managed to consume three goldfish bowls, before moving on again to Jabez, this time having to physically move G Man past the bus stop to prevent his escape home. Lots more alcohol followed with Squirrel going on a run of drinking five consecutive pints of Stella in the down in one mode. Dancing until getting kicked out they staggered to the bus, where some random woman got on the bus and started sucking the face off the G Man, and then got off the bus. Kebab and taxi followed.

Sunday saw Hopalong off to visit his gran in hospital in a somewhat worse for wear state, which prevented coherent speech and actions. Squirrel and G Man did absolutely nothing apart from slob in front of the TV. Monday saw, somewhat surprisingly everyone managed to turn into work, BUT it did take its toll, with a very early night being taken by Hopalong, probably helped by Squirrel starting on the Jack Daniels on his arrival home from work, G Man also retired early, BUT Squirrel stayed up til the early hours and finished the bottle. The remainders of the week saw very little action, apart from loafing round the house and watching football. Strange that.

The Six-Month Anniversary Edition

Somewhat of an extended week this week, starting with Squirrel, G Man and Hopalong watching the Arsenal Vs Man Unt game, and Hopalong trying to empty the baby. Garden arrived shortly after G Man had gone to bed for an extended temporary stay at Chez Didsbury. (Ricky Organ is still in SARS stricken China.) Thursday saw Squirrel and Hopalong taking it easy doing not a lot, but with the holidays coming G Man went out with Asset, Palindrome and Jack, for a few quiet drinks in Didsbury, however, as is normally the case things got out of hand quite rapidly, XS beckoned and a weed deal followed, which left G Man leaving his neighbours in the early hours, and the door open. Once back in the safe confines of Chez Didsbury he proceeded to look suspiciously at the crutches in the corner (that did have a tablecloth on top of them) as if they were another person, before asking Squirrel how many people were in the room, before disappearing off to puke again.

Friday saw Hopalong off for the weekend to sunny Swindon, and G Man and Squirrel doing absolutely nothing.

Saturday morning saw breakfast in Didsbury with Garden and Chip, before another day of lounging doing nothing, before being persuaded to go out into town. Garden went to her cousin's hen party, while Squirrel and G Man had a few quiet ones in Sinclair's Oyster Bar, before meeting up with Garden to go to Walkabout. Stella's, VB's, Vodka and Cokes, Wine, and Tequila followed. G Man pulled, but this was somewhat tarnished by repeated clarification of her name, plus on a visit to the bar he tried chatting up the barmaid and the girl was stood next to him. Therefore it was of no surprise when she refused his invitation for an assignation in the toilets. She did take his number, after he had to ask Squirrel what it was. The casino (Viva Las Vegas) followed for G Man and Garden, but Squirrel wasn't having any of it and hid behind a telephone box to prevent conscription. Therefore after losing (only £20) G Man and Garden were somewhat surprised to find themselves at home before Squirrel, who had stopped somewhere for food.

Sunday brought about a promise of lounging, but no football forced G Man into putting his CDs into alphabetical order (oh, and generally tidying his room), whilst Squirrel went to the Friendship, where he bumped into Sally, and met up with Kissme, her house mate Vek, Garden, and Chip. Various other prior arrangements meant that only Squirrel, Kissme and Vek were left in the pub at closing time.

Monday really did see some serious lounging time and lots of football watching, and the normal attempt at a Sunday night film (yes it was Monday, but we're not going to quibble over minor details such as that). Hopalong arrived home, with Lamb in tow, and immediately disappeared to his room.

Tuesday saw back to work for most, but Sally came round to see Squirrel during the afternoon, and the evening saw G Man and Hopalong meeting straight from work in the Parrs Wood, for a few quiet ones and a few games of pool. Squirrel met them later, but decided that soft drinks was the sensible option. Garden arrived later, and before closing time Squirrel and Garden decided it was home time. However Hopalong and G Man saw going drinking in town as the sensible option, and off they went. Unsurprisingly they found themselves in the casino (Viva Las Vegas), where contrary to their recent form both came up with reasonable wins, G Man £40, and Hopalong somewhere in the region of £2-300, however due to a shoe defect, G Man spent most of the evening walking and talking like a pimp.

Wednesday, however, they paid for this, and despite getting an early morning call from Squirrel neither of them made it into work. Both went for the two days are more convincing than one route of illnesses and had Thursday off as well with some decidedly spurious excuses. Wednesday night saw everyone watching the masterpiece game of football that was Man Unt Vs Real Madrid.

Thursday morning, saw Blondie in demand from Galaxy 102, where after an e mail to them the previous week in response to the "What would you give up to get tickets for Justin Timberlake?" competition their breakfast show was running, had said she would give up her job, led to her being on the air. After giving initial details and agreeing to hand in her notice live on air, she was live on air, telling the boss various, Nicksy prompted, things. First of all demanding four weeks paid holiday immediately. Then onto calling her an orange faced madam, then a bag, then Saddam Hussein, then the piece de la resistance, "You can stick this job up your arse, Justin Timberlake is more important than you, so stuff your job." It must be said that her boss played her part quite well being in on the situation. Then after an agonising twenty-minute wait, Blondie was back on air to be asked what had happened, to which she replied I've just been sacked, brought about the words Blondie and Spiderwoman wanted to hear, "You've just won Justin Timberlake tickets." Cue absolute fucking pandemonium. Basically anything after that was flat. Just one note, the entire recordings of Blondie on air will be available on the web site as soon as possible, at www dot Blondie makes a goon of herself dot com.

The Bank Holiday Bonanza Edition

Where to start this week? Well it's best to rewind to the early hours of Easter Monday to point out that Hopalong managed to puke into the cupped hands, and all down the front of his girlfriend while staying in Swindon, it might explain his absence from most of the action this week. Of course, of course, everyone knows that you came here to open the box and see what happened on the first ever Surerandomality night out, and therefore let's get down to business.

Hopalong had skived off work again and was hiding out at Lamb's house in the fear he may be dragged out. So, the only two residents of Chez Didsbury still in residence, Squirrel, and G Man, aided by the visiting Me Laird, started on the Stellas early. Squirrel and Me Laird, joined by Morning, got the first taxi to Scubar to start the proper drinking. By 9.30, everyone who was coming out had arrived in Scubar, giving a grand total of eighteen brave souls, they were: Squirrel, G Man, Me Laird, Morning, Garden, Blondie, Rah, Asset, Mogadon Man, Sally, Dylan, Lovelace, Shan, Kissme, Vek, Ven, Omi, and Ven (yes, a different person). Pints, wine, goldfish bowls, shooters, and champagne followed, some in copious amounts, before the first casualty of the evening was found to have disappeared home at 10 (Mogadon Man, so no great loss really).

The main party then set off to wind their way to 5th Avenue, but they had to make a stop at the cash point nearby, where, somewhat earlier than usual, the familiar tones of Gold were heard, much to the bemusement of anyone passing by. Shan, Kissme, Vek, Ven, Omi, and the other Ven had remained behind in Scubar, and except for Omi and Ven, stayed there for the remainder of the evening, before having to carry the seriously worse for wear Kissme home.

On the way to 5th Avenue, the party managed to temporarily lose Sally, Asset and Lovelace, to some unknown dodgy drinking establishment, but ploughed ahead relentless. Once inside, the vodka – red rooster combination kicked in, along with masses of various bottles, and the dance floor was hit virtually straight away. Sally, Asset and Lovelace caught up with the rest soon afterwards, and then Omi and

156

Ven arrived, but before Omi could continue, a puke stop was required. Lots of dancing and vast amounts of alcohol followed, interspersed with photos from funny angles. The first to leave 5th Avenue was Me Laird, who headed off back to Chez Didsbury with Squirrel's keys.

However, he didn't have the alarm code, and 20 minutes of the alarm going off followed, during which time phones calls were ignored (well, they couldn't be heard), and text messages were laughed at and then deleted. Squirrel managed to hit the deck twice in quick succession dancing to out of space, and Blondie managed to fall over at the top of the dance floor steps. Morning was the next to depart, feeling worse for wear, something that continued the next day, with a near all day puking bout. Blondie and Rah headed off to Sankey's, though not for very long. Sally, who had spent most of the evening being chatted up by one of the bouncers, disappeared at some stage, before Squirrel, G Man, Garden and Asset got a taxi back to Chez Didsbury, leaving only Dylan and Lovelace in 5th Avenue, where they were til the end cos Dylan managed to lose his cloakroom ticket.

Back at Chez Didsbury, Squirrel wouldn't behave, at all. Jumping round the house, shouting "Sip Bacardi like it's your birthday" and generally being a pain in the arse, before going out for a walk. Meanwhile G Man and Asset were laughing on the floor in one of the rooms, before heading next door for the night. Garden went to bed and Squirrel returned to occupy his favourite sofa.

Saturday morning brought fun and games, as Squirrel crawled off the sofa in search of other people. Garden was asleep in bed, but was the only other person in Chez Didsbury. Me Laird had left at about ten, and G Man was still next door. A quick role call got things moving again, and G Man poured vodka shots at midday, which everyone refused except Squirrel. A lift into town with Asset from Garden, led to more mayhem. After dropping the camera in from the night before, Squirrel and G Man moved to Sinclair's Oyster Bar, for a couple of breakfast beers. Then it was shop, pub (pint & tequila shot), shop, pub (Stella and double JD's), then strolling up to the Train station in T shirts and sunglasses in the pouring rain, singing "Cos I Got It Like That", and getting strange looks from everyone they passed, who were trying to get out of the rain.

They later found out that they had narrowly avoided bumping into Mummy and Daddy G, who were on an unexpected visit to Manchester. Back at Chez Didsbury, the Vodka came out again, along with bottles of Stella, as they tried to persuade Hopalong to come out drinking. Hopalong was going out for a meal, but his departure was hurried along by Squirrel and G Man attacking the vodka with such gusto. Then at 7.30 disaster struck, after a vodka and Red Rooster, G Man came to an abrupt and alcoholic stop, and refused to move, not even the taking of his phone could persuade him to move.

So Squirrel headed to the Friendship, knowing that Dylan was out. Also out was his girlfriend Lyem and several of her friends. One of them mentioned that they were going to go to friends and family at the Roadhouse, so Squirrel got himself invited, as Dylan wasn't going anywhere due to the effects of the previous night, and being out drinking since one had caught up with him. So, Squirrel, El, Caz and Shiv went to Revolution, and then Glass, where some pissed up muppet came over to Squirrel and asked him whether he was Johnny Vegas, much to the obvious embarrassment of his girlfriend. Then to friends and family, before leaving at 2 for the long bus journey home, via a kebab shop. Garden meanwhile was also trying to get back to Chez Didsbury from work, but managed to get bumped on princess street, and then pulled by the police for being on the phone to Squirrel, ordering Kebab.

Sunday saw Squirrel get up with a bad back, probably caused by repeated falling on Friday, but not noticed due to the alcoholic anaesthetic that he'd been under since. G Man and Hopalong refused to leave the house, so Squirrel and Garden went to the Friendship for Sunday dinner and met up with Dylan, Lyem, El and Caz, all of whom started the afternoon off on soft drinks. Despite protestations to the contrary, Squirrel finally cracked just before 4 and had a Stella. They were joined briefly by Kissme, who was still feeling the effects of Friday. When the football finished Squirrel got a lift back to Chez Didsbury, and Garden went back home for the first time in ages. It must be said that for the remainder of the week, Chez Didsbury could hardly be called a hive of activity. So much so that there were stages where the residents couldn't even be bothered to get up and turn the lights on, and so sat in the dark.

Amazingly everyone made it to work on Monday, and G Man went down to London for a course. Ricky Organ arrived back in the country and is currently serving a 10-day quarantine from work, to preventing him from possibly passing on any SARS bugs he managed to catch in China. So, although he is back, he hasn't managed to make it back to Chez Didsbury yet. Rumours are that Thursday night might get messy, but Squirrel won't have time to update you on that this week, but if the casino (Viva Las Vegas) does beckon then it will be here next week.

The Days Later Edition

Again, where to start this week? Where else but last Thursday night, which missed being reported due to the sheer chaos, and the fact that there was somewhat of a blackout in the communication process, meaning the details filtered through too late to be included. Squirrel arrived home, and got ready to go in a rush, and he was joined by G Man in a drinking quest, Hopalong was hiding out at Lamb's to avoid being dragged out (again). After visits to the Dog and Partridge, Pear Tree, Slug and Lettuce, and XS, it was on to 5th Avenue again, where things really got messy. Armed with a fair amount of money, and all drinks being a pound, they managed to work their way through numerous rounds of double vodka and red bulls, and bottles of Stella down in the down in one style. At this point events started to lose focus, and have only been pieced together in the days since. On leaving 5th Avenue at about 1.30, a cash point and a taxi ride took place, and on their arrival back at chez Didsbury, they proceeded to open the tequila and drink from the bottle, Bgerk Hopalong, and play random shit on the stereo.

Focus returned at 8.30 the next morning where the constant ringing of the house phone prompted G Man to get up, and he woke up Squirrel, who realised he was late for work, he rushed dressed and stumbled to the bus stop, once in town, the unbelievable happened. Squirrel stood in St. Peter's Square and puked. It was by all accounts his worst state ever, as it turns out that at some stage during the night he had got up, and pissed on his bedside cabinet, shorting his alarm out, which was part of the reason he didn't wake up in time. He sat at work most of the day still pissed. G Man did find this amusing until he got up and found that he too had puked, using the bath as his target this time.

Destroy had taken the day off work to go to Alton Towers, and by all accounts had a fun time, so much so that once bevvied up, he thought it was a good idea to strip naked and streak, the only problem was that on redressing he seems to have lost his boxer shorts. Friday night saw Hopalong eager to go out, but Squirrel and G Man were having none of it, and they stayed in watching lots of videos. Hopalong however went out by himself, going to Squirrels and then onto the casino (Viva Las Vegas), where he spent the best part of 6 hours, getting himself to a position where he was £800 up. Most people would leave at this stage, but no, Hopalong had to keep going, and left the casino £50 down, fucking goon.

Saturday saw the return to Chez Didsbury of Ricky Organ, and by the time Squirrel had got back from work, all the residents were sat round drinking. Plane was also there, and they were joined by Sally, before getting a minibus round to Dylan 's for his housewarming party. After copious amounts of alcohol, and chatting to various people, the crowds of people there started to disperse, and just before 1 G Man, Hopalong, Ricky Organ and Plane were in a taxi heading off to the casino (Viva Las Vegas) again. By this stage there were only a few people left drinking at the party, and people were starting to crash out. Wes's missus, Lyem was one of the early casualties, going to bed at 11 complaining of feeling unwell. By about 3 Squirrel and Sally were crashing out on the sofa in Dylan's room, and Ricky Organ, who was £200 down, and Plane were just leaving the casino (Viva Las Vegas). On arrival back at Chez Didsbury they realised they didn't have keys, and tried ringing the rest of the residents to come home and let them in. G Man and Hopalong were in a no coverage zone, and Squirrel who had just dozed off, got up and moved to a sofa downstairs in Dylan 's house, point blank refused to come home and let them in, even after being offered the taxi fare to do so. G Man and Hopalong left the casino (Viva Las Vegas) at 4 when it shut, and were £100 and £400 up respectively at the time, despite the frantic efforts of Hopalong trying to place bets in panic when finding that it was about to close, and being refused. They arrived back at Chez Didsbury to find Ricky Organ and Plane christening the porch. The two of them stayed up drinking until it got light and then headed to the garage to get cigarettes and ask for donkey porn. On their way back they rang Squirrel, who once again disturbed from sleep moved to another sofa, while being in the process of being Bgerked.

Sunday saw a quiet day of relaxation in Chez Didsbury, with a new temporary resident arriving in the form of Melvin, who was going to be starting temporary work at Astra Zeneca. Meanwhile, Dylan woke up in his bed with Lyem, and somewhat surprisingly Sally, who it turns out was there before him. After dragging himself off the sofa Squirrel joined him in wandering around the house. Cans of Red Stripe beckoned, and whilst Squirrel and Dylan attempted to cook breakfast sausages on the barbeque, they started on the beer, much to the obvious disgust of the rest of the party goers that were getting up and trying to pull themselves together. They then sat in the lounge drinking beers with fluorescent Velcro hats on, with felt balls stuck to them. Geezer came to pick Sally up, and most of the party goers left. After a couple of hours of Lyem puking and pulling herself together Dylan and Squirrel headed to the Friendship for Sunday lunch and to watch the football. Once that was finished, they headed to Squirrels for more beers and some games of pool, by this stage Dylan was feeling the effects, and a taxi to the Metropolitan in Didsbury to meet up with Lyem and some of her friends. On last orders, everyone headed home, with Lyem having to help Dylan to get home. Squirrel stopped for a kebab and wandered back to Chez Didsbury, where everyone else was watching Pulp Fiction.

Monday saw relaxing big style, Ricky Organ and Plane went down to London for the day, Hopalong went out to meet Lamb and her friend. Squirrel and G Man watched a film, before G Man met up with Hopalong to go to see X2, however it was sold out, so they ended up watching Welcome to Collingwood (which is a pile of shit by all accounts). Then back home, fajitas and doing sod all. Tuesday night saw Squirrel getting pissed off with the length of his hair, and the lack of opportunities to get to the hairdressers, and therefore shaved his own hair, thus leaving it at its natural colour, which is the first time most people have seen that. Not only that but we've found out that Radio has shaved his mullet off and is now sporting a number 1. Wednesday saw Ricky Organ at some celebration party to do with work, whilst everyone else relaxed, and this week, there were no Thursday night excursions.

The Superfortress

It would appear that there are grown adults (well perhaps that's stretching a point a bit, it is the residents of Chez Didsbury) who really shouldn't be allowed out without qualified supervision. It must be said that the portents of disaster were in evidence from an early stage on Friday. Squirrel was supposed to be meeting up with other residents in town straight from a late finish at work, and with Kissme, was going to be starting on the wine early. Things weren't going to plan elsewhere. G Man had sloped off early from work again, and had persuaded Hopalong to meet him for a quiet drink in the Parrswood.

It does need to be pointed out, that there has never previously been a quiet drink at the Parrswood, and tonight wasn't going to be an exception. Squirrel and Kissme, met Vek and Buster in Athenaeum (or however the fucking place is spelt), and then moved onto the Sawyers Arms. Vek had to puke, and went home (after two abortive bus journeys and a long walk) with Kissme. Squirrel meanwhile decided that XS hadn't been visited for quite a while and off he went. Once there he bumped into Sally, Dylan and Lyem, and found that G Man and Hopalong had moved from the Parrswood after Karaoke, and a mini lock in. After more mad Out of Space dancing by Squirrel and G Man, G Man and Hopalong headed to the casino (Viva Las Vegas) again. Everybody wandered off, leaving Squirrel by himself by chucking out time. After food he got home about three and crashed out, G Man got home just after 4, after losses of £100, and a failure to get Hopalong to leave the casino (Viva Las Vegas), even though he was £400 up.

Squirrel got up just before 8 on Saturday morning, to find Hopalong just coming back in. He had left the casino (Viva Las Vegas) at closing time £300 pounds down, despite being level quarter of an hour before. On his way home he decided it was a good idea to go and dump Lamb.

G Man and Hopalong started early on Saturday, by going for food, and ending up in the Clock Tower all day. Squirrel met Kissme in the Friendship, but Kissme had been drinking Whiskey since the morning, and was somewhat worse for wear. Dylan and Lyem arrived to watch Wolves. At half time Kissme had to go home, and after the match, Lyem went off to a party with friends. Ricky Organ was off roller skating with the Cheshire set with Plane and Melvin. Squirrel and Dylan went to Squirrels with the intention of playing pool, but with no free tables had a few pints and moved onto the Orange Grove, where they eventually played some pool and had some more pints.

On the bus journey to Jabez, Squirrel attempted to chat some random female up with little success. Meanwhile G Man and Hopalong were queuing to get into Tiger Tiger, but were getting bored, so walked up to the VIP entrance and confidently walked in, claiming they were with the girls in front. This being despite the fact they were in shorts, trainers, and t-shirts. Ricky Organ, Plane, Melvin, and the Cheshire set had more difficulties getting in, despite being suitably dressed, and were somewhat amazed to find G Man and Hopalong drinking champagne at the bar in the VIP area. In Jabez things were getting cloudy, and not long after Lyem and her friends turned up (though it could have been ages), Squirrel headed off for food, and went for a curry.

Once there he continued in the theme of the evening by trying to chat the two women on the next table up, and failing miserably. The mystical beer scooter then took him home. Meanwhile Hopalong was having a similarly unsuccessful time at Tiger Tiger, after losing G Man to another mystical beer scooter, he left at closing time and after trying to find his way home, and ending up at Victoria, decided the only way for him to get to Piccadilly Gardens would be to follow the Tram lines.

Sunday saw all the residents of Chez Didsbury, watching the final games of the premiership, before Hopalong left to go and repair things with Lamb. The evening saw the normal mix of smoothies and DVDs before the back to work slog.

Monday saw Hopalong off to Bracknell for a four-day course, and Squirrel off to Squirrel's to pick up the stuff he'd left there on Saturday. Back at Chez Didsbury it was DVD time again. Tuesday and Wednesday saw the usual lounging and watching football. Thursday saw Hopalong returning, and a planned excursion out by Squirrel and G Man, to meet the girls whose party they'd missed on the previous Friday. Whatever happened was too late for the deadline for this issue, but it's worth remembering that the last time this pairing went out on a Thursday night, it got very messy.

164

Me Laird's Addition To The Superfortress

Now then folks, Northeastern/West Coast of Scotland Update!!!

Actually not much to say, except for I RESERVE THE SOFA for the next night out and Sports Day. THIS TIME I intend on being one of the last home and, therefore, do not care if I know the alarm code or not [not that it ruffled many of my feathers last time].

I do have occasional pangs of guilt for having secured Hopalong's membership to the casino (Viva Las Vegas) for a random night out which I guess took place almost a year ago. Having said that, he does make me feel better about my own gambling misfortune, which usually run to being twenty quid down, gutted and walking home. Anyway, trust all are well, have yet to hear how the prospective SARS patient is doing so I guess he is fine in his tent in the back garden of chez Didsbury.

I would update everyone on my activities for the past few weeks, but to be quite honest they would probably bore even the most devout Methodist minister, this weekend does, however, promise to be a great deal messier as I am going to Amsterdam for the weekend, digital camera at the ready.

Finally, an appeal for information, you may remember a few weeks ago the 'TRUE' Blondie won tickets for Justin TrouserSnake's UK concert from Galaxy, I have been trying to get the DAB recording from them so we can all share this moment of Radio history but need the date the piece was broadcast to give the impish albino version of ook at galaxy a chance!!!! Answers on an e-mail please........

Keep smiling.... Me Laird

The Half A Crown

Thursday night, it got very messy. That was the prediction from last week's issue. How little did anyone know, and although the borderline was run it didn't quite descend into the realms of two weeks before. G Man's outstanding luck and resilience at work finally ran out, when he was called into the office by the Aussie BQFH that masqueraded as his boss, and was handed his marching orders for his dedication to slacking.

The evening saw Squirrel and G Man take a short train journey to Deansgate Locks and into Baa Bar, where they weren't the only black sheep there, as Howard Marks was sat in there drinking. With a shooter menu longer than that of Scubar, and bottles of Stella for only a quid, there was enormous potential for things to get messy quickly. But the arrival of Sop and Sallythree (yes folks, yet another Sally) did calm things somewhat, and they were able to get out, in a better shape than expected. It wouldn't have been a Thursday night without a visit to 5th Avenue, where the all drinks a pound should have kicked in, but strangely didn't. Sop and Sally found that 5th Avenue wasn't really their scene, and Squirrel and G Man left them for the dance floor as the first strains of Out Of Space were heard. Mad dancing didn't last long, as within thirty seconds Squirrel had slipped and hit the floor hard, damaging his knee, and taken out some random female in the process. The injury didn't stop him dancing, and at some stage Sop came onto the dance floor and led G Man away to a cosy corner somewhere. Some silly bitch nicked Squirrels sunglasses, which led to more drinking.

On closing Squirrel and G Man got a bus to Fallowfield for kebabs, after Sop and Sallythree had got a taxi. On arrival back at Chez Didsbury, a brief rendition of Gold was considered appropriate to celebrate their arrival home (after a Squirrel rendition of Straight Outta Compton on the bus to ward off scallys). Ricky Organ was still up and joined them in emptying the baby and making as much noise as possible before heading off to bed in the early (or should that be late) hours.

Friday saw Squirrel struggling to walk after the alcoholic anaesthetic wore off and the full extent of knee damage was found out.

The evening saw very little being done, except lounging and watching Tarantino films.

Saturday saw FA Cup final day, and first in the pub were Dylan, Lyem and Nat. Eventually Squirrel finally managed to pry G Man and Ricky Organ out into the rain (though both had to bring umbrellas) and they were the next to arrive. Melvin arrived just before kick-off, and then Radio, with shaved head and attempted goatee, turned up during the match, but left just after the final whistle. At about seven (ish) everyone left, which included Sther who had arrived at some stage, moved over to the Orange Grove to play pool.

Things got hazy from this point, and G Man and Sther disappeared back off to Chez Didsbury early. Ricky Organ took a short flight across the room, courtesy of a hip toss from Squirrel. Melvin decided to lose the plot and started calling everyone cocks, and then had a go at Lyem, at which point Dylan had to step in and threaten him, and Melvin and Ricky Organ left not long afterwards. On the way back to Chez Didsbury they nearly got involved in fights twice, once with a car full of scallys that they were baiting, and then with a taxi driver that Ricky Organ was poking with his umbrella.

Everyone else left the Orange Grove, leaving Squirrel asleep in the corner, when he woke up, he finished all available drinks, and moved over to XS, where it seems, somewhat surprisingly, that they have a dress code!! No jogging bottoms allowed. Unperturbed by this Squirrel went in anyway, where he bumped into Sally and Geezer, and had another nap, before being woken up by Sally as she was leaving. Food and a bus home followed.

Sunday morning saw Squirrel get up at the ungodly hour of eight, and was shortly joined by G Man and Sther (who someone reckons is from Kentucky!?). One by one the residents got up and just sat watching MTV, the last to rise was Ricky Organ, who looked rough as fuck after the previous night. Sther left just after midday, and while G Man was cooking breakfast it was mentioned to Ricky Organ that the paper had had a cup winners supplement in.

This had already been hidden to prevent him gloating about the fucking north London red scum winning. Squirrel, G Man, Hopalong and Ricky Organ took a trip to the Trafford centre after the GP, and then settled at home for an evening of film watching. During the evening

Ricky Organ became increasingly agitated about the missing supplement, and whined continuously for it to be given to him. Then after one of Squirrel's special chilli's, he became more childish, and kept changing the channel while Melvin, G Man and Squirrel were trying to watch a film, before completely throwing his toys out of his pram, and removing the main fuse from the fuse box, thus cutting power to the house, and continuing to whine about the supplement's whereabouts, whilst prodding people with a golf club.

Squirrel point blank refused to tell him, G Man got his guitar and started playing, Hopalong and Lamb nicked his passport, and all refused to give into his childish attempt at terrorist tactics. Squirrel had dumped the supplement out of the window of the downstairs bathroom, and it had fortuitously fallen into the sink outside as so couldn't be seen from any window or door. Melvin got his portable speakers and plugged them into a Sony Discman and so everyone was still listening to music, and candles were busted out, and so after a couple of hours Ricky Organ put the fuse back in, only to find that Squirrel still wouldn't tell him where the supplement was.

Hopalong and Lamb had taken the power cut as a sign they should eat all the ice cream in the freezer, and when the power was back on Hopalong called Ricky Organ a pussy for giving in and turning the power back on. So, as people went to bed Ricky Organ thought he's try carrying on annoying people and would slip his hand inside a door and turn other people's lights on. Only for Squirrel to use Ricky Organ's pellet gun, which had confiscated and hidden earlier, to fire at and hit Ricky Organ's hand as he reached for the light switch. And finally there was peace in the house.

The most important take away from the football at the weekend was that Dylan ended up finishing third overall in the Sun's fantasy football league and won himself ten grand in doing so.

Monday saw Ricky Organ off on another work trip, this time to Prague, and Melvin moved out of Chez Didsbury, and into a flat in Alderley Edge. G Man has been job hunting all week, Hopalong had Tuesday and Wednesday as study leave for accounting exams that he took on Thursday, and he was going out that night to celebrate Lamb's birthday which had been the day before. The week had seen lots of films, and a fair bit of football watched, and lots of lounging around, which was greatly appreciated after such a quiet weekend.

The Baskin Robbins

A quiet weekend would be somewhat of an understatement. Friday saw G Man join Hopalong, Lamb and one of her mates to see the Matrix Reloaded, in the meantime Squirrel started his weekend long sit in at Chez Didsbury, and started watching DVD's. After the film G Man returned to Chez Didsbury and Hopalong went to Lamb's. Meanwhile Kissme had gone drinking straight from work, and ended up at a Morrissey night at the Star and garter, where she ended up snogging some random bloke. Upon leaving in the early hours and a lot worse for wear, she rang Squirrel. An hour and a half later she finally managed to get into a taxi after wandering round aimlessly, with no idea where she was most of the time. During this time she was warned off by a prostitute who thought she was trying to muscle in on her patch, and was asked how much she charged by a random bloke passing by. She obviously must have had the look of a tart about her.

Saturday saw very little motion at Chez Didsbury, with the watching of football and films. Hopalong went out with Lamb and one of her childhood friends, and was subjected to an interview style evening.

Sunday was much the same, with the tedium being broken up by the return of Ricky Organ from Prague, armed with a bottle of potential messiness called Absinth.

Monday saw virtually no motion again, just more football and films.

Tuesday night saw Squirrel and Hopalong drinking at Chez Didsbury straight from work, and failing in their attempts to get G Man to join in, as he was claiming that with a job interview the next morning and a shopping trip with Mummy G, there was no way he could have faced the day with a hangover. A taxi to 5th Avenue brought about the shock of a lifetime, it was closed. As it would seem was most of town. Squirrel and Hopalong wandered up to Springbok for a few swift drinks, before going to Brannigans, for some expensive ones. With the impending Champions League final, most of the people in town were Italians.

On Brannigan's closure at 1 they wandered out to see where else was open, and were asked by an Italian where else was open to which Hopalong tactfully replied, "Dunno, everywhere seems to be closed, it must be because of all the foreigners." They did however manage to find somewhere else open – Teasers, where more expensive drinks were purchased. After leaving they got a bus back to Didsbury, where a dangerous precedent was set by them going into the open all hours Tesco's, before arriving back at Chez Didsbury to continue drinking.

Wednesday night saw Ricky Organ off on his travels again, this time to Chicago. Meanwhile the remaining residents cabbaged in front of the telly to watch the somewhat tedious Champions League final. Elsewhere Destroy was in the process of getting quite a shock. Entrusted with the task of keeping an eye on his dad's house whilst he was on holiday, he made a visit, and thought that the place had been burgled, due to the considerable number of smashed ornaments and mess around the house. He did however find the culprit and found there had been no burglary. In his previous flying visit, he had failed to notice that a crow had sneaked in, and he had locked the crow in the house. The crow was found dead at the top of the stairs, but had managed to find the strength before death to shit on the beds.

Thursday saw Squirrel and Kissme going out straight from work to meet Omi, but details from that aren't in yet, but it had the potential to get messy.

The Freezing Point

It started, as so many weeks' tales with another Thursday. Needless to say that a few drinks (as was the plan) got slightly out of hand. Squirrel and Kissme met up with Omi, straight from work in the Square Albert, and despite Omi going early, they continued drinking til chucking out time, and then headed to XS, where they met Comi and others, with Comi being the proud possessor of a baby Guinness fridge that he'd won earlier. Kissme left sometime after midnight, and Squirrel and Comi left at chucking out time.

Despite this both Squirrel and Kissme thought it would be a good idea to go out straight from work again on Friday, and met up with The Nolt, Vek and Ven to sit outside the Slug and Lettuce on Canal Street. The Nolt left to get his bus just before midnight, by which time Ven had stopped drinking, and Vek had been and puked. By midnight Kissme was in a state where she couldn't even speak, and after smashing a glass was led to get a taxi home. Having dropped Kissme and Vek off near home, Squirrel headed on to XS and when he arrived was greeted, with "Sorry mate, we're closed." Meaning they were full, in a repeat from a scene a couple of weeks earlier the response was "you are having a fucking laugh, aren't you?" Once in Squirrel bumped into Sally, and after a few more drinks, closing time arrived, they went for food and crashed at Sally's.

This did lead to Squirrel getting into town too late to pick up his new bank card, and eventually arriving back at Chez Didsbury mid-afternoon. The evening saw Squirrel, G Man, Hopalong and Lamb having a miniature barbeque in the garden, and a lounging night at home.

The next excursion by anyone from the house was Wednesday when Hopalong managed to tempt G Man into meeting him straight from work at the Parrs Wood, which normally gets messy, but it was restrained and they headed back to Chez Didsbury, where Hopalong continued drinking, and failed to get G Man to do the same, as he was off to an interview in the morning.

The Double Carpet

The second Surerandomality night out was a strange affair, with plenty of people out and about, but not necessarily in the same place at the same time. First out of the trap could have been Hopalong and G Man who met up at the Parrs Wood, just after them would have been Squirrel, who had a quick drink at the Paramount before meeting up with Kissme at the Peveril of the Peaks. Some of the more eagle eyed of the readers may notice that there appeared to be no food stop mentioned, and this comes into play. After a couple of swift drinks Squirrel and Kissme headed to Kro 2 where they met up with Ven and Onle, and somewhat later Vek. After a couple more drinks they headed off to Scubar, where over time they were joined by Hopalong, G Man, Dylan, and Lovelace. It's at this point that the lack of a food stop began to catch up with Squirrel, and his memory of events began to get hazy. After a few drinks he began to lose the plot and after chasing Kissme around the pub, and getting kicked in the bollocks by Hopalong, he stormed off, not to be seen for the rest of the night.

Not long after that Kissme, Ven and Onle headed off to town, and then for a curry, while Vek headed off home. G Man, Hopalong, Dylan and Lovelace headed to Jabez, meanwhile Squirrel was on the wrong bus and heading to West Didsbury, and therefore a long trek back to Chez Didsbury. In Jabez they met up with Sally and Geezer, and much drinking was done. Squirrel arrived back home in a bad mood, and Ricky Organ, who was having a quiet night in could get no sense out of him before he went to bed (fucking lightweight). In Jabez, Dylan and Lovelace seemed to be hitting it off, but Hopalong and G Man were getting bored and headed off into town to go to the Casino (Viva Las Vegas), where they met up with Asset, who had been out in town. As usual things got messy, G Man finished £110 up, whereas Hopalong and Asset were both losers, to the tune of £70 and £50, respectively. A taxi home followed, where Hopalong and G Man stayed up drinking until just after 6 in the morning before collapsing in heaps on various living room seating.

Saturday saw Squirrel up early to go to work, and G Man and Hopalong off into town at a ridiculously early hour to do pissed up shopping. While out they bought a barbeque and then spent the afternoon constructing it while lounging in the grounds of Chez Didsbury and drinking. The evening saw them heading off to Deansgate locks and the Fat Cat Café to meet up with another of those random females that G Man had met while travelling, in this case one called Less. After a few pints Less and her friends headed off to the Fab Café, whereas the Chez Didsbury residents were going to meet up with some of Ricky Organ's friends, they just didn't know where yet. As it turned out it was Via Fosa, and after spotting someone they went to school with G Man and Hopalong made a sharp exit and headed off to try and get into Fab Café.

This left Ricky Organ and Squirrel to meet up with Hary, Shan, Lene and others, and then after what seemed like about two days, they eventually moved on to meet up with everyone else in Fab Café. However there was a one in one out policy and when they rang G Man it turned out that him and Hopalong had moved to Walkabout, therefore Squirrel, Ricky Organ, Hary, Shan and Lene went to join them. After half an hour's fruitless searching for them, Squirrel got pissed off and went home (yet again lightweight behaviour). The rest never met up, and all left separately to go home. However Ricky Organ bumped into G Man in Subway, and then along with Hopalong headed to the casino (Viva Las Vegas). Again it got messy, and G Man was £60 down, Ricky Organ about the same, and they left having failed to drag Hopalong out, though he did leave 5 minutes later £200 down, but that wasn't the end of his losses for the evening. On the way home in the taxi he managed to lose his wallet, and thought he'd lost his Zippo (though this was found later in the week in bed).

Sunday saw the vast majority not wanting to do anything; however, this was destroyed when people started arriving at Chez Didsbury for an impromptu barbeque. Asset and Mogadon Man arrived from next door, and Ricky Organ arrived back with Ness, and then later Hary and Shan turned up, peace was returned by about ten, just in time to watch a DVD to end the weekend. The week didn't see much motion at all, with the normal lounging, and watching of football, and Squirrel showing signs that he must be an Irish squirrel, as he seems to want to hibernate during the summer, as he was in bed before half ten every night of the week, definite strange behaviour for the nocturnal one.

Quotes of the week started to be noted, and so will feature from now on.

Ricky Organ - Have you put on weight?
Squirrel - Yes Mate.
Ricky Organ - Doing what?
Squirrel - Absolutely fuck all.

Extra-Curricular activity.

This week saw an example of the editing that went into some issues of Surerandomality to protect the residents of Chez Didsbury from potentially irate other halves. Ness was an American woman who wasn't Plane (Ricky Organ's girlfriend). And it led to the regular chants of USA, USA, USA, a la the American Mosconi Cup team, in Ricky Organ's direction whenever Plane wasn't around.

The Selenium

Once again it was an early start on the Friday with Hopalong wangling a half day off, and being joined by G Man at lunchtime. After an extended spell at the Cock Inn, they moved to the Clock Tower, and then at half ten they staggered across the road to meet up with Squirrel, Ricky Organ, and Asset, who had only just managed to make it out, outside the Dog and Partridge. After last orders at the Dog, they went to get drinks from the Hogshead, but lost Hopalong and G Man along the way, but still managed to walk out with five pints of Hoegaarden in the special Hoegaarden vases, and proceeded to wander around Didsbury drinking them while trying to find the other two. Unsurprisingly they were found in the kebab shop, where upon leaving they bumped into Mad Dof, someone Hopalong and G Man knew from Harrogate, who proceeded to rip the shit out of them. Back to Chez Didsbury where some Stellas saw virtually everyone asleep in the living room.

Saturday saw the day of the Chez Didsbury Barbeque, and somewhat surprisingly it didn't rain. The visitors started arriving early, with Baby G, and Sargin the first ones to arrive, but not before the arrival of the bouncy castle war zone, complete with fugal sticks. This set up the start of a long day of violent fun, which saw some fierce rivalries taking place, and only one draw all day, in the can't be arsed match between Squirrel and G Man. Further guests arrived and the drinking started in earnest, with both Wen and Pugh (the cousins G) arriving, and Lem, Expire, another Ven, Asset (a different one), and Rory coming up from Bedford. The bouncy castle by now had become a large sun lounger, and football was being played, and still people were arriving. Lamb turned up, and shortly after so did Dylan, armed with Swingball, which turned out to be another half an hour fad. Late arrivals were Melvin, and then Garden. Food and drink were constantly on the go, and another bout of battle drome bouts broke out which were fuelled by alcohol.

Time flew as people were enjoying themselves, and it was soon time for the first victims to be leaving, with Garden escaping into Manchester just before midnight, then real violence flared as Hopalong and Dylan squared up on the bouncy castle, and Dylan took exception to a cheap shot and squared up without accessories. After a few tense moments peace broke out and eating and drinking resumed. The cousins G departed, and the spirits started, but by now Dylan had been lost to sleep, and the deep grass.

Of course once the spirits started things got a bit hazy, alcoholic smoothies were started on. G Man became monkey boy and climbed up the outside of the house and in through Hopalong's window, ripping his jeans in the process. Squirrel passed out in the music room, only to be woke up by Hopalong, he got up, and walked straight into the wall mistaking it for a door, and knocking the notice board onto the floor. The alcoholic smoothie shots weren't exactly going like hot cakes, probably cos people weren't sure about the colour. As people began to crash out, Hopalong and Lamb went to bed only to find Dylan in it, after they managed to get him up, he moved to Ricky Organ's bed only to be removed again when Ricky Organ made it to bed, after an argument where Dylan swore he was in his own bed at his own house, only to look out of the window and realise he wasn't, and he eventually found a resting place on the now deflated bouncy castle.

Sunday morning saw the landlord of Chez Didsbury turn up with a strimmer. Melvin opened the door, took the strimmer off him, and closed the door again without saying a word. There was the slow dispersal of guests during the day, not before another round of swing ball and bouncy castle battles before that was taken away at about four in the afternoon. Squirrel finally surfaced at 7 in the evening, after seriously considering not getting up at all. The absinth smoothies were not a clever idea.

Monday saw Hopalong take the day off work due to the after effects of the weekend, and general weariness all round from everyone else, this continued through the week, until Thursday when G Man met daddy G for a drink, and Hopalong was drinking at home, they then went to the Parrswood for a while and then returned to Chez Didsbury to make an attack on the remains of the Smirnoff Blue.

Quotes

Hopalong (to Ricky Organ) - Why won't you let me kiss you?

Hopalong (to some random person) - That's Asset, she fancies him (pointing at G Man)

The Millimetre Camera

What a surprise, the plan to do absolutely fuck all went out the window very early on the Friday night, as when Squirrel returned home from work, he found G Man, Ricky Organ, Plane and Melvin already drinking, so in a typical display of willpower he joined in. Hopalong and Lamb had travelled down to Milton Keynes during the day in preparation for the Eminem gig on the Saturday. After a few cans of stella in the house they were joined by Asset and Mogadon Nan, and then headed into Didsbury for a few drinks. After a couple in the Dog and Partridge they headed to the Hogshead for more glass pilfering, but were somewhat disappointed to only get one Hoegaarden vase, Mogadon Man was left in the Hogshead, and was last seen trying to get a 20p for a load of change. After a quick stop at the kebab shop, they headed back to Chez Didsbury to re attack the Stella. After nearly everyone had taken a turn at falling asleep in the lounge, and Melvin had tried the not-so-subtle approach with Asset, people headed off to bed.

Saturday saw Squirrel meet up with Kissme and Vek in the Fringe Bar, while in the meantime G Man was out in Didsbury with Asset. Squirrel and G Man arrived back at Chez Didsbury within a few minutes of each other and had the same thing in mind - empty the baby, however due to the efforts of the night before this wasn't going to be an arduous task as there were only three cans of stella and four Archer's aquas. Ricky Organ rang to ask if they wanted anything from Sainsbury's but the plea for more alcohol fell upon empty wallets. The idea of raiding the spirits was toyed with, but eventually dismissed, and they sat in watching films.

Sunday saw another late rising by Squirrel, just managing to see four o'clock, the late evening saw Hopalong and Lamb return and very little motion by anyone.

The same thing continued for Monday and Tuesday with basic cabbage behaviour in the confines of Chez Didsbury, just without the dribbling.

Wednesday was a different matter entirely. Despite being a sneaky fucking Russian about it and not mentioning it, it was Squirrel's birthday, and in keeping with the low-key behaviour, the plan was to nip into Didsbury and have a few quiet pints. Yeah, like that's likely to happen where Squirrel's concerned. A few shots of Smirnoff Blue before going out kicked things off in the right mode, then to the Dog and Partridge where Ricky Organ, G Man and Squirrel entered the quiz. They were joined by Gopher and Inane who were stopping over in Manchester at Chez Didsbury, on their way down to Glastonbury from Glasgow, and then by another female who they knew and lives nearby. After winning the quiz and the gallon of beer that accompanies it, they headed to the Hogshead, where they successfully managed to get four more Hoegaarden vases. Then back at Chez Didsbury the fun began, with Squirrel attacking the spirits with an enthusiasm seldom seen within those hallowed walls. With very little help from anyone else, Squirrel managed to kill the end of the Smirnoff blue, and make very large inroads into the Bombay Sapphire gin, and Absinthe, before wandering off to bed somewhat unsteadily.

Unsurprisingly he had some problems rising for work the next morning, managing to sleep through his alarm. However G Man wasn't so fortunate, and got up to turn it off and wake Squirrel up, having got a response he went back to bed. However Squirrel wasn't so easily woken from his alcoholic stupor, and it took a second attempt to wake him a couple of hours later, and he polled into work two hours late still under the influence, and somewhat confused. Thursday saw another bought of taking it easy, to recharge before the weekend kicked in.

Quotes

Ricky Organ - And so what was the name given to me that day?
Squirrel, G Man and Melvin (in unison) - TWAT

The Bottom Of The Barrel

A few quiet drinks, doesn't anyone know the meaning of these words? It would appear not, from work Squirrel met up with Shan and Kissme in the Peveril of the peaks, after a few drinks they were joined by G Man and Asset, and then just after last orders Hopalong arrived, having escaped from the packing duty Lamb had assigned him. From there they moved on and ended up at Northern Funk at subspace, however it was established along the way that Shan had been out earlier, and was decidedly worse for wear upon arrival there. After a single drink Shan headed off, and a couple of drinks later Kissme began to show signs of losing the plot, and eventually left carrying her shoes and sat outside talking to Squirrel. With G Man and Asset on the dancefloor this left Hopalong at the bar with four drinks, which he could just about cope with. Hopalong and G Man did however manage to get their photos taken, and as it would turn out a couple of days later it was for the Manchester online busted web site. (so you can check out their ugly mugs for a while). Feeling like a third wheel Hopalong left, only to virtually trip over Kissme and Squirrel who were still sat outside talking. The three of them got a taxi, and after dropping Kissme off, Hopalong decided it was a suitable time to ask Squirrel about Excel formulas. Thankfully, Squirrel was rescued by the return of Asset and G Man, and yet again Asset managed to fall asleep in one of the Chez Didsbury lounge chairs, before going next door for the last time. Squirrel thought it was a good idea to stay up watching baseball and made it to bed at about seven.

A couple of hours later and Hopalong was up, just before being descended on by Lamb and her mum. Squirrel got up just before noon and headed straight out to meet Kissme and Vek in the Friendship for breakfast and was joined not long after by G Man. A somewhat surprising mid-afternoon return to Chez Didsbury followed shopping, and all four residents spent the afternoon lounging and generally (verbally) abusing each other. Plane arrived somewhat to the surprise of Ricky Organ, and by the time it was starting to get dark, Squirrel, G Man and Hopalong headed into Didsbury, first stop, somewhat unsurprisingly was the Dog and Partridge, where they had the misfortune to be collared by Mogadon Man. Normally this would lead to quick drinking and escape, but the trio just ripped the ginger misfit to pieces to such an extent that he sneaked off. After that they headed to the Clock Tower, which just got messy, especially when the flaming sambuca girl came round. Hopalong tried first (on his second attempt after drinking the first one straight down). Now it's not sure whether he quite grasped the concept of flaming sambucas but once lit he managed to spit it out all over Squirrel's jeans, complaining it was burning his lips. After a couple of drinks they managed to clear the dancefloor, and then did more flaming sambucas and tequilas before heading to XS. Once in XS they bumped into Lyem, Kat and Sther, which led to Squirrel dancing with them, G Man trying to keep a distance profile, and Hopalong trying to get G Man and Sther in close confinement (mmm that might be a bit harsh, not all monkeys are in captivity). Upon staggering out G Man leaped in a taxi with two females and persuaded them to let them all share their taxi by claiming Squirrel and Hopalong were famous rugby players (right build, wrong fitness level). After the females got out in Withington, the trio decided that the garage was the place to go and cause havoc. Yes, that's right Hopalong and G Man went on a half hour mission to find the secret garage supply of donkey porn. Squirrel got bored, bought food, and went home, where G Man and Hopalong joined him nearly an hour later.

Sunday morning saw a true return to form with Squirrel doing a fry up, followed by lounging and watching sport in the afternoon, fajitas, and the Sunday night film.

Monday brought about a working week with a twist. For a start G Man had found someone mad enough to employ him for the week, and therefore spent the week working with Squirrel. Monday evening saw them meet Kissme and Vek in the Square Albert after work with the promise to do a different pub each night, however this fell by the wayside due to excessive overtime. It did however take Destroy four days to realise that he was sitting next to G Man, and despite not exactly being Mr current affairs, the reaction was dramatic. Having already spoken to Shaun Goater on Monday night, he was somewhat starstruck, which just went up a gear when he realised he was in the presence of yet another Surerandomality A list star.

Thursday night had the promise to get messy with Hopalong and G Man out and about in Didsbury, but you'll hear about that next week.

Quotes

Hopalong (to Ricky Organ) - Shut your bitch up

Mogadon Man – I'm thinking where I'm going to move to next.
Hopalong – Down south would be good.

Mogadon Man – I'm hoping to get a government job in Amsterdam.
Squirrel – Have you tried the Dutch Government?
Hopalong – Why don't you get a flight tonight?

Ricky Organ – It's been a quiet week.
Squirrel, G Man and Hopalong – What?

Short And Sweet

Not a great deal. G Man left work early on Friday, to go to the Slug and Lettuce with Garden, Blondie, and Rah, and were joined by Spiderwoman and Night, but all the women had left G Man by the time Squirrel managed to get out of work, though it seems his arrival was only moments after G Man had texted him to say there was a strippogram. They moved on to Sinclair's Oyster Bar for a few Weiss beers, and got some Ayingerbrau vases, before heading home early.

Saturday saw nothing being done at all by the residents of Chez Didsbury, and the vaunted triple birthday bash turned out to be a single birthday bash as Asset and friends went to Funkademia, whereas a mix of lack of funds and general apathy meant that the Chez Didsbury residents didn't leave the house, or even have any beers.

Sunday saw more of the same, with chilli and a Sunday night film that no one could be arsed to watch.

Monday and Tuesday saw G Man going into Didsbury to meet BB, though the proximity of Sther on Tuesday may cast doubts on this.

Wednesday saw Squirrel, G Man, Ricky Organ, Plane and Asset going for a couple of quiet ones in Didsbury, having one in the Station, before heading to the Dog and Partridge for a couple and to win the quiz.

Thursday saw some of the Chez Didsbury residents going to the cinema, but who cares, the week has been boring as fuck.

The Tonne Maximum Load

A quiet weekend is in store, they were the words to hit the presses this time last Friday, just goes to show what Squirrel know. First out of the blocks was G Man who after finishing work at just after 3 headed to the pub with his new work colleagues. Then at half four Blondie, Morning and Rah rushed out of work and headed to the Slug and Lettuce where they were joined by Squirrel and Garden (only briefly) just after six. To say things got messy quickly is somewhat of an understatement. Despite the fact he claimed he was only out for one drink, Squirrel took little persuading (and a sub) to stay out, and it was sealed by starting on Tequila shots before 7. Rah suggested that they weren't drinking quickly enough and asked if anyone knew any drinking games. Unsurprisingly Squirrel did and suggested I have never. Word had reached G Man of this and after a brief pitstop at Chez Didsbury to pick up his gear for Harrogate and Ricky Organ they arrived in town. More Tequila followed which led to Morning having to rush and puke, and Blondie accidentally (well so she says) flash Squirrel and Ricky Organ.

At around nine G Man had to rush off to get his train to Harrogate, which after all he missed and had to go home ready for the early morning train on Saturday. Morning had to go off to meet her other half, but in the process managed to bang Rah head in hugging goodbye. At some stage after this Squirrel, Ricky Organ, Blondie, and Rah wandered off to Jar Bar and despite how they were dressed they got in. After a few more drinks Ricky Organ went to the toilet only to find everyone gone on his return. Rah had gone for fresh air, Blondie had followed her, and they'd gone to Walkabout, where Blondie later fell down the stairs.

Squirrel had wandered outside thinking everyone had gone and Ricky Organ found him leaning on the railings outside. They started to walk off home, when Squirrel remembered he'd left his bag in Jar Bar with his latest expensive eBay purchase in it. Ricky Organ went back to get it and after difficulty getting back in managed to retrieve it. Next stop was KFC where they thought it would be a good idea to start chatting to the two oldest ugliest married women in there. (And at that time of night that is a seriously stiff competition to win) Despite efforts to the contrary it inevitable got messy and the polite chatter turned to abuse.

From there it was onto a bus for what should have been a simple journey home, however Ricky Organ hadn't envisioned the nightmare on Squirrel Street. As soon as the bus hit Rusholme, Squirrel decided they were home and jumped up and staggered down the bus, despite the protests from Ricky Organ that they weren't in Didsbury. Only after other (laughing) passengers joined in did Squirrel grab a pole to stop and turn round, however doing so meant he swung round and about knocked some poor bloke through the window as he hit him with his arse. Squirrel sat back down, only to jump up again in Fallowfield and escape from the bus. Ricky Organ finished his food and got off a couple of stops later to try and find him, which he managed as Squirrel was quite happily sat in Happy Daze eating a burger. A further (uneventful) bus journey saw them get to Didsbury, where Squirrel fell asleep in a chair for a change.

Saturday morning saw Squirrel awake in bed with little recollection of how he'd got there and with his sleeping T-shirt on inside out and back to front over the clothes he'd got back in the night before. G Man managed to get up and go to Harrogate, and Squirrel managed to get to work. By the time he'd sobered up, Kissme had joined him, and it was time to go to the pub again. They met with Vek in Albert Square and then went to the waterside Pitcher and Piano, where they met up with Omi and Ven on her Farewell to England tour. Others joined them and they sat outside drinking for the rest of daylight hours. Just after 10 Kissme and Vek went home, and after last orders the rest of the gathered wandered off to go home. However Squirrel had other ideas and yet again his bus journey home was interrupted by a stop in Fallowfield. Off the bus and straight into XS where a few drinks with the regulars and a look at what was on the dancefloor prompted him to go home, which he eventually did, only to fall asleep in the chair again, before dragging himself to bed at 6 in the morning.

Sunday saw Squirrel and Ricky Organ relaxing and doing absolutely fuck all. G Man rang just after ten begging for a life as he was on the train journey from hell back from Leeds, as the train stopped at every little armpit and hell hole between Leeds and Manchester. How little did we know.

Monday was supposed to be an easy night; however G Man rang up and got Ricky Organ to stoke up the Barbecue as BB had insisted on one (and a barbecue). After some food they retired to his room, only for Daddy G to ring up with expert timing. Meanwhile Hopalong rang, and it was discovered the real train journey from hell starts in Swindon. A one PM journey start had progressed to Gloucester by ten, due to points problems caused by excessive heat. He was at least on a moving train by then on the way to Birmingham, where he eventually got a taxi back to Manchester (paid for by Virgin) and arrived home at just after two in the morning. This is what you get for attending a festival of speed, "the longest delay I've ever seen on a Virgin train", and that was a quote from a train employee.

Tuesday saw Ricky Organ's birthday, and with it Ricky Organ and Hopalong attacking the baby with gusto. Ricky Organ decided that playing poker on Yahoo was a good idea and was soon joined around the computer by G Man and Hopalong. Who needs the casino (Viva Las Vegas) when you can gamble online, as the night went on Hopalong put $200 in as stake money from his switch card and was $55 up when Ricky Organ persuaded him to cash in his initial $200, which he did, but it didn't take long for him to lose the $55.

G Man must think he's landed his ideal job, it was someone's birthday at his work on Wednesday, and therefore the place shut down at one and everyone went to the pub. Ricky Organ, with Melvin in tow were off to a barbecue, and made a fleeting stop at Chez Didsbury. After quite a few beers G Man managed to meet up with BB in the Clocktower and they headed off to her house. Some hours later they were interrupted by her boyfriend banging on the door and shouting slut through her letterbox. Ejected from the house quite quickly G Man arrived back at Chez Didsbury just before midnight without any keys, without his cash card, pissed and attendance at work the next day compulsory.

Thursday - another day, more drinking, after finding out that BB's boyfriend had threatened to get the bouncers at the Clock Tower to kick his head in, he decided that meeting Hopalong for a few quiet ones in Sofa in Fallowfield was a good idea, just how G Man is managing to do a full week's work attendance on this kind of drinking schedule is anyone's guess. Furthermore, phone calls at eleven o'clock at night asking if a pin number for a credit card had arrived in that day's post is not a good sign, and would suggest that a trip to the casino (viva Las Vegas) was underway.

Overall it's been a tip top week.

Quotes

Various – I have never....

Ricky Organ - they were very nice, almost perfect.

The Steps

A quiet weekend would be somewhat of an understatement. Friday saw Hopalong out with Lamb who was up for the weekend, Ricky Organ was with Plane in his room, and Squirrel and G Man just sat round watching TV.

Saturday saw Ricky Organ head down to Bedford for Rory's birthday. Hopalong and Lamb stayed in his room, Squirrel and G Man were sat in front of the TV again, and were joined by Garden and Chip for the evening.

Sunday again saw a severe lack of motion, with Hopalong and Lamb going out, and Ricky Organ returning from Bedford. The week continued in much the same fashion with very little motion from anyone, until Wednesday when the residents of Chez Didsbury were boosted by the arrival of The Chemist, who is starting his new job on Monday, and along with other conscripts they went to play their first Powerleague fixture (more details later). Upon return The Chemist and Hopalong sat up drinking until the very early morning, and Hopalong was showing signs of wear and tear all day Thursday. That evening saw G Man out and about somewhere, but it has been a quiet week, where basically any rumours of activity have been spurious, not genuine, and worth fuck all.

Yes, strange activities going on. The residents of Chez Didsbury have taken up playing five a side football in an organised league. Their efforts at playing in the back garden leading them to believe they can play football.

And with The Chemist now at Chez Didsbury, the famous five were now all together on a permanent basis. (The Chemist staying was supposed to be a temporary arrangement, but it wasn't, he was there until the bitter end.)

Quotes

Rah (Talking about homeless people) – They always claim to have no money, yet they always have mint sleeping bags

Hopalong & Ricky Organ (Separate occasions, but both talking about joining the Wednesday power league) – What day do we play?

Life Begins At

Just a little more happening this week than last week's half a dozen lines, and not all of it has been tip top, but there has been some inspired cheekiness, though the long-term effects aren't good. Squirrel wandered out of work to the Rising Sun (surprising some, who thought I was just another hum drum), where he met up with Kissme, The Nolt, Ven, and the celebrating birthday boy Vek. They were joined by more people later, and somewhat unsurprisingly Kissme's words of I'm just having one, and Squirrel's I'm not drinking both flew out of the window. The rest of the residents of Chez Didsbury were safely ensconced at home with little hope of movement, however by the time the Rising Son was kicking out, rumours of XS were starting to circulate, and Squirrel, Vek and Kissme got a taxi there, only for Vek and Kissme to refuse to get out cos there was a queue. Undeterred by this Squirrel went in anyway and was joined by Hopalong. Things got a bit blurry as many pints of Stella and bottles of reef followed, and were shaken up by dancing, before heading to Abduls at kicking out time. They blagged sharing a taxi back with some bird from Cheadle who when they arrived back at Chez Didsbury got out and went in the house and proceeded to talk utter shit at high volume for the next hour before going home. Well at least it saved one of the residents doing it.

The next morning saw a gas safety engineer arrive while the residents were less than Mr current affairs. While he was still there, Squirrel and G Man ventured into town, with Squirrel in one of the lariest moods ever witnessed, as he found words of abuse for nearly everyone they encountered. On arrival back at Chez Didsbury they found that the boiler had been condemned which left the house with no hot water. Hopalong went to the gym to get a shower, G Man went to meet BB in Fallowfield and Squirrel got ready to go out.

Now the sneaky fucking Russian was going on a date, however with the lary mood he was in things were likely to get messy and being Squirrel he wasn't going to disappoint. (The rest of his housemates did try and persuade him to postpone, but Squirrel was having none of it.) On his dates arrival (15 minutes late – not bad for a woman) his first words were "Have difficulties finding the place?" (She worked in the same building as Squirrel, and they were meeting in the bar on the ground floor of the building.) Things weren't going particularly well, when Squirrel went to the bar and realised the woman next to him was his ex-wife's matron of honour. Unable to keep his mouth shut he asked, "What the fuck are you doing in Manchester, I thought you were quarantined in Leicester." He went to sit back down and a few minutes later the bridesmaid came over and started giving him shit, to which the standard reply was "fuck off". At which point she went to throw her drink over Squirrel, missed and covered his date. Squirrel did what any self-respecting date would do and burst out laughing. At which point the glass was thrown at him. This also missed, but didn't miss the plate glass window behind him, and went straight through. His date went home, and so after going to the restaurant by himself he started to head home as well.

Squirrel was under the impression that the Residents of Chez Didsbury and Asset were meeting up to go to friends and family, and so headed home. He got there and was surprised to find that Hopalong and the Chemist had been too lazy to go, and were sat watching DVD's. Meanwhile, Asset had also pulled a no show, which left G Man and Ricky Organ out of control in a strange environment, and they both managed to get trolleyed. Ricky Organ, by all accounts left just after two and G Man at sweeping up time, whereupon he got to Fallowfield for a kebab and shared a taxi with two fare dodgers from Withington, however in their haste to get out of the taxi without chipping in they left their unopened pack of Mayfair, which G Man claimed as a trophy. They still sit untouched in the lounge of Chez Didsbury. When G Man got in Squirrel was still up, and questioned him as to the whereabouts of Ricky Organ. G Man was surprised that Ricky Organ had not got back yet, and he was too pissed to negotiate the journey home in a timely manner and arrived back at some stage after everyone else had gone to bed.

Sunday didn't see Ricky Organ in the best shape and with Squirrel and The Chemist in danger of getting cobwebs, G Man and Hopalong went out to play pool and watch The Hulk.

Monday saw Ricky Organ out with Plane.

Tuesday saw G Man and Hopalong make an extended stop at the Parrswood.

Wednesday saw the 5-a-side night, and the start of work on getting a new boiler. Thursday saw the completion of this work, and after nearly 6 days Chez Didsbury has hot water again, though the time without it has been less than tip top.

Quotes

Squirrel (to random woman struggling with heavy bags at Piccadilly) – Do you want a hand with them?
Random Woman – Yes please
Squirrel starts clapping as wandering off.

Big Issue Seller – Big Issue?
Squirrel – So, What is the issue, and what's so big about it.

Squirrel (to bloke wearing a hat with corks hanging from it) – Is that the equivalent of a big game hunter's hat, you display the corks from the bottles of wine you've conquered.

The Return of Fantasy Football

Another Friday came along and in a regular occurrence Squirrel was out straight from work, this time for The Nolt's birthday. Meanwhile Hopalong was in Cheltenham to meet up with Lamb, and the remaining residents of Chez Didsbury were emptying the baby and contemplating going out. Back to town, and the Slug and Lettuce, where Squirrel, Kissme and Kol decided that it was too pricey and moved next door to Churchills, they were joined by Ven and Onle, and then moved on to the Rembrandt. Meanwhile Dylan was out drinking in Chorlton, and arranged to meet Squirrel in XS later. After a stop in Baa Bar for shooters the townies moved onto Spirit, and the Chez Didsbury residents had moved into Didsbury and the normal stop of the Dog and Partridge. They too arranged to meet Squirrel in XS, therefore Squirrel left town to move onto Fallowfield. Back at the Dog the regular pisshead was just warming up for his latest virtuoso performance of singing and dancing with a full pint balanced on the top of his head. However the performance never got started as some dick of a rugby player flattened him with a wheelie bin (having a wank). XS saw Squirrel there, but no sign of anyone else. Dylan had gone to the Orange Grove to play pool as XS was a bit dead, and the Chez Didsbury residents had gone home. Undeterred Squirrel continued drinking and dancing til chucking out time, and Dylan couldn't get back into XS at 1 cos it was crammed.

Saturday saw much lounging at Chez Didsbury, and when Squirrel arrived back from work, G Man, Ricky Organ, and the Chemist were going out to the Comedy Store. From the Comedy Store they moved on to the casino (Viva Las Vegas), where it was a low-key night by normal standards, there again there wasn't any Hopalong so that might help explain things. G Man lost a tenner, Ricky Organ was £25 up and the Chemist was £30 up, so not bad overall.

Sunday saw Squirrel working again, and saw G Man, Ricky Organ, and The Chemist off on a road trip for the afternoon, with a stop in the Lake District, and at Morecambe, before Ricky Organ's car suddenly cut out at 80 on the motorway. More laziness followed, and after only two hours' worth of train delays Hopalong made it back from Cheltenham. The week seems to have blurred together, with not a lot being done except lounging in front of the TV. Wednesday saw Hopalong escape on a corporate golf day, which he managed to win, and after the five a side football saw the residents sit round talking shit and abusing people until the early hours. Thursday saw Ricky Organ off on another work jolly, this time to Vancouver, and it also saw another temporary resident arrive at Chez Didsbury.

The Level Answer

Another Friday came along and in a regular occurrence Squirrel was out straight from work, This time with Kissme, Jobs, Garden and Chip in the Rising Sun (surprising some who thought I was just another humdrum). Kissme and Jobs went off to meet Vek, Ves and others, before returning to the Rising Sun (surprising some who thought I was just another humdrum) and then heading off to the Morrissey night at the Star and Garter. Squirrel, Garden and Chip returned to Chez Didsbury, where Garden got changed before going out for the weekend with Chip. Squirrel got changed while the rest of the residents present, plus BB, were lounging at the bottom of the estate drinking. He then went to meet Asset in Kro2 where they caught up before heading to XS to meet Dylan and Hopalong. Lots of alcohol later, they staggered out of XS and got a taxi back to Asset's new pad. Dylan came in, sat down, got up and left. The rest started drinking wine and crashed out.

Saturday morning was bright and warm, and after finally managing to drag Hopalong from his slumber Asset drove him and Squirrel back to Chez Didsbury where they had breakfast on the lawn. Meanwhile G Man had headed off to the Lake District with BB. Saturday was hot as fuck and apart from a trip to the bookies there wasn't much motion in Chez Didsbury, except to open the baby, and throw the occasional dart. The Chemist opened the football season successfully winning on two lines on his betting slip, and Pizza Hut all round was ordered.

Sunday saw the same lack of motion with another fried breakfast and football watching. G Man and BB returned from their weekend away, and nobody was up for much DVD viewing. Just before lights out, Garden returned from her weekend.

Monday saw some motion, with Squirrel and Garden going to see Terminator 3, The Chemist going into Didsbury with The Quiet Man, and BB turning up at Chez Didsbury at an extremely late hour.

Tuesday was back to no motion with the most interesting visitor being a Hedgehog (oh yeah BB came round again). It was decided to feed the Hedgehog with milk, which Hopalong put at the wrong end. It was pointed out that milk shouldn't be fed to hedgehogs, as their digestive systems haven't got used to dairy products yet.

Wednesday saw Hopalong off to Bracknell for a remarkably interesting finance meeting, and Garden out with Chip, which left Squirrel, G Man and The Chemist to watch the football again.

Thursday however could have got messy. Garden was out with Chip again. Hopalong returned from Bracknell, and immediately rounded up G Man and headed to the pub where they were joined later by Squirrel, who had every intention of hitting 5th Avenue. However they managed to avoid this and wandered back to Chez Didsbury after chucking out time at the Slug and Lettuce, via the kebab shop and a couple of amazing bgerks before settling back down to watch Snatch.

The Chickens and Elephants

Another Friday came along and unsurprisingly it saw Squirrel in the pub straight from work, though slightly later than normal due to a few minor problems. When he eventually got to Simple in the City, he met up with Kissme, Vek, Jobs and others, though most left not long afterwards. Meanwhile the remaining residents of Chez Didsbury were having a Grolsch extravaganza at home. At closing time Squirrel, Kissme and Vek got the bus back towards Fallowfield, though Kissme and Vek got off and went home leaving Squirrel to go to XS by himself.

After a few pints whilst chatting to the XS regulars, some random female came over and started talking to Squirrel. After a few more pints, Squirrel accepted the offer to go back to her bedsit for a coffee. Once there, and in normal light, she seemed to be less certain that it was a clever idea and taking the hint, Squirrel left rapidly, and proceeded to walk all the way up Burnage lane to Chez Didsbury, where on arrival he was surprised still to find life. Squirrel had woken G Man before getting home by singing Gold at the top of his voice on the walk back to Chez Didsbury. G Man got up to look out of the window at where Squirrel was and was confused at not seeing him in the cul-de-sac. Only for Squirrel to turn the corner into it and for the singing to get louder with his approach. A lot of people will have been woken up on that walk home. Hopalong and Ricky Organ were still up and about drinking Grolsch and choosing fantasy teams. One by one they went to bed until Squirrel finally managed to find his pit at about half seven in the morning.

Saturday saw Squirrel somewhat unsteadily weave his way into work before midday, before not staying long before to go and meet Kissme in the Friendship. Ricky Organ had got up and met Plane to go down to Birmingham for the weekend. G Man met up with Daddy G and Baby G to go and watch the football. After the friendship Squirrel got back to Chez Didsbury to watch the results come in with Hopalong and The Chemist, and were joined by Dylan. When G Man returned from the football they sat drinking and discussing going out, until they eventually got a move on between Simpson's episodes and got ready before heading to the Parrswood to play pool. The Chemist left early complaining of weariness, and the remaining three walked into Didsbury and got a bus into Fallowfield and headed to XS.

After much drinking and dancing they headed to Abdul's in what would normally be considered a textbook manoeuvre. However once in there G Man got involved in a scuffle with one of the other customers and punches were exchanged. This calmed down and they left to get transport home. Hopalong was calming things with the other scuffler, and G Man and Squirrel were stood by the side of the road, when 4 random Muppets came over and started beating on G Man, as soon as Squirrel pulled or pushed one off then another took their place until someone from XS came over at which point the 4 Muppets disappeared as quickly as they had appeared. After statements to the police it was off to MRI to have a look at the damaged state of G Man's head. Once there the long wait began. Squirrel wandered off and was found wandering aimlessly by the security guard and pointed back in the right direction. At half 6 G Man gave up hope of being seen and they got a taxi back to Chez Didsbury.

Sunday saw the minimal movement possible, with watching football, eating pizza, and lounging the order of the day. Ricky Organ arrived back from Birmingham and was quickly drawn in. The working week saw G Man take most of the week off to recover.

Monday saw another opportunity to lounge and watch football, with Ricky Organ out with Plane for her birthday, and The Chemist out to meet up with The Quiet Man at the Didsbury.

Tuesday saw Plane come round for a bit, The Chemist was out again at the Didsbury, this time with Last, and there was more football viewing.

Wednesday saw Football being played by some and watched by the others, and general sleep deprivation causing The Chemist to hallucinate and to claim that he'd seen a white horse while playing football.

Thursday saw Squirrel take a rare day off work, which he used constructively by meeting Kissme in the Friendship for a few drinks. The evening saw very little motion from anyone, somewhat of a recurring theme.

QUOTES OF THE WEEK

Hopalong - Are you alright?
G Man - Yes Mate, I'm Tip Top, I'm just not sure about the colour of
my eye.

The Chemist (In the lounge of Chez Didsbury) - Where's the telly?

The Droopy Draws

Friday night did not see a straight to the pub venture, for quite possibly the first time in living memory. However the temptation to drink was too much to resist and by the time it got to eight the raping of the baby in Chez Didsbury was well underway. Squirrel and Hopalong moved to the Parrswood to play pool, and after a few pints headed into Fallowfield and their usual pissed end of night location of XS. Once in XS lots of Stella's, reefs and other drinks flowed, along with dancing and talking to the locals. By kicking out time Squirrel was asleep on the comfy sofas and therefore missed the all action brawl that was taking place outside. After waking up he headed to Abdul's for kebabs with Hopalong, but when the bloodied victims came in to get kebabs Hopalong headed home, and Squirrel did likewise once he'd finished eating to arrive back at Chez Didsbury just behind Hopalong and to fall asleep on the Sofa, until waking at half seven in a dazed state and wandering off to bed.

Saturday saw Ricky Organ off to Cork for the weekend, and BB had come up to see G Man. Hopalong and the Chemist had watched the football in the morning, been to the bookies and were settled down for the afternoon by the time that Squirrel emerged from his pit. Despite lack of food they started on the baby again, until it was time to scrape themselves out of the chairs and back to the Parrswood to play pool again. The Chemist headed home before eleven again, but not before producing a toxic gas alert, which was an indication of the remains of a small dead mammal, and despite everything Squirrel and Hopalong didn't have the common sense to go home as well. Instead they got a taxi to Jabez.

At this point Hopalong did have the good idea of stopping drinking, but it didn't prevent a bit of follow through and the loss of his boxers because of it, (is Squirrel glad that he doesn't have that job at Jabez). Squirrel was thwarted while things were looking good by an untimely arrival of a guard dog, and later managed to find Hopalong just before closing time. Despite various requests there were no takers to go for a curry, and despite good Chinese torture work, there were also no takers for the Chez Didsbury late bar experience. Therefore kebabs were in order before arriving back home just after four.

Sunday saw more football watching, and a general apathy to do anything that might involve the slightest amount of movement, however, there was a brief journey into the estate for a small barbecue, before settling down to a night of random shit viewing.

Bank Holiday Monday brought movement by Hopalong and The Chemist to the Trafford centre, and somewhat more surprisingly to the gym. G Man and BB headed for a random trip around north Wales taking in Llandudno and Betws y Coed. Meanwhile Squirrel did absolutely, positively fuck all, so no surprise there.

Tuesday saw suffering back to work for everyone (except holiday boy Ricky Organ who was still in Ireland), and the evening saw more lounging in front of the telly and darts.

Wednesday saw G Man off to Old Trafford with various other G Family members, while Hopalong was off to his CIMA course, and the rest of Chez Didsbury went to play five a side, and somewhat unsurprisingly things got messy from this point. Hopalong came straight out of his lecture and into the Springbok to watch the end of the football, and by the time G Man had joined him, he'd got a tab going. From Springbok they headed to Teasers, where Hopalong managed to have a discussion with the manager overpaying by credit card. After being told that they don't take credit cards, he piped up, "What, so we get them for free then?" The drinks were confiscated until he could get to the cashpoint and back. Upon leaving Teasers at chucking out time they got in a taxi, however as the taxi rounded the corner into Portland Street, they spied the Casino (Viva Las Vegas) and ordered the taxi to stop. They jumped out and ran into the casino (Viva Las Vegas), but in doing so Hopalong managed to leave his rucksack, with all his CIMA notes and books he'd just got that night, and his mini disc player in it. Things didn't improve once in the casino (Viva Las Vegas), and they came out to get a taxi home with Hopalong £250 down, and arrived back at Chez Didsbury just after 3.

Thursday saw very little movement, with recovery on the agenda, with the Hopalong birthday weekend on the horizon, with just Ricky Organ out, after returning from Ireland the night before.

QUOTES OF THE WEEK

The Chemist (In the lounge of Chez Didsbury) - Where's my phone?
Squirrel - Just there on top of the baby.
The Chemist - No, where's my phone?
Squirrel & Hopalong - It's that one there, on top of the baby.
The Chemist - No, I want my phone.
Pause
The Chemist - This one's mine (picking up the one off the top of the baby as pointed out by Squirrel and Hopalong)

The Chemist (after an ear shattering sneeze) - My farts don't normally make a noise.
Squirrel - No Mate, that was a sneeze.

The RPM

This will get messy was a prediction for this weekend, and looking at the state of the bodies in the Chez Didsbury living room on Sunday afternoon, the prediction wasn't far wrong. It's half past three Friday afternoon and Hopalong is already at the bar in the Old Cock Inn warming up for his birthday weekend, when who should turn up, but G Man and most of the people from his work. Therefore the drinking starts early. After a mass wimp out by all his work colleagues, Squirrel joins them just before seven.

It can be seen at this early stage that things are getting messy, so they move to the pool table where they are joined by Dylan. Hopalong and G Man head to subway for food and are collected by Squirrel and Dylan, and even at this pre 9pm stage it is clear to see that the boy G Man is worse for wear, and it's in this kind of state that he's got to meet up with his work colleagues again later. Squirrel and Hopalong manage to shepherd G Man past his instinct of running up to the door of the Clocktower and Bgerking the bouncers and hustle him into a waiting taxi.

Next stop The Printworks, where they meet up with Ricky Organ, The Chemist and The Quiet Man, before heading for Waxy O'Connor's. They are then joined by Asset, and just after midnight head to Tiger Tiger. At this point things could have taken a turn for the worse as the bouncer's initial reaction was to turn the birthday boy away for being inappropriately attired. This was a funny situation because he'd told everyone else to dress smart. Anyway after much whining (and turning his trousers up, and taking his jumper off) they were let in. After a quite normal round of drinks Hopalong lost his mind and bought everyone out (including G Man's work colleagues who happened to be in Tiger Tiger) champagne, blowing nigh on one hundred and fifty nicker. More drinks and dancing followed and somewhat unsurprisingly G Man was the first casualty, sloping off unannounced to get a taxi home.

At kicking out time, The Chemist and The Quiet Man got a taxi together, Squirrel, Dylan and Asset got a taxi, and despite some vigorous window knocking left Hopalong and Ricky Organ to get their own taxi. With Squirrel making a food stop in Fallowfield, he was the last to arrive back at Chez Didsbury, where the drinking continued and the boisterousness continued with the result that Hopalong pushed Squirrel into the wall, which turned out not to be a wall after all, and a sizeable hole was put in the plasterboard.

The movement on Saturday wasn't the most it could have been. After football bets and the first live game, Squirrel finally managed to crawl from his pit to watch Soccer Saturday. Dylan came round to Chez Didsbury, but apart from that there wasn't much movement. In the evening, The Chemist went over to St Helens with The Quiet Man, and Ricky Organ went to hibernate in his room with Plane. The baby was attacked with gusto, until just after a showing of The Two Towers, Squirrel left the house and went to XS. After a chat with the usual suspects there, he went to get a kebab (Abdul's again) before wandering off home. As he walked up, he thought he was seeing things, but as he got closer it was true, Hopalong was walking the other way, as he went to meet Emerald whose taxi driver was somewhat retarded and was having difficulties finding his arse with both hands. A few minutes later, Squirrel had resumed his customary position on the sofa and Hopalong has taken Emerald to his room.

Sunday saw the big twenty-five of Hopalong's birthday, and the news that he had secured himself a birthday shag. The rest of the day saw watching football and films and large helpings of pizza hut. Monday followed on, as did Tuesday, and not long after that came Wednesday, soon after came Thursday with the only thing to differentiate between the days was 5 a side football and Squirrel having a few drinks with Kissme.

The Sea Knight Helicopter

In true horoscope style, the only two things predicted with any certainty last week, both failed to materialise. Due to an internet booking / credit card fuck up, G Man failed to make his way down to Essex for the weekend, and instead came and met Squirrel straight from work. After a couple in Simple in the City they managed to drag a snoozing The Chemist from his evening nap and got him to collect them from town, amazed that they had secured a lift they hurried across town and downed a quick drink in the Paramount, before The Chemist turned up, and taxied them back to Chez Didsbury, where there was a full house with all the residents being there, plus Plane. Lots of bottles from the baby and comedy video watching saw a drift off to bed by everyone, leaving Squirrel asleep on the sofa for a change.

Saturday saw most residents out, betting and doing the normal glued to the TV afternoon. Squirrel meanwhile headed to work, and then into the Rising Sun (surprising some who thought he was just another hum drum) to watch the England game. The Chez Didsbury residents stayed at home and raided the baby again. After the England game, Squirrel found out that he wasn't going to the 40th birthday thing, and headed to the Friendship to watch the Wales game, and after this into his usual haunt of XS where he had a few with the locals before being joined by Dylan, and then more beer, and dancing followed, before staggering out at closing time and going their separate ways. After food Squirrel headed home and found himself asleep in the lounge of Chez Didsbury at seven in the morning again.

Sunday saw all the residents of Chez Didsbury (except Squirrel) going to the driving range to whack a few golf balls. Squirrel emerged from his pit at about five and there was the normal lack of motion in the evening.

Monday saw Hopalong at college, The Chemist at Tae Kwon do. Tuesday saw the return from work after holiday by Destroy, who in true fashion had an exceptional tale from his time off. After an extremely heavy night on the piss he fell asleep and started snoring heavily, and in doing so kept his girlfriend awake, after a couple of sleepless hours she headed to the balcony and set herself up a makeshift bed using seat covers and the like.

Later in the night Destroy rises from his pit in need of the toilet but due to the pissed-up senses mistakes the balcony for the bathroom and starts to piss on the makeshift bed, narrowly missing his girlfriend who had woken at the last moment and scrambled to safety.

Anyway back at Chez Didsbury Tuesday saw football watching. Wednesday saw Hopalong at college again, the five a side team headed to the Dog and Partridge after the game, and Squirrel watched the England game in peace at home. He also went to bed straight after the game in a somewhat unprecedented move. The rest of the residents arrived home sometime after eleven from their various locations under the impression that Squirrel was out presumed whoring. Thursday saw The Chemist at Tae Kwon do again and G Man out with the returned BB.

QUOTES OF THE WEEK

Morning - There's no fat in Ice Cream

Morning (To Squirrel) - I've bet you've got a Stanna Stair lift installed

The Chemist - I forgot that there was a day today.

Unidentified voice from Chez Didsbury living room - Where's Squirrel? Hopalong - Dunno, Probably gone whoring. (pause) He might be in bed though. (another longer pause) No, no that's not likely, The first one.

The AK

What do you think is going to happen when all the residents of Chez Didsbury are at home and the words 5th Avenue are mentioned? Ricky Organ goes to bed, The Chemist curls up in his chair, and Squirrel starts gibbering like Gollum, and we are sure that he mumbled about his precious before succumbing to temptation and joining Hopalong, G Man and BB in going out.

Things were likely to get messy. First stop was the Pitcher and Piano for some overpriced drinks before a taxi to 5th Avenue, where the drinks were in a more reasonable price band. Lots of vodka and red roosters and dancing later and it was at the unbelievable time of three in the morning and time to leave. No one is ever sure of how time goes so quickly whilst in 5th Avenue, except for the time flies when you're enjoying yourself thing. A taxi back to Didsbury and a kebab, and another taxi home saw them get in just after 4, and in true style Squirrel woke in daylight hours asleep in the chair, having managed to wake The Chemist up at half five by full volume MTV.

Saturday saw a lot of promise of movement with not a lot of substance to back it up. Squirrel made it his mission to spend the entire day torturing Hopalong who was suffering from a monster hangover. Plane came round, and hid in Ricky Organ's room, and everyone wandered off to bed having not done a great deal. Except for the Chemist that was, who had gone into town to meet up with The Quiet Man and others. They went for a Thai (not a bride) and then headed for Tribeca. After a lot of beers The Chemist headed for the Ibis that he'd booked as he was too fucking lazy to get a taxi back to Chez Didsbury.

Sunday saw Hopalong and G Man head out early to hit a few golf balls in the company of Emerald, and saw them arrive back at Chez Didsbury late in the evening in a somewhat pissed state. The Chemist went to Buxton for some bizarre reason, almost as if he's doing a delayed reaction follow G Man round the country. Squirrel didn't move from the house, and there wasn't a lot of movement on the Ricky Organ front either.

Monday saw Squirrel with a rare day off, only to find that the other residents had set the alarm, and taken his keys with him, therefore preventing him from really doing anything, so it was a day of tidying and watching MTV. It turns out that G Man had accidentally picked up Squirrels keys in his hung over state, and the day for him and Hopalong was a bizarre one. Hopalong got to work, after not being able to find his wallet before leaving, and found he hadn't been paid, and upon ringing the wages department was asked "Do you work for us?" With his boss abroad on holiday it looked like they'd sacked him on the sly, but they did pay him eventually.

He met up with G Man to go to the gym, and after the circuit training while G Man went for a swim Hopalong tried to get into the locker using the code G Man had given him, but it was the wrong code, so he had to wait 45 minutes for G Man to finish his swim. That evening G Man had to go out with BB and went to Greens to try and make up for his Sunday on the piss session. Emerald came round to see Hopalong, The Chemist went to Tae kwon do, and Ricky Organ worked late, while Squirrel didn't move from his chair in front of the telly.

Tuesday saw G Man round at BB's, still grovelling for Sunday. Hopalong was out for a few Stella's with Emerald at the Slug and Lettuce, while the other residents watched the football at home. Wednesday saw Hopalong at college and the rest of the resident out playing football and watching the second half of the great Arsenal humiliation.

QUOTES OF THE WEEK

The Chemist (5 minutes after coming out of the shower and wrapped in towels) - Why aren't I dry yet?
Hopalong and Squirrel - Have you ever thought about using the towels to dry yourself?
The Chemist - No I just usually wait til I'm dry

Another Hours

Overall a more relaxed kind of weekend, with Ricky Organ, living the lifestyles of the rich and the famous again off to Copenhagen for a business trip. Squirrel, Hopalong and The Chemist refused to move from the comfort of the Chez Didsbury lounge. It left just G Man, aided and abetted by BB to fly the flag, with a half-hearted effort, just doing a standard Didsbury run of the Dog and Partridge and the Slug and Lettuce.

Saturday saw football watching during the day and in the evening, Hopalong, G Man and BB went out for a curry, while Squirrel and The Chemist again refused to leave the house, Ricky Organ returned from Copenhagen, bitching about his hard life, but there wasn't a great deal of sympathy going around. Quite right too. After the curry Hopalong, G Man and BB headed off to the casino (Viva Las Vegas), where after many hours of gambling they emerged a fiver up between them. The next step was to try and negotiate the journey home. Their first thought was to ring the Chemist for a lift, but the fact that they woke him up in doing so, and the number of Stella's he'd had ruled that out. The next suggestion was to try the same trick on Emerald, who much to their surprise agreed, and then stayed at Chez Didsbury.

Sunday saw the usual lounging around watching the box. G Man went to meet Mummy and Daddy G to watch the football, and the evening saw Hopalong out with Emerald for a few drinks at the Parrswood, and Ricky Organ deserted Chez Didsbury for the week to stay at Plane's.

Monday saw Hopalong at college and G Man at the gym.

Whereas Tuesday saw G Man out with BB in Fallowfield, with stops at Something Blu and Glass, and Hopalong out with Emerald straight from work. Both nights saw very little movement from either Squirrel or the Chemist.

Wednesday brought about five a side football again, but Squirrel stayed at home complaining of ill health, and Hopalong was at college.

Thursday saw G Man and Hopalong playing five a side football again, and then saw Hopalong going into Didsbury with Emerald for a few drinks.

QUOTES OF THE WEEK

The Chemist (talking about Shakira) - Hasn't she got something serious? Like Cancer.
Blank looks from the rest of Chez Didsbury residents.
The Chemist - It might not have been that serious, it might have been a cold.

The Chemist (while watching a Pink video) - Is that her real name?

The Chemist (while watching a Dannii Minogue video) - Is that Pink again?

Morning (while talking about suitcase weight for her impending holiday) - I know how many kilos I can take, but what is that in Kilograms?

The ..ers

Well the votes are in and it's official, it is likely to get messy, as Squirrel is out to get absolutely, positively more pissed than any other muthafucker in Manchester over the weekend, which isn't going to be pretty, especially if, as normally happens, he drags someone else down with him. Elsewhere there are various people thinking up various excuses not to go out drinking with Squirrel for their own health and general mental state. They were the opening words from last week's crystal ball.

How true, and people managed to devise a shift system to get round the problem. Friday night saw Squirrel out straight from work to meet up with Kissme and Vek in Anthaeneum. Meanwhile G Man was claiming illness and was refusing to leave the house. Hopalong had done the impossible and persuaded The Chemist to move and they met up with Squirrel in Squirrels to watch the football, after quite a few pints Squirrel wandered off to go to 5th Avenue. This left Hopalong and The Chemist to go to The Queen of Hearts, where somewhat unsurprisingly Hopalong managed to get into an argument (not the bouncers this time), but was rescued by The Chemist. Meanwhile Squirrel arrived at 5th Avenue somewhat worse for wear, and can remember little after this until waking the next morning. However BB and her friends were there, and they report that although there in body, the mind and spirit had vacated the building. Squirrel even managed to throw one of his drinks all over McCarthy for no apparent reason. The next memory is being in the kebab shop in Didsbury, and somewhere along the way managed to fall heavily after twisting his ankle.

Saturday morning saw everyone in Chez Didsbury up at unreally early hours for them on a Saturday. Hopalong went out before noon with Emerald, and The Quiet Man came round to meet The Chemist so that they could go flat hunting. Squirrel managed to coax G Man from his sick chair and into going to the Friendship to watch football, have all day breakfast and drink. Just after five BB joined them and then took G Man away to go and get ready to spend the evening at a private party in Baa Bar, where he managed to bump into Mogadon

214

Man. Squirrel went and had another drink with Lyem, Tak and Tan, before doing some drunken shopping in Sainsbury's and getting the Chemist to come pick him up. Back at Chez Didsbury, Emerald was just leaving, and Hopalong and The Chemist were in no mood to join in drinking with Squirrel, and suffered several hours of torture before Squirrel went to XS. In XS they were some of the usual suspects, and Squirrel managed to stay off the dancefloor, before leaving at chucking out time to hit Abdul's for a kebab. Back at Chez Didsbury there were no signs of life, so Squirrel sat watching MTV and drinking.

Half seven Sunday morning and Squirrel goes to bed, but peace doesn't last long with early risers in the house. Granted the cause of the noise to wake everyone was from a strange source as some goddamn scout marching band was warming up in the next cul-de-sac. After a fry up, The Chemist gave Squirrel, G Man and BB a lift into town, whereupon Squirrel realised he was supposed to be in Didsbury. He met up with H (no not the one from steps) and another mate in the Clocktower for an afternoon of football watching, which was followed by an evening of more pints in O'Neill's before getting back to Chez Didsbury and a night of total non-movement.

Monday saw Squirrel go to work, decide that it wasn't the wisest thing to do on a weekend of drinking like that and went back home again.

Tuesday saw G Man at BB's for some quality soap watching, and Hopalong was out in town with Emerald, hitting, Bar 38, Square Bar and Rain Bar, before deciding that the trip back to Didsbury would be too much and staying at the Ibis in town. Anyone would think that the residents of Chez Didsbury were living the lifestyles of the rich and famous and had money to burn.

Wednesday saw Hopalong take the day off work with a classy Mickey Mouse, spurious and non-genuine excuse, and then complain he was too tired to play five a side in the evening even though the Chemist and G Man both made it while ill.

Thursday saw Squirrel, Blondie, and Garden planning to go to 5th Avenue, so god only knows what time that session went on til, but if the normal pattern is followed, things will have got messy. Overall a Tip Top week.

215

QUOTES OF THE WEEK

Who else but The Chemist (watching MTV again, Madonna is on) - Who's this?

Hopalong and Squirrel - You are joking aren't you.

The Chemist - I've got a good idea, but I'm not sure.

Hopalong and Squirrel - Tell us who you think it is then.

The Chemist - No, I'm not sure.

Hopalong and Squirrel (eventually after the video has finished) - It was Madonna.

The Chemist - That wasn't who I was thinking of.

Hopalong and Squirrel - Who were you thinking of then?

The Chemist - (after a long silence) I'm not saying.

Squirrel - You were going to say Kylie, weren't you?

The Chemist (somewhat sheepishly) - erm, yeah.

Not published at the time.

When Squirrel, Blondie, and Garden got home from 5th Avenue, it wasn't a quite arrival. The record player went on, and loud music woke the entire house, and probably half the street. There was more drinking, and Blondie, who had long had a crush on G Man, decided that she was going to go and sleep in his single bed with him rather than sharing the double with Garden.

In Da Club

Friday morning saw some very unsteady forms leaving Chez Didsbury, after the shenanigans of the night before. Suffice to say there is no way on god's green earth that Blondie should have been driving and reversing up Scarisbrick Avenue at thirty miles an hour. Garden wasn't fairing much better, but at least she didn't have to have a couple of hours kip at work. Meanwhile Squirrel was annoyingly chirpy. After work saw G Man leap into action at half three, on a freebie booze session with his work colleagues. Hopalong and The Chemist were entrenched at Chez Didsbury and seemed reluctant to move or drink, and Squirrel went to meet up with G Man, however G Man's phone took that moment to complete its journey to no power.

This meant that Squirrel was left with the task of trying to find G Man in a pub somewhere in Didsbury. Thus began the quickest ever completion of the Didsbury dozen. (With the exception of the Clocktower, who wouldn't let him in cos he was wearing trainers. How come the pub that is scally central in Didsbury is the only one with a dress code? Yes mate, come in, fight, and smash the place up, you're OK, you've got shoes on. Fucking dicks.) Granted there were no drinks taken on board. He should have known he was up against mission impossible. Have any of you tried finding a midget in a packed pub? After a fruitless search, Squirrel then headed to the safe haven of XS, and got talking and drinking to the regulars, and therefore failed to meet up with Dylan and Lovelace in Jabez. Kicking out time saw the normal journey over to Abduls, and then the bus ride home, where there was someone else up.

Saturday saw most of the residents head out early to get Subway, however this soon led them to the Olde Cock Inn to watch the football. The Chemist and Squirrel went to pick Mate and met the rest of them in the pub. They were joined by Dickie Boy, Iel, and BB, and more drinks were taken on board. G Man and BB were the first to leave, and the rest left in dribs and drabs, with Hopalong and Squirrel going to do pissed shopping at Tesco. Back at Chez Didsbury the drinking restarted, and soon there was just Hopalong and Squirrel there as G Man and BB were still out and the other residents and guests had gone to a party, (and not the animal fancy dress one that had been suggested the day before). Emerald came round, and at some stage G Man and BB came back. This prompted Squirrel to stop being a gooseberry and go to XS for a change. More dancing and drinking followed, and the closing time exit and trip to Abduls followed. Back at Chez Didsbury, Squirrel's rest on the sofa was ended with a forcible ejection, by the return of the party goers.

Sunday came with no one in a particularly tip top state, after all the weekend to this point had got messy. The promise of fajitas subsided with the fact that Squirrel wasn't functioning properly. Not much motion, football watching, and a DVD was the order of the day.

Monday saw lots of work, and not much after.

Tuesday was much the same, but with Squirrel and Garden going for a curry, and Hopalong taking it on himself to cook the fajitas, and the Chemist leaving the house to go to Tae Kwon do, and a stop in Squirrels.

Wednesday saw a night off from football, and very little motion. Somewhat unsurprisingly.

Thursday was a little different, with Emerald coming round to see Hopalong, G Man out with BB for a curry and The Chemist at Tae Kwon Do.

QUOTES OF THE WEEK

First let's draw the scene. Morning is on holiday with her other half Monis (pronounced as if he was Spanish). They are stood outside a restaurant looking at the menu.

Monis - Do you want to eat here then?

Morning - Mmm, I don't know, I fancy Mexican.

They are stood outside the biggest Tex Mex restaurant in the resort, complete with large sombreros on the wall.

Area

The Friday was going to be a quiet night, and certainly Hopalong and The Chemist were sticking to the plan. G Man was out to see Athlete at the Academy with BB and her housemates, and they had mentioned 5th Avenue as a destination, so this had aroused the sense of drinking in Squirrel and after a few at Chez Didsbury he went and met Dylan in The Garrett, for a drink before hitting 5th Avenue. Pretty soon G Man, BB and her housemates arrived, which allowed Squirrel to apologise for his drink throwing of a couple of weeks prior. You never quite believe just where the time goes, and soon it was three in the morning, and everyone had got separated and wandered off home. Squirrel bumped into Dylan at the bus stop and though there was talk of curry they headed home.

Saturday saw Hopalong, G Man and BB in the Olde Cock Inn early on to bag the best seats in the house. They were joined by Squirrel, who bought an emergency change of clothing for G Man, who had unwittingly come out wearing a T-shirt that looked suspiciously like it was written in Turkish. As the afternoon continued, then so did the arrivals. Dancing made it just after 3, and was soon followed by Ricky Organ, The Chemist, Hary and Turkish. Lots of beers and England qualification for the European Championships followed before the decision to move on was taken.

Next stop was The Famous Crown, where Shan and others joined the crowd. G Man and BB deserted to go for a curry, and on leaving Hopalong went home, whereas everyone else headed to the Hogshead, where shooters, aftershock, and whiskeys did Squirrels mental health no good at all, and he headed off to XS. Everyone else went for a curry, before wandering back to their homes or Chez Didsbury. Squirrel reverted to his traditional round of drinks in XS, of Stella, Reef, and Tequila, before hitting Abduls on the way home, where he managed to make bed, probably since Hary was crashed on the sofa.

Sunday saw BB leaving early to go to work. Squirrel surfaced just as Hopalong and The Chemist were visiting Burger King for themselves, Ricky Organ and Hary. G Man surfaced mid-afternoon, and went to the driving range with Ricky Organ. Emerald came round and hibernated with Hopalong in his room all afternoon. Pizza hut was ordered, though not finished, and sport was watched all day, with the rugby world cup, snooker, F1, football, American football and baseball watched before the last of the residents had crawled to bed.

Monday saw very little motion in the house with what appeared to be illnesses creeping in everywhere.

And true to form Tuesday saw G Man off with flu type symptoms (and just after finishing his probation period), and Hopalong coming home from work at dinner as well with the same symptoms.

Both were off on Wednesday as well, and whether they made it to work on Thursday is under debate as well. This meant that neither of them were fit enough for 5 a side football, though the Chemist managed to make it after Tae Kwon Do the previous night, and that Squirrel made it despite the continued attempt to cough part of a lung up. After the football it was the normal loafing in front of the telly talking crap.

QUOTES OF THE WEEK

The Chemist - You're Idle!!!!! (How the Chemist can possible say that about anyone else just beggars believe)

After the evening's five a side game
Squirrel - Next week's game is a ten o'clock kick off
Dickie Boy - What, at night?
Ricky Organ - No in the morning, we're all taking the day off work

Ricky Organ (Holding bright red Happy Garden menu) - I'm going to ring up and order now
Dickie Boy - Ask them to deliver a menu, so I can tell you what that dish is called
Ricky Organ - I'm holding it
Dickie Boy - I need a menu to be able to tell you
Ricky Organ - I'M HOLDING IT - COCK!

Ricky Organ (trying to suggest that Squirrel is a Country and Western Fan) - So I suppose you like Dolly Parton as well, and that other bloke, erm what's his name…. Yeah Elvis Brooks

The Chemist - Where was Zen?
Ricky Organ - He's in Nottingham
The Chemist - Where's Nottingham?

The Deck of Cards

Friday night started early, with Squirrel meeting Kissme and Vek in Simple in the city, and overall, he was taking things easy. Meanwhile back at Chez Didsbury the entire resident's association were in full effect, and were getting ready to head into Didsbury to meet up with Plane. After a few beers Squirrel left Kissme and Vek in Simple in the city and headed to Kro2 to meet up with Asset. At the same time, Hopalong, G Man, The Chemist, Ricky Organ, and BB were getting to the Pitcher and Piano, where they seemed to stay for the rest of the evening. After a few beers Squirrel and Asset headed to XS as a kind of nostalgia thing, and met with the usual locals in the corner. Asset left after a couple as she had a journey to Suffolk early on the Saturday morning. Squirrel left at throwing out time to head over for the obligatory Abdul's, before heading home.

Back at Chez Didsbury Ricky Organ, for some inexplicable reason was asleep on the sofa, and Squirrel couldn't resist the temptation to put on MTV at a very loud volume and then ask Ricky Organ "Why don't you go to bed then." What Squirrel didn't know until the day after was why Ricky Organ was there in the first place. While at Plane's, the arrogance kicked in again and he took it upon himself to criticize her taste in music. This led to a bit of an argument, which led to the attempt by Ricky Organ to flush Plane's CD's down the toilet. This, somewhat unsurprisingly, didn't go down too well, and after copping an elbow in the face from Plane, he was ejected by her parents and had to return to Chez Didsbury, where he found that the Chemist, for the first time ever, had taken up the invitation to use his bed.

Saturday saw most of the Chez Didsbury residents up and around early on, and heading to the new Saturday afternoon location of the Olde Cock Inn to watch the football. The notable absentee was Squirrel who despite phone calls from Hopalong and G Man and text messages from Dylan decided it was best to stay in bed til half four. The residents returned from the pub, along with The Quiet Man after the football had finished and proceeded to attack the baby. The Quiet Man left in the early evening, and the residents had a return to the old-fashioned days of sitting around drinking, watching shit TV, and playing poker and shithead. Ricky Organ went to try and apologise but was turned away.

Sunday saw various things happening. An afternoon visit to the driving range by everyone apart from Squirrel. Lots of watching football, and basically a lot of lounging.

Monday saw more football watching and lounging.

Tuesday saw Squirrel punish the other residents with the chilli from hell. G Man managed to avoid the brunt of this by going to Greens with BB, and The Chemist resisted, since he was going to Tae Kwon Do.

Wednesday saw visitors to watch the United game, with Dancing round before going to play football, and Dickie Boy. It led to an hour during which, there was the strangest echo sensation, with most of the conversation being repeated twice, due to the fact no one was listening to what had just been said. After the match everyone went to play late night football, and then returned and watched late night poker.

QUOTES OF THE WEEK

The Chemist - If you spray anti-freeze on your windscreen when it's not frozen, will it clean the windscreen?

The Anniversary Issue

Friday night saw G Man and Hopalong in the Parrswood straight from work (after G Man had had a five o'clock finish on a Friday - poor lamb). They were joined by their other halves (BB and Emerald respectively). After a while they returned to Chez Didsbury to find Squirrel, Ricky Organ, and The Chemist lounging, drinking beers, and playing Tekken bowl. Little did they know then that the game was going to heat up. From the dusty archives of Chez Didsbury the Tequila roulette wheel was found and was filled with the remnants of the Absinthe and Bombay Sapphire, plus Vodka, Irish Cream, Stella, and Blackcurrant juice. Every strike in Tekken bowl meant a shot decided by fate and a loss meant two. But this tip top idea led to things getting messy. The Bombay Sapphire disappeared quickly and was replaced by more vodka, the absinthe wasn't far behind with more Irish Cream taking over. Then disaster struck with the last of the blackcurrant going, which meant replacing it with more Stella. Hopalong was extremely tempted to join in, but, probably the best in the long run, decided to go back to his room with Emerald. Just after midnight the first victim was claimed with The Chemist having to retire to his comfortable floor. However it wasn't early enough to stop him puking into his suitcase and over his jeans and pillow. Regardless Squirrel and Ricky Organ pushed on, only for Ricky Organ to pass out in his chair, and Squirrel to eventually crash out on the sofa, performing his usual trick of sleeping and holding his beer upright. Ricky Organ awoke in the daylight hours and gave his moisturiser to Hopalong, though the reason for the need is unknown.

Saturday came with G Man up early and out and about. Squirrel woke still holding his beer, finished it in traditional style and then cleared out the remaining shots on the roulette wheel. He dozed as everyone else surfaced, and football was watched. Movement was not the highest priority and the only person to leave the house for any great length of time was G Man who went to watch football and then spent the night at BB's. Hopalong surfaced mid-afternoon demanding a fry up, and then went back to his room. Lots of shit telly followed all the way through to Squirrel going to bed after the clocks went back and after watching the final game of the Baseball World Series.

Sunday came with more sport watching and most of the residents going to the driving range again.

Monday saw little motion, and Plane coming round to see Ricky Organ.

Tuesday saw Hopalong and G Man in the Parrswood straight from work again. Ricky Organ then joined them, and Squirrel met up with them when he eventually got out of work. BB arrived later, before everyone wandered back to Chez Didsbury, most of them via Happy Garden. The Chemist meanwhile was doing the normal Tuesday night thing of Tae Kwon Do followed by Squirrels.

Wednesday saw an early kick off for the five a side football, and another lifestyles of the rich and famous outing, this time to Luton. It also saw the first trick or treaters brave enough to tackle the door of Chez Didsbury. Somewhat surprisingly, they didn't go around empty handed as G Man gave them the tin of shortbread biscuits that were in the house. However, this isn't the generous act it would appear. The tin had been lying around the house for well over a month and only had one extremely soggy biscuit in it. The tin was found discarded a few yards down the road on the way out to football.

With the anniversary night out coming up, Thursday should have been one of the quietest nights in history, but does anybody listen. Straight from work it was Morning, Spiderwoman, Blondie, Destroy, Squirrel and Bert (no idea), and a 5pm start in Brannigans. Alcohol, that early in the proceedings on any night in living memory is going to mean that things get messy, however because everyone except Squirrel had left by half seven, there was still the possibility of a quiet night. Especially seeing as G Man was going to BB's and Hopalong was waiting for contact from Emerald. The Chemist was off to Tae Kwon Do, which left Ricky Organ alone at Chez Didsbury, desperately ringing housemates up asking for peppers. After a monumental effort in Brannigans to secure a pink item, Squirrel headed to Fallowfield and managed to blag a pink fan in the friendship, before meeting up with Comi and the other cronies in XS, and a post-midnight return to Chez Didsbury, chilling before a mad Friday out. Meanwhile Hopalong and

Emerald had headed to Deansgate locks and hit Baa Bar and Loaf, before arriving back in the early hours.

Me Laird Re: Surerandomality The Anniversary Issue

Is this rumour about a meteorite hitting Manchester related to sunspots, or is Gonfer coming back for the weekend?

Anyway, moving on, would be very remiss of me not to send a "Reply All" message on such an auspicious (special to you Hopalong!) occasion as the first anniversary of this delightful publication and even more remiss for me not to thank Squirrel for his efforts.

This would also probably be a suitable time to get the residents of Chez Didsbury to text or e-mail me the alarm code as we don't want a repeat of last time now do we!!!!

Anyway, if I can haul my ageing ass from Hull for the occasion then, as I see it, nobody has an excuse for not turning up (sending apologies due to the stress of moving house WILL NOT BE TOLERATED)

Look forward to seeing you lot again, and remembering nothing tomorrow other than my name, and how many places Squirrel and I go window shopping, Amsterdam stylie!!!!

A Little Interlude To Try And Prevent Squirrel Going Totally Bat Shit Crazy

There was a lot of work involved in putting out an edition of Surerandomality every week, especially as it had grown arms and legs, a second head, a tail, fins, and several tentacles by this stage, and Squirrel was feeling under pressure churning out ten thousand words every week.

So he made the decision to go to a fortnightly issue to try and alleviate some of that pressure.

Did it?

Not really. It just led to Surerandomality expanding even more to more like fifteen thousand words every issue.

It was a bit more organised now however and not only was every day covered in the lives of Chez Didsbury, but there are dates included as well. So the format changes a little bit from this point forward.

Gotta Have Teeth

Friday 31st October - Where else to start a new year off, than with the Surerandomality first birthday party. As well as all the residents of Chez Didsbury, the house also saw visitors from far off parts of Yorkshire in the shape of Me Laird and Zac. After a couple of beers, the first taxi departed Chez Didsbury to Scubar, containing Squirrel, G Man, Hopalong and Me Laird. They were joined just after arrival by Morning, and then Blondie. Then after the arrival of Turkish, the second taxi containing Ricky Organ, The Chemist, Turkish and Hary was on its way to Scubar. The early arrivals had gone for the goldfish bowl route, and by the time Dylan and Lovelace turned up, the drinking was well under way. As time seemed to fly by, Destroy, after weeks of hyping up the event, bottled it and decided not to come out. Pretty soon the suggestion of playing "I have never", was made. It was a roaring success, and many revelations were made (a lot were old news to some though), and came to an end, with the call for movement being made, despite a plea from Morning to stop when Monis arrived.

The next destination was Northern Funk, and somewhat unsurprisingly the journey saw the group split into three, but everyone made it, but by this early stage some people were already getting an early form of memory loss. Once there, the party were joined by Asset and one of her friends, and at some stage an unwanted guest moved into the group of people talking. Hopalong inadvertently bumped into the blonde bombsite called Frost, and told her loads of others were there. Elsewhere there was lots of drinking, and eventually some dancing, and out on the floor, Ricky Organ spotted what many seem to believe is the doppelganger for Squirrel, and managed to get a couple of photos. As alcohol kicked in people began to wander off. Squirrel and Me Laird were first to go via taxi to Chez Didsbury. Next would have been Turkish, but how and where is unknown. Ricky Organ and The Chemist went for the bus, kebab, and taxi route home, where The Chemist found Me Laird sleeping in his room, using his only clean towel as a pillow. Morning, Monis and Blondie were next to go, with Blondie eventually being picked up by her other half, while Morning and Monis heading off to continue drinking. Hopalong supposedly left next, but must have had a bit of Hue & Cry trying to get home as he was the last to arrive back at Chez Didsbury. G Man, Hary and Asset were last to leave, and chose the bus route home. G Man thought he'd left this phone on the bus, but it was on him, it just took him 5 minutes to find it. Asset meanwhile, must have forgotten that she didn't live next door anymore, and had to get a taxi back home from Chez Didsbury.

Saturday 1st November - Saturday saw the somewhat worse for wear Ricky Organ up and out early to meet Plane. G Man, Hopalong, The Chemist (who somewhat unsurprisingly not made it to the Tae Kwon Do seminar) and Hary headed to Burger King, with Hary holding his head out of the window all the way as a dog would. Me Laird left after suitable recovery time, and left Squirrel at Chez Didsbury, to await the return of the rest from Burger King. Hopalong went and met Emerald in the pub, as the other three came back to suffer for most of the afternoon. When Hary got up to go back to Leeds mid-afternoon, he still didn't look in tip top form. Hopalong returned about sixish, while G Man and Squirrel started on the baby before going out to meet BB, McCarthy, and her sister for a curry. But, typical of women, they managed to pick the only curry house in Rusholme not to serve alcohol. After a speedily eaten curry, McCarthy and her sister headed off to a party, and Squirrel, G Man and BB went for a couple in The Whitworth, before bringing carry outs back to the dead zone of Chez Didsbury.

Sunday 2nd November - Well, the pace certainly hadn't been picked up, and a bit of golf was the only non-TV related activity.

Monday 3rd November - G Man went round to BB's, but from the rest of the inhabitants it was a textbook evening of doing absolutely fuck all.

Tuesday 4th November - Motion everywhere. C-Bitt was visiting to cheer on his beloved Rangers, and early, G Man, Hopalong and C-Bitt, were in the Parrswood, Despite a late panicked call to The Chemist, they managed to get to Old Trafford before kick-off. Ricky Organ had Plane round, and The Chemist headed for the normal Tuesday of Tae Kwon Do and Squirrels. After the match, the trio searched somewhat in vain for a drinking establishment that was open in Manchester and ended up having to go to the Casino (Viva Las

Vegas) to get a drink. After about four hours they wandered out, with the virtually unknown situation of Hopalong been up £200.

Wednesday 5th November - Wednesday saw a very early five a side kick off, and with so much of the evening left, Hopalong went round to Emerald's and the other talked absolute shit while watching late night poker.

Thursday 6th November - The Chemist headed for the normal Thursday of Tae Kwon Do and Squirrels, but wasn't the last to arrive home. G Man had gone straight to the Olde Cock Inn with Topher from work, and after about seven pints, met BB and her mate for a meal in the Didsbury. After going back to The Olde Cock Inn, BB and her totally non-speaking mate went home, and G Man and Topher arrived back at Chez Didsbury. Halfway through his second bottle Topher started falling asleep and within a few minutes had slumped all the way over so that he was asleep on G Man's lap. Something which was last seen when the Blonde Bombsite did the same in the days of Chez Rusholme.

Friday 7th November - Topher the sneaky fucking bastard had failed to mention that he didn't have to go to work, which left G Man feeling a bit ropey at work all day, and with BB back home in Essex for the weekend, decided the best way to deal with this was to meet Squirrel straight from work and sample a few pubs. First up was the Slug and Lettuce, followed by the Ape and Apple, and then onto the Giraffe and Grapefruit. (Whoops, sorry that last one isn't really a pub name, got carried away there.) Next up was Mr Thomas' Chop House, and then to Sinclair's Oyster Bar. Food followed on the way back to Chez Didsbury, and the total lack of willing volunteers to continue drinking. Undeterred Squirrel, headed to XS to meet up with Dylan and his housemate Sofi. After the usual Stellas, Reefs and Tequilas they headed out at closing time. While stood outside waiting for Sofi to come out a bitch fight kicked off, and as Dylan tried to stop it, he got a slap for his troubles. Things kicked off big style and Squirrel managed to get Dylan out unscathed, and everyone wandered home when the police turned up.

Saturday 8th November - Another Saturday morning and another daylight waking for Squirrel while sat in the Chez Didsbury lounge. Football watching was the order of the day, then when Ricky

Organ returned from town with Tiger Woods golf for the play station, the inevitable happened, five in the morning came before playing finished.

Sunday 9th November - Little motion again, with a rip-roaring football double on, but Hopalong who had been at a revision lecture, went straight to Yates for a few afternoon drinks, argued with some Aussies, before heading to Emerald's for the evening. Meanwhile a DVD viewing was followed by the residents of Chez Didsbury getting sucked into watching the one hundred greatest number ones.

Monday 10th November - G Man was straight round to BB's but managed to make it home just before Hopalong, who after a day's hard revising had gone to meet Emerald in Didsbury, before coming back home and continuing drinking, meanwhile Tiger Woods was back.

Tuesday 11th November - The Chemist headed for the normal Tuesday of Tae Kwon Do and Squirrels. Hopalong was at Emerald's, Ricky Organ was on another lifestyles of the rich and famous trip, this time to Bonn, but only for a day. G Man had BB round, and for the second night on the trot when Squirrel arrived home, it was like walking onto the Marie Celeste again.

Wednesday 12th November - The tedious latest possible kick off meant a late night for all, but didn't stop the late-night poker again.

Thursday 13th November - The Chemist headed for the normal Thursday of Tae Kwon Do and Squirrels. Everyone else just chilled, in preparation for the weekend. Hopalong at Emerald's, G Man with BB, and Ricky Organ with Tiger Woods.

QUOTES OF THE WEEK

The Chemist (watching the credits to Get Carter) - Britt Eckland? Is that the same one?

Squirrel (discussing the effects of Stella) - Well, it's not really a case of wife beater, it's more a case of eggbeater.
The Chemist (as Homer Simpson) - Mmmm Eggs.

Squirrel - Are you growing your hair then?
Frost (the blonde bombsite) - Yeah!

Squirrel - Is that so you can sweep it over your face then?

The Chemist (during a conversation about the royal family) - So does anyone know what the story is about Prince Charles?
Ricky Organ, Squirrel, & G Man (pointing out the front-page headline in the news of the world right in front of The Chemists face) - What? That one?

Hopalong & Emerald (Looking at Prince - Hits 1) - What's the name of the track that has the line about When Doves Cry.
Ricky Organ & The Chemist - Don't know.
Hopalong & Emerald (Eventually) - Would it be "When Doves Cry"?

The Speed Limit

Friday 14th November - In a remarkably quiet evening for a Chez Didsbury Friday, the only absentee from the house was G Man who was out for a quiet meal with BB. Meanwhile Hopalong was working at doing some revision. After much cajoling Ricky Organ managed to persuade Squirrel to break with tradition and play a PS2 game, in the shape of Tiger Woods. Little did he know what he was starting. Four in the morning and still playing is a rough indication.

Saturday 15th November - The day started off from where the night before left off with Tiger Woods playing. Meanwhile all the residents of Chez Didsbury assembled and smartened themselves up, and were joined by Dancing, and it really was a case of everything going to the dags. Two taxis to Belle Vue followed and after going for the tokens off the local scallies it was off and betting. Squirrel and The Chemist won on the first race, but generally things went downhill from there. Hopalong did win a tricast, but it only returned £14 the lowest of the night, to rub things in the next race's tricast would have brought in £187. Leaving before the end of proceedings, there were two taxis to the Printworks, and the "pre" queue for Lucid. However this brought about the zone of narrow minded dumb sexist muthafuckers that were masquerading as bouncers. The six usual suspects were told there were too many lads. They headed to Tiger Tiger and split up, but were turned back cos it was couples only, despite letting a group of eight girls in just in front of the lead two. Somewhat disgruntled they headed for a quick pint in Sinclair's Oyster Bar, and the decision was then made to head to the casino (Viva Las Vegas), and after a calm start the wheels fell off after the free buffet, and everyone headed home reasonably sober and with Hopalong bringing his gambling losses for the evening to a round £400.

Sunday 16th November - Sport watching in all forms. The England game was the main thing, with BB taking G Man to Old Trafford to watch the England game, while everyone else watched it at home. Squirrel managed to put in another 6 hours of Tiger Woods.

Monday 17th November - Squirrel had the day off, with only one possible outcome. The house was quiet, but meanwhile, in Cambridge Destroy was causing chaos, after nicking the hotel bar / restaurant sign and running round the hotel being chased by the night porter with it, before finding his room. The only problem being that he forgot to remove the evidence in the morning and got rumbled.

Tuesday 18th November - Another day off for Squirrel, and Hopalong was on more Study leave. The evening saw little motion except for the Chemist going to Tae Kwon Do.

Wednesday 19th November - Hopalong had a day filled with exams, The usual suspects had another 10pm football kick-off, which meant watching late night poker on their return. Meanwhile continuing the great week of work trips May managed to fall and scrape her nose while completely bladdered.

Thursday 20th November - The following morning saw May wake with no memory of the cause, but with a bright red swollen nose, but did manage to pull two decent excuses to tell people. Slipped while on the Treadmill - yeah right, that's even less likely than Squirrel on a treadmill. The second was the kind of genius that even G Man would be hard pushed to beat. Excess fumes from hairspray caught alight when she lit a fag and burnt her nose. Hopalong finished his exams, which led to drinking and going to the dags with Emerald. G Man was out in Didsbury with his cousins, and it was generally late nights all round.

Friday 21st November - More Squirrel days off, joined by The Chemist, Ricky Organ, and Hopalong, leaving the somewhat unlikely position of G Man being the only worker, something that not even the casino (Viva Las Vegas) would have given you odds on. Hopalong and Emerald headed off to Edinburgh for the weekend mid-afternoon, and Ricky Organ and The Chemist went to the driving range. Meanwhile the stress of being the only worker led to G Man going straight out from work, though the drinking came to an abrupt halt, when BB turned up unannounced and dragged him out for a curry. Ricky Organ had Plane round, and Tiger Woods figured alongside some rather poor TV.

Saturday 22nd November - The Rugby World Cup final saw The Chemist in agony as he had to go to Tae Kwon Do just as extra time started. G Man had to rush to Old Trafford after watching the end, and Squirrel got up mid-afternoon oblivious to everything. Meanwhile after the match G Man headed to Bradford to pick up his car, and thinks that he got pictured speeding within the first 20 minutes. Severe lack of motion except for Ricky Organ who was with Plane.

Sunday 23rd November - Well the day came and went, and nothing memorable happened.

Monday 24th November - Football watching, after another Squirrel day off.

Tuesday 25th November - G Man went to get fed at BB's, Hopalong went to college then had Emerald round. The Chemist went to Tae Kwon Do, and the football was watched.

Wednesday 26th November - Blondie managed to run out of petrol on the way to work. Hopalong absconded for the evening, as everyone else played footie, and then watched it, before progressing to the late-night poker scene.

QUOTES OF THE WEEK

The Scene - Morning and Blondie had been bitching about their other halves all afternoon, and had moved on to talking about the rampant rabbit.
Squirrel (Sarcastically) - At least you won't get shit back from it.
Morning - Depends which hole you use it in.

G Man (at the dags.) - It tells you which number they are, but how do you know which trap they've been drawn in?

Bouncer at Tiger Tiger - Sorry lads, but it's couples only.
Hopalong - So, that huge group of girls you've just let in are all lesbians then.

Everything's Gone Green

Thursday 27th November - Despite a vigorous recruitment campaign, Squirrel only managed to persuade G Man that it was a good idea to go out drinking, and even that didn't last very long. They got dropped off at the Slug and Lettuce, and after a couple of pints headed back to Chez Didsbury after finding that the baby had been freshly restocked. Hopalong decided that he'd rather go round to Emerald's than continue drinking and got a taxi round there after midnight. Ricky Organ arrived back from work just before 1 and had a couple of beers before heading off to bed, as did everyone except Squirrel who continued drinking until falling asleep on the sofa.

Friday 28th November - In a somewhat bizarre turn of events Ricky Organ was up and out of the house before 7.30 instead of his normal 10.30, Squirrel woke G Man at just after 8, and G Man just rang up work and asked for the day off. Just after 9 Hopalong rushed in and ran about as he was supposed to be at work, and managed to persuade G Man to give him a lift in. After a day of shopping Squirrel arrived back at Chez Didsbury to find that BB was round. Hopalong went out on a leaving do straight from work, starting at the Didsbury before heading into town. Ricky Organ and The Chemist went to see Eddie Izzard at the MEN before ending up somewhat surprisingly in the casino (Viva Las Vegas), where unsurprisingly both came out down. G Man managed to drag himself off the sofa and go to Revolution for another leaving do, along the way depositing BB back at home. He then managed to finish the night off by going to a house party in Swinton, and managed to christen another house with his puke. Squirrel, after being left alone at home, suddenly remembered that G Man had invited the neighbourhood weirdo Wayout to over for a drink, and therefore exited sharply for the bright lights of Fallowfield. A quick stop in the friendship was followed by a large amount of alcohol in XS before transporting home via a kebab shop.

Saturday 29th November - Squirrel was awoken from his slumber in one the chairs by the movement of The Chemist in the living room. "What are you doing up at this time?" was answered by "It's half eleven." Next to surface just after midday was Hopalong who was somewhat put out to find Squirrel and The Chemist consuming food from Gregg's. If he looked rough it was nothing compared to G Man when he arrived home shortly after. After waking in Swinton just before midday he got a taxi back to Chez Didsbury, and proceeded to crash on the sofa, with one arm of his shirt rolled up to hide the puke marks. Ricky Organ was the last to surface, and was soon travelling with Squirrel to Blackburn to pick up decks.

There was a severe lack of motion from most residents, with G Man still motionless on the sofa, and Ricky Organ and The Chemist back in their rooms. Hopalong went out with Emerald into town and was impressed by M2 before going for a Cantonese, then a brief stop at the casino (Viva Las Vegas) to get a taxi, but Hopalong couldn't resist £40 on black, and having won returned to the waiting Emerald. Meanwhile Squirrel was heading to Chortlon as Dylan and Sofi were having a house party, as a joint birthday / housewarming bash. Revise and The Bar (yep that really is the imaginative name) were pre party locations before things kicked off just before midnight. Lots of people and lots of alcohol. A little siesta for Squirrel was to be expected after mainlining spirits, and the last to leave left at 6 in the morning, with no major bust ups, and no major liaisons.

Sunday 30th November - After a party finishing at 6 in the morning there is absolutely, positively no facing need for someone to be cleaning up, opening curtains and windows at 9. Unperturbed by this Squirrel found any remaining punch and started drinking again. By half eleven everyone else was in the process of moving, and after a couple of refresher beers, Dylan and Squirrel headed to the Royal Oak to watch the football, though at half time Squirrel headed home to watch the rest of it.

Monday 1st December - A quiet day, and with the residents of Chez Didsbury taking it easy, Squirrel went round to see Garden's new flat. Meanwhile, still feeling the effects of the flu, Kissme managed to puke all over some unsuspecting woman on the bus home from work. Now that would be messy.

Tuesday 2nd December - This is where things start to blur into one with late nights blending into each other. Football was on the TV,

238

and The Chemist was at Tae Kwon-Do. Hopalong was down in Bracknell for a meeting, or a course, or something.

Wednesday 3rd December - 5 a side football except for Squirrel and Hopalong, who through work both made it back too late to play

Thursday 4th December - G Man had the day off so that he could travel down to Essex with BB for a wedding over the weekend. Meanwhile Ricky Organ was also heading down south, first to pick up Plane from Luton and then onto see his family in London. Hopalong stayed at Emerald's which left just The Chemist and Squirrel watching shit TV.

Friday 5th December - Ricky Organ and G Man still being away, the only person out was The Chemist, who along with The Quiet Man was out on the Tae Kwon-Do social at the Footage. Meanwhile Hopalong was raiding the baby, and Squirrel embarked on a tidy up / move around to accommodate his decks and this led to the unearthing of the Christmas tree and disco ball, which were both set up in the lounge.

Saturday 6th December - G Man was at the wedding with BB feeling like a spare part not knowing anyone, Ricky Organ and Plane were seeing Phantom of the Opera. Squirrel had his hair dyed green, and got back to an empty Chez Didsbury after working for most of the day, with Hopalong being out and about in town with Emerald, and The Chemist being out and about with Iel, Dickie Boy and others from his course. They did have similar problems to a couple of weeks before, being unable to get into Lucid (Iel wearing trainers), but did manage to get into Tiger Tiger by smuggling him in the middle of a group of girls. Squirrel headed for Fallowfield for a change and after a quick one in the Friendship, headed to XS for a few, speaking to the regulars, and then Dylan and Jobs when they arrived from playing pool in Chortlon. With it being Dylan's birthday they then headed off to Jabez, where things got a little bit hazy and messy. Squirrel woke up to find himself on the bus at the terminus.

Sunday 7th December - Hopalong and The Chemist combined to cook a fry up, and Squirrel managed to drag himself from his bed (which he found the night before for a change) to eat it. The Chemist went to Tae Kwon-Do, and Hopalong went to Emerald's which meant they both missed the rescheduled 5 a side, which Ricky Organ managed to get back in time for, but G Man didn't as he had more difficulties with the traffic.

Monday 8th December - Hopalong went straight out from work with Emerald and had a somewhat unsuccessful attempt at the quiz. Everyone else was just lounging at home.

Tuesday 9th December - Squirrel had a day off playing loud music and fucking with the decks. Meanwhile Destroy had a few public transport problems and ended up walking in from the Kellogg's factory in Old Trafford to work, this was because his train couldn't get into Manchester, and he had no cash, cash card or phone credit and so was an hour and a half late instead of his normal half an hour. The Chemist had Tae Kwon-Do, and football watching was the main evening theme.

Wednesday 10th December - 5 a side in the evening against the little scallies, and more lounging watching shit TV. Hopalong was working late again and then was out with Emerald.

Thursday 11th December - All quiet on the western front, with everyone reserving their strength for the partying ahead. That is except Garden and Blondie (amongst others) who were at the Justin Timberlake gig.

QUOTES OF THE WEEK

Morning (talking about printing off pictures on the printers at work) - I've managed to get them, so they are full page, but they still print off in black and white.

Blondie - Is Essex in Cambridgeshire?
Morning - Isn't Essex in Essex?

Destroy (upon seeing Squirrel's green hair) - It's Afro turf

During a discussion on drinking milk.
Destroy - I don't like sterilised milk, it's like water.
Squirrel - No, that's Skimmed milk.
Blondie - So what is sterilised milk then?
Destroy - Isn't that what comes out of women's boobs?

Blondie - What date is it on the 17th?

The Heinz Variety Passenger

Friday 12th December - They let G Man out early from work and along with Pain and Topher an all dayer was started on. Works parties were the order of the evening, and the first out for theirs were Squirrel and Destroy, who started at 6 in the Square Albert. They were joined after 7 by the already somewhat worse for wear G Man, Pain, and Topher. After a couple more drinks they headed to Brannigans. Next to turn up was Spiderwoman, which was shortly followed by Topher puking on the dance floor, and then proceeding to dance in it. Garden and Blondie then turned up, and then Morning and May. Entrance to the VIP area and food followed, and Topher was at the food before it was even on the table. For some reason, a bloke making stuff out of balloons was wandering round, and Destroy wandered round for quite a while wearing a balloon gladiators' helmet. After food came dancing, with Destroy getting up on the stage to twirl round like a dervish. First to go were Morning and May, and G Man wasn't far behind them, though the 10pm deadline he'd been given to be at BB's was a distant memory, and it was after midnight when he arrived there, where he managed to crash out in the starfish position almost straight away. Back at Brannigans, Chip arrived, and the drinking continued, and things became a bit hazy. Elsewhere Ricky Organ and Turkish were getting hammered at the AZ do and were trying to track down and other Chez Didsbury residents to meet up with. Hopalong and The Chemist were keeping a low profile at home, G Man had passed out, and Squirrel wasn't ever going to hear his phone in a club, so they headed home instead. For some reason Brannigans closed at 1, Destroy had already left, though Blondie saw him in Teasers. Spiderwoman fell into the car of her lift. Garden and Chip went to queue for a taxi. Squirrel took quarter of an hour to get from Brannigans to Teasers, where he was refused entrance, partly because of his green hair, and partly because he was completely wankered. Blondie left Teasers and found Garden and Chip still queuing for a taxi, and went back with them.

Saturday 13th December - Somehow Destroy managed to make it to the airport to go to Dublin without any hitches, something that

Squirrel, who woke in the chair at 8 with no idea of how he managed to get home, might have had difficulties with. G Man was off to the football for the Manchester derby. Everyone assembled in the lounge in the evening, but the previous day's exertions meant that the full Chez Didsbury Christmas party wasn't going to be moving much. There were a few beers had, and the boxing was watched, though the night was a bit of a damp squib. Squirrel though did manage to continue watching boxing from the states until 6 in the morning.

Sunday 14th December - The roast didn't materialise either as Hopalong was working. Sport watching was the main occupation for the day, with the 5 a side cancelled cos the opposition pulled out, early nights all round followed.

Monday 15th December - No idea, Squirrel's brain is so addled by this point that he hasn't got a clue what's been happening

Tuesday 16th December - Nothing immediately strikes Squirrel as happening. G Man is in the middle of an extended period off work this week, and therefore is likely to have been with BB. Hopalong will have been working late.

Wednesday 17th December - An early 5 a side kick off was done without Ricky Organ, who was away on another work jolly, with drinking til five in the morning at some plush hotel somewhere in Cheshire.

Thursday 18th December - Quiet night in, except for G Man who was out somewhere with BB.

Friday 19th December - Squirrel had the day off, and G Man had only half a day (the only half-day he'd been at work all week), and used to time to get ready for his forthcoming holiday and for his work do which was at The Moat House that evening. One by one the residents came back home, and the beers were started on, while watching the pool. There was a Christmassy feel in the house, and it is quite difficult to try and describe just what it was like. A game of family fortunes was started, the TV was turned off, and some quality mellow music was put on, with Frank Sinatra, Elton John, The Beatles, and The Rolling Stones providing the soundtrack. The lights were turned off, with the Christmas tree lights, the spinning disco ball and outside lights providing a very homely feel. More drink was consumed, Scrabble was played and a very civilised evening (and so far removed from the image of Chez Didsbury it was quite spooky) followed as the residents waited for G Man to come home so that the present opening could take place. At 3am that was a lost cause, and everyone traipsed off to bed but within half an hour G Man arrived back in, and was intent on causing chaos and mayhem, wherever he'd been things had obviously got very messy. He'd been in two minutes when there was a knock on the door. It was the taxi driver who was waiting for G Man to return to pay him. Squirrel paid the driver, and along with Hopalong sat while G Man opened his presents. G Man had failed in his attempt to get Ricky Organ and The Chemist up again to join in. The Surerandomality album went on at a loud volume, and G Man passed out on the sofa just after 4.

Saturday 20th December - Early morning and Squirrel is trying to get G Man to get up as his parents are arriving to take him to the airport for their holiday to the States and Caribbean. Despite repeated efforts nothing moved G Man until his dad arrived, and shouted at him. With G Man still being pissed as a fart a bit of a slapdash packing followed, during which it is quite possible that there was no underwear packed, and certainly the cutlery put in his case by Hopalong the night before wasn't removed. It was also discovered that he's left his jacket, phone, and keys at The Moat House the night before (and there had been an unscheduled trip to Pandora's as well). To say his dad wasn't impresses was somewhat of an understatement. Little movement in the house during the day, with only Ricky Organ exchanging and opening presents, as the last evening they would all be there together. No late nights, meaning a quite weekend all round.

Sunday 21st December - Hopalong was off to Emerald's for the day and night. Ricky Organ was out shopping again, this time with Plane. The Chemist and Squirrel didn't do a great deal. Another late-night watching sport followed.

Monday 22nd December - Hopalong was at Emerald's again, which left The Chemist, Squirrel and Ricky Organ watching football and other random TV.

Tuesday 23rd December - Hopalong went to Edinburgh for Christmas. The Chemist and Ricky Organ were spending their last nights in Manchester before going off home for Christmas. Ricky Organ went out for food with Plane, and then came back to watch a DVD. The Chemist and Squirrel watched more boxing.

QUOTES OF THE WEEK

Blondie - When they have the boxing at the MEN, do they put the ring in the middle?

G Man - I'm ready
G Man's Dad - No you're not, you're still in bed.

Welcome to 2004

Wednesday 24th December (Christmas Eve) - The Chemist made his way home for Christmas, which left Squirrel to his own devices and after getting out of work early he made good use of his time by heading to Fallowfield early, and got a few in the Great Central, before heading over to the friendship, where he later met up with Kissme and Vek, and consumed large amounts of alcohol, before managing to get home somehow.

Thursday 25th December (Christmas Day) - A quiet day all round, with recovery time and lots of random film watching, and playing with decks.

Friday 26th December (Boxing Day) - More of the same except replace films with sport.

Saturday 27th December - Hopalong sneaked back to Manchester, and hid out at Emerald's. Squirrel managed to leave the house, first there was the sales, and then there was drinking, and the destination was Fallowfield for a change. First stop The Friendship for a couple, before heading to XS, where there was lots more alcohol, some dancing, before a kebab and the beer scooter home.

Sunday 28th December - Early AM and guess who wakes in the chair in the Chez Didsbury lounge? If you said Princess Leia, you need your head looking at, however if you said Chewbacca then you were a lot closer. With more football than you could shake a stick at, what did the Chemist find when he got back mid-afternoon? Loud music and Tiger Woods.

Monday 29th December - Doh, back to work. Ricky Organ arrived back, and Hopalong dragged himself back to Chez Didsbury. Drinking started early in the evening, and within a couple there was big talk of going out. Squirrel, Hopalong and Ricky Organ were up for it, but The Chemist wasn't convinced, and despite cajoling, begging, violence and threats, held firm, and left the trio to head into town. Brannigan's was the somewhat random destination, where cheap drinks led to ordering taxis for The Chemist. They hit the dance floor, where Ricky Organ managed to attract a munchkin, that he brushed off. On closing time they went to get Hopalong's coat, but found it impossible because someone had collapsed on the stairs, and everyone was waiting for the ambulance. In the meantime Hopalong decided he was going to abuse the biggest honey monsters he could find, but found that they had lots of friends and so ended up having to talk to them. On leaving Brannigan's they looked for somewhere else to go, and Fantasy Bar was decided on. They got another taxi number and ordered another taxi for The Chemist. The Fantasy Bar was closed, so they headed to Teasers, and got turned away. The bouncers suggested that Long Legs might be open. They flagged a taxi, only to be told that Long Legs shut at 11 as well, despite this they made the driver go past it. Home was then the venue, however Fallowfield kebab shops called, and kebabs were bought, and Hopalong abused the server. Then another flagged taxi, where Hopalong abused the taxi driver, and as the trio exited at home, they were advised that they would be remembered. Once back at Chez Didsbury they banged the music on loud, and Ricky Organ tried to get The Chemist out of bed by prodding him with a golf club, and eventually succeeded.

Tuesday 30th December - Who's bright idea was it to go out on a Monday? Squirrel, Hopalong and The Chemist all suffered all day at work, while Ricky Organ did fuck all at home all day, which would explain why he was so keen to go out the night before.

Wednesday 31st December (New Year's Eve) - Tiger Tiger was the suggested location, and Ricky Organ, Hopalong, the Chemist, Plane, Dancing and Ant were amongst those who got tickets and went. Squirrel meanwhile refused to pay £25 for a ticket, and went to Fallowfield instead, and started off in the Great Central, before heading to XS. Tiger Tiger was getting messy quickly, with Plane feeling worse for wear before Midnight, and had to be taken home just after by Ricky Organ. Even worse off was Ant, who was doing a good impression of the exorcist and projectile vomiting everywhere, to such an extent that even the bouncers wouldn't go near him to throw him out, and he had to coaxed out by Dancing. Not much after one Hopalong and The Chemist left and got a taxi back, and tried to get hold of Squirrel, but without success. This would have been because he was busy dancing and chatting up women, with mixed results. The first attempt was going well, until some older Irish women had a word and scared her off. This led Squirrel to their niece, who come closing time he was getting off with, but the five minutes it took him to get his coat and say his goodbyes to the regulars, meant he got back to see her leaving with someone else. A bus followed, then Kansas fried chicken to arrive back at Chez Didsbury and join Hopalong and The Chemist in drinking pints of vodka and red bull.

Thursday 1st January (New Year's Day)- Recovery, somewhat unsurprisingly. Hopalong went to Emerald's and for some bizarre reason everyone else watched Legally Blonde

Friday 2nd January - Doh, work again, except for Ricky Organ, Hopalong went round to Emerald's in the evening, and Plane came round. Tiger Woods and late nights followed.

Saturday 3rd January - Lots of sport on TV, Hopalong went round to Emerald's in the evening, Squirrel headed to Fallowfield, with a quick stop in the Great Central, before quite a few in The Friendship, where he bumped into Tak, Tan, Lyem and Sther. Meanwhile Ricky Organ and The Chemist headed into Didsbury, for a cultured evening in The Pitcher and Piano, and the Slug and Lettuce. Meanwhile Squirrel was back in XS, consuming the normal mix of alcohol, and doing the normal amount of dancing, before the obligatory trip to Abdul's and a taxi back to Chez Didsbury, where Ricky Organ was still up watching the American Football.

Sunday 4th January - Half seven and Squirrel goes to bed, eventually gets up for some of the football, and the overall level of movement in the house was minimal, Plane was round for a bit, and the night was polished off by the spectacular darts final.

Monday 5th January- No Monday night football, meant shit TV and no movement. Ricky Organ went out for a drink with Melvin.

Tuesday 6th January - Hopalong went round to Emerald's, and Plane was round for a bit, leaving Squirrel and The Chemist watching football.

Wednesday 7th January - G Man eventually returned from his trip to the States and the Caribbean, retrieved his belongings from The Moat House and stayed over at BB's. Hopalong was absent presumed at Emerald's again. Squirrel, The Chemist and Ricky Organ watched football.

Thursday 8th January - Hopalong was lounging on the sofa suffering from going out the night before. G Man was looking forward to a quiet night recovering from his jet lag after a torturous first day back at work, but that illusion was shattered when BB rang and summoned him round to hers. The Chemist, who had joined the gym the day before, went to the gym. Ricky Organ was working late.

QUOTES OF THE FORTNIGHT

The Chemist (50 minutes into the film) - I've just worked out why it's called Legally Blonde.

It's chucking out time at Brannigans, and there is a crowd at the top of the stairs preventing access to the cloakrooms and toilets.
Hopalong - What's the hold up?
Random person - Someone's collapsed on the stairs.
Squirrel - So? Just step over him.

E-Mail conversation. Squirrel has just forwarded a holiday update from G Man.
Hopalong's reply - Friggin' hell - how long's he there for - do we know yet?
Squirrel - He's put "Back Wednesday" in the e-mail.
Hopalong - OH, I though he meant back Wednesday (for the second division title).

2003 SPECIAL AWARD ZONE

Below you will find the 2003 Surerandomality awards. Under no circumstances will Squirrel waste his time explaining the reasoning behind any of these awards. If you don't know what they've been awarded for then you've not been paying attention over the last year, so basically, unlucky.

The "Stella Live" event of the year - Chez Didsbury Barbeque.
The "Tone Deaf" Karaoke anthem of the year - Jungle Brothers - Because I Got It Like That

The "Dancing Bear" dance anthem of the year - The Prodigy - Out of Space

The "Bryan Adams" Waking up the neighbours' award - Squirrel

The "Sunken Battleship" award for most alcohol (total volume) consumed - Hopalong

The "Pavement Pizza" puking champion of the year - G Man

The "Armitage Shanks" award for mistaking a girlfriend as a toilet (1) Pissing - Destroy

The "Armitage Shanks" award for mistaking a girlfriend as a toilet (2) Puking - Hopalong

The "Thomas Cook" award for Suitcase Packing (1) When pissed - G Man

The "Thomas Cook" award for Suitcase Packing (2) With Puke - The Chemist

The "Good Charlotte Lifestyles Of The Rich And Famous" award for most countries visited - Ricky Organ

The "Dennis Norden, It'll be alright on the night" award for least successful date - Squirrel

The "Anne Widdecombe" award for biggest minger pulled - Dylan

The "David Attenborough" award for what species pulled? - G Man

The "It's good to talk" best comedy misdial / text at 3am award - G Man & Hopalong

The "Fuck off Santa" award for most embarrassing moment at a work do - G Man

The "Ray Stevens - The Streak" award - Destroy

The "Eminem Guilty Conscience" award - Hopalong

The "I know a shortcut" most torturous route home from Bolton award - The Chemist

The "David Bailey" where's my camera missed photo opportunity award - Anyone, on the Names have been changed to protect the innocent night.

The "Red Light District" award for getting warned off a patch - Kissme

The "Gill's Taxis" are you sure this is a cab award - Pecs

The "Kronk's Gym" best punch bag award - G Man

The "Keith Gillespie" gambler of the year award - Hopalong

The "Ernie, Fastest Milkman in the west" award for outstanding timekeeping (1) Accidental - Hopalong

The "Ernie, Fastest Milkman in the west" award for outstanding timekeeping (2) Purposely - Ricky Organ

The "Dog ate my homework" award for most original excuse for being off work - G Man for A Cricked Neck

The "Domestos" Blonde of the year award - Blondie

The "Star Spangled Banner" award - Shared by Ricky Organ and Nick "Art Garfunkel" Varner

The "Couldn't score in a brothel" award for pulling - Squirrel

The Brighton Line

The beginning of the end, when the shit hit the fan and things began to fall apart.

Friday 9th January - A quiet night in was the forecast, however it must be said that Squirrel failed to recognise the correlation between a quiet night in and what happened. First though, Squirrel, Karen, Blondie, and Garden went to the Hogshead at lunch for a few drinks for Karen's birthday. Then in the evening, with all the Chez Didsbury residents in residence for the first time in a long time, the baby raiding started early. In addition to the residents Emerald was also there. After much discussion taxis were booked, but in line with previous form The Chemist was refusing to leave the house. Therefore it left Squirrel, G Man, Ricky Organ, Hopalong and Emerald to head to 5th Avenue after quite a few, Squirrel was the first the hit the dance floor (and for a change not literally). Everyone else soon followed. Hopalong got into a bit of an exchange with a random on the dance floor, and turned to G Man and said what a tosser the guy was. This prompted G Man to punch the random and knock his glasses off. Squirrel was torn between keeping an eye on this and the woman he'd been talking to. Eventually he went and dragged G Man to the bar to buy drinks. After things had calmed down everyone went back to dancing, and Squirrel went back to chatting the woman up, this was going well until her mate ran in and dragged her out saying their lift was there, a typical kind of guard dog move. Not long after the famous five left (It was a surprise they got in, with them all being under age, and the fact that Timmy's a dog), then Squirrel, G Man, Ricky Organ, Hopalong and Emerald left and got a taxi to Fallowfield for the customary kebab, and then another taxi back to Chez Didsbury, where for the first time in quite a while Snatch got an airing, while at the same time the baby raiding started again, and the mainlining of spirits started. Elsewhere it wasn't such a good night for Pugh, who got pistol whipped and robbed in Fallowfield after an argument with the occupants of a passing car. Back at Chez Didsbury, the alcohol was beginning to take serious effect and Ricky Organ was passed out on the kiddie's chair in the corner, Hopalong went to bed, and after Snatch, some loud volume Beastie Boys videos was a tip top idea to round off a textbook night.

Saturday 10th January - What is all that fucking noise? It's a muthafucking ridiculous. Sleep. Noon saw Hopalong, Ricky Organ and The Chemist in the Parrswood, they were joined mid-afternoon by Squirrel and G Man. Not long after Ricky Organ left to go and meet Plane, and The Chemist left to go to the gym. Before you all die of shock it must be pointed out that he didn't end up going as the car park was full. G Man then left to go round to BB's. This left Squirrel and Hopalong having a few beers, watching football, playing pool and darts. Emerald arrived just after 6, and then left with Hopalong before 8. Squirrel, still suffering from that last three quarters of a bottle of tequila from the night before decided solo drinking in the Parrswood wasn't the way forward, and headed back to Chez Didsbury. A night of NFL playoff followed for Squirrel and The Chemist, with Ricky Organ and Plane in his room, and Hopalong and Emerald coming back later, and hiding out in his room. Elsewhere, after a night out, Blondie managed to slip over whilst showing off, landing on her arse and banging her head and getting a nice egg-shaped swelling. Quite possibly the only time ever that Blondie could be referred to as an egg head.

Sunday 11th January - Emerald and Hopalong were back in the Parrswood soon after opening time. The Chemist made it to the gym. G Man arrived back at Chez Didsbury, and picked up Squirrel and Ricky Organ and went to see United. After the match G Man went round to BB's, and Ricky Organ, The Chemist and Squirrel watched the quintessential Sunday night film in Irreversible and more NFL playoff action

Monday 12th January - G Man went to BB's, and Hopalong to Emerald's, the others, for a change watched shit TV

Tuesday 13th January - See above, the only difference being that Squirrel had had the day off.

Wednesday 14th January - Hopalong was at Emerald's yet again, as the rest of the residents headed to their late 10pm kick off in the 5 a side league, and then came back and lounged and had the Surerandomality album as the celebratory soundtrack.

Thursday 15th January - Basically see Monday and Tuesday. The only thing of note was the rare sight of Ricky Organ dragging his carcass out of bed and out of the house before 7 in the morning.

Friday 16th January - Ricky Organ worked late and went out with Plane. Hopalong completed the set for the week and was at Emerald's. Squirrel went straight from work to Moss O Growlie to meet Kissme and Vek. Meanwhile G Man and The Chemist headed to the Woodstock to meet up with Zen, Wen, Pugh, and Topher. Squirrel joined them later after leaving town, and they all stayed there until kicking out time, when the route back to Chez Didsbury involved a surprising stop at a kebab shop.

Saturday 17th January - Squirrel went to work, and met up with G Man, Ricky Organ, and The Chemist, who were in town shopping. A trip to Sinclair's Oyster Bar quickly followed, and after a drink there they headed to the comfort of leather armchairs in Waxy O Connor's. It was a dangerous period which could have led to a messy unplanned evening. However they all headed back to Chez Didsbury. G Man went straight back out to pick BB up and headed to the Didsbury for something to eat. Ricky Organ also went straight out to meet Plane for something to eat, which left Squirrel, The Chemist, and Hopalong sat around watching films and DVD's.

Sunday 18th January - G Man and BB were in and out all day, and went to see the Last Samurai. Hopalong went out in the afternoon to view a flat with Emerald, and didn't return. There was the usual watching of football. The Chemist went to Tae Kwon Do, there was a Sunday night film, and then NFL playoffs. Overall a textbook Sunday.

Monday 19th January- In somewhat of a rarity, everyone was in Chez Didsbury at the same time, though Ricky Organ was in his room with Plane while everyone else watched football.

Tuesday 20th January - Ricky Organ was off on another jolly, this time though, only to London. G Man went to BB's, and Hopalong went to Emerald's after watching football.

Wednesday 21st January - Hopalong went round to Emerald's and Ricky Organ came back from his latest jolly in time for five a side, another late-night watching shit TV.

Thursday 22nd January - A quiet nigh, with Hopalong round at Emerald's, and Plane round to see Ricky Organ, The Chemist was out with The Quiet Man, and yep rubbish TV was watched.

QUOTES OF THE FORTNIGHT

The Chemist (talking about American Football) - I quite like the Cowboys, but I wouldn't want to go to Tesco's. (He meant Texas)

Destroy - Is there anyone else except City playing tonight
Squirrel - Yeah, Watford-Chelsea
Destroy - Who are Chelsea playing?

Destroy (one can only hope sarcastically, as Karen and Garden were talking about Avon prices) - God, I wish I was a girl.

Random Man in The Post Office - Do you sell stamps?

Cabbage (as response to a Wedding invite from Gonfer) - Sorry, but I'm in Barbados then. (A rival to the cricked neck excuse!)

What Really Happened?

That first Friday night out of the fortnight was all fine until everyone got home. The bottles of spirits had been cracked open and there may not have been a lot of glass usage in taking swigs of tequila, vodka, rum, etc, and well as drinking beer. People were falling asleep in the chairs, on the sofa, on the floor and started to go off to bed.

Hopalong came back down to the living room where there was now only Squirrel passed out in a chair as the daylight was coming in through the conservatory and patio doors. Hopalong woke him up. "Have you seen Emerald?" Squirrel hadn't seen a thing as he was passed out. And now, just awake Squirrel dragged himself out of the chair and headed to bed. Hopalong continued his search.

This involved the conservatory, shower room, deep dive in the living room, including behind the sofa, the music room, the kitchen, under the stairs, a look into The Chemist's room, and the upstairs bathroom. Hopalong then woke Squirrel up again, this time in Squirrel's room. "Have you seen Emerald?" "Not since the last time you woke me up and asked me?" "Is she in here?" "Not unless she's in the wardrobe."

Hopalong continued the search, checked Ricky Organ's room, and finally into G Man's room, where he finally found Emerald. And that's when the shouting started. She was naked. In G Man's bed. G Man was partially clothed, and denied even knowing she was there before Hopalong came in. Hopalong was shouting for Emerald to get out of G Man's bed, but she was saying "No, I want to stay here," and cuddling up to G Man.

Later, before Hopalong, The Chemist, and Ricky Organ headed to the pub, Ricky Organ and Squirrel were finding articles of Emerald's clothing in various rooms in the house (music room, hallway, living room), which would suggest gradual de-robing. With Hopalong rampaging around the house, it was decided that this kind of evidence shouldn't be made public at that time.

It would be a bit icy in the house until they left, and from that point until after this book ends, the only people who knew anything about what happened that night were the six people in the house. People knew Hopalong and G Man (lifelong friends) had had a falling out and weren't really speaking to each other. But no one knew why, and no one was telling anybody why either.

The Minutes

Friday 23rd January - A quiet night in was the forecast, however it must be said yet again that Squirrel fails to recognise the correlation between a quiet night in and what happened. After a couple of quiet beers from the baby, Squirrel, G Man, Ricky Organ and The Chemist headed into town, with first stop Bar 38, after a few in there they headed out, and met up with BB, McCarthey and Oj, and headed to M2, however entrance was denied due to Squirrel not being dressed funkily enough and the fact he has green hair, after a short pointless exchange, they all headed to Teasers, which for some strange reason had the upstairs dance floor bit shut off, and therefore left no dancing room. Therefore another location was sought, and found in Barracuda (Springbok, by a new name, but with the same décor). After a few more drinks, the strains of Out of Space were heard, and Squirrel and G Man were off, and when they finished dancing, so were McCarthy and Oj, which probably says a great deal about Squirrel and G Man's dancing. Just before last orders Ricky Organ, The Chemist, G Man and BB rushed round the corner to the Casino (Viva Las Vegas), to try and catch the end of the free buffet, leaving Squirrel to finish all the drinks. When Squirrel arrived in the Casino (Viva Las Vegas), he found that they had been denied food cos they were too late, and that the others were all on losing streaks. With a combined £150 loss they headed off, with G Man going to BB's and the other heading back to Chez Didsbury.

Saturday 24th January - The concept of taking it easy is a difficult one to comprehend, and after a Gregg's breakfast, and bets, Squirrel and G Man headed to the Clocktower to meet up with Wen, Zen, and a whole host of their mates. Again, there is a failure to recognise the correlation between a few quiet drinks and what happened. Ricky Organ and Plane joined them in the pub briefly before heading off, and despite G Man heading back to Chez Didsbury under orders, Squirrel was going to continue. When it came to time to leave the Clocktower, Wen headed home to smoke, but everyone else headed into Fallowfield and for the nice cheap drinks in The Great Central. Then it was across the road for a few more in Revolution, and in what was probably a mistake some Tequila Slammers. At this point, Squirrel got separated from everyone else and the homing beacon set in, and he went to XS, meanwhile everyone else was off to Robinski's. The XS odyssey didn't last long, as the beer scooter came and took Squirrel home not long after midnight, but not before he downed his own pint, then someone else's and donned his sunglasses and headed to the dancefloor.

Sunday 25th January - Hopalong was out early to view flats, which was interspersed with visits to pubs, of which the Clocktower was one. Elsewhere Ricky Organ was out with Plane, The Chemist went to Tae Kwon Do, G Man went to the cinema with BB, and Squirrel did absolutely, positively fuck all.

Monday 26th January - Ricky Organ was off on his travels again, this time the warmer climes of Lisbon were the destination, meanwhile everyone else was just chilling.

Tuesday 27th January - With expert timing, G Man and BB left the restaurant just as the heavy snow fall started, and were therefore covered in it by the time they got back to Chez Didsbury, much to the amusement of Squirrel. Apart from that another quiet night in.

Wednesday 28th January - No football, meant there was the rumour of going to the Dog and Partridge to do the quiz, however the afternoon enthusiasm had subsided by the time it was dark and cold, and a few quiet drinks in followed.

Thursday 29h January - Speaking of a few quiet drinks, why does it never seem to happen whenever Squirrel and Kissme meet up. One drink turned into "a couple" turned into three bottles of wine and ten Stellas, and being ushered out of the Square Albert as the staff attempted to lock up. After three quarters of an hour just sat in Albert Square, they managed to get a taxi to their respective homes, and all without falling on the icy snow once.

Friday 30th January - Squirrel and Destroy (who had also been on the piss the night before) thought it was a good idea to hit the pub at dinner and had a few swift ones in the Waterhouse. G Man escaped early afternoon, and headed to Scotland to get a weekend's snowboarding, meeting up with Gopher amongst others. The Chemist was in a non-movement mode for a change, and with Ricky Organ on his way back from Portugal, it left just Squirrel and Hopalong to do the drinking. The Parrswood was the first destination, where quite a few beers accompanied the watching of the Sheffield Wednesday game, before some more accompanied some pool playing. At last orders they got a taxi to Fallowfield and a trip to XS, where lots more beers, a few tequilas and some reefs accompanied quite a bit a dancing before heading to Abduls where Hopalong refused to get food, and managed to get in an argument with some random before they got a taxi back. Once in the taxi Hopalong started to beg for some kebab, but Squirrel point blank refused to give any away, so once back at Chez Didsbury Hopalong found some microwave pasta meal in the fridge and proceeded to cook and eat that.

Saturday 31st January - After finding bits of pasta all over the floor of his room Hopalong realised that he'd nicked The Chemist's pasta, but there wasn't a chance of replacement before going out with Emerald, as they headed to the Golden Lion to watch the football. Squirrel found bits of his kebab on the floor, and was tempted to eat it, but thought better of it. Ricky Organ had gone into work and made it back for the start of the football. Hary made it over from Leeds and after the football him and Squirrel headed to O'Neill's in Didsbury to meet up with a whole host of people, with Dancing and Ant being among the 20+ people who were out (the rest allegedly being Shan, Ander, Buzz, The Quiet Man, Ory, Moyet, Zil, Cork, Artois, Texas, Emerald, Roof, Drew, Carbony, Trebor, Welsh Hard, Perhaps, & Wonder). The Chemist was at the same time heading to Tae Kwon Do, and Ricky Organ was staying in "working" before going out with Plane in the evening to a birthday party of one of her friends. Meanwhile in O'Neill's there were plenty of jugs been drunk, and some pool playing going on, until just after 7 everyone headed to OP bar, where even more people (Hara, Brown, Othy, Omi, Stinky Belle, Shuv, & Artois's brother), as well as Dylan joined up. After quite a few more Dylan and Squirrel headed to XS, while everyone else was heading into town, using a mixture of taxis and good old UK North, they headed for Walkabout, but whilst those that were walking there from the bus stop, met the ones that had gone in the taxi walking back having been put off by the size of the queue. Unfortunately, the point at which they met was where they ended up... the scally-ridden Square Bar. Meanwhile The Chemist had met up with Tyka and Iel, and they ended up in One

Central Street. In XS Dylan and Squirrel met Sally, who had made it back to the country, and was looking remarkably well considering how ill she had been. After a couple of drinks in XS Dylan and Squirrel headed to Jabez, where lots more drinks, and a little bit of dancing followed, before heading home. Back at Square bar, after a couple and just after midnight, Dancing, Moyet, Artois, and Texas headed home, and at some stage a host of others, including Hary and Ant, headed to Rusholme and Al Bilal, where for the second time on the trot Ant managed to fall asleep. Squirrel headed to Fallowfield and Abdul's again, and was waiting for a taxi when Hary rang, to say he was on the way back. However it seems that Hary's journey wasn't the easiest as he didn't arrive back at Chez Didsbury until half five, after managing to puke five times on the way back, this despite the fact he left Rusholme in a taxi heading to Didsbury with several others. However he jumped out at some point on the journey home, after giving the impression he knew where he was going.

Sunday 1st February - Not a great deal of early motion, with Hopalong back from Emerald's early, and Hary managed to drag himself up to start the journey back to Leeds just after midday. Both Ricky Organ and The Chemist got up during the football, and Hopalong went out just after the first match with Emerald. G Man got back after missing an afternoon's worth of Football in time to inspire a Wicker Man viewing, before The Superbowl, and another extremely late night started.

Monday 2nd February- Quiet night in, with G Man round at BB's.

Tuesday 3rd February - As above but BB in with G Man and Hopalong out at Emerald's

Wednesday 4th February - The Chemist point blank refused to play 5-a-side and stayed in with Hopalong to watch football, and when the rest of the residents got back from 5 a side, Hopalong was preparing to go to Emerald's. The euphoria of the win wore off, and the rumoured drinking spree failed to materialise.

Thursday 5th February - Absolutely anything could have happened, but due to work commitments, I'm not exactly Mr. Current Affairs myself, and can't with any degree of certainty tell you exactly what has gone on.

QUOTES OF THE FORTNIGHT

Bouncer (To Squirrel) - You're not dressed funkily enough.
Ricky Organ - Did you say Funky? What do you want us to do? Time warp back to the seventies and come bouncing back on space hoppers?

Ricky Organ (during the same conversation) - What does it take to get in? A rub down and a Shiatsu?

Blondie - Can we accept a change of address?
Long pause, expecting something else to be said before,
Spiderman - That is what we do.

Jose Reyes (Arsenal's new signing) - I am joining the best club in England.
Followed by - To be honest, I know nothing about English football.

Hary - So what date is Valentine's day then? 15th? 18th? 12th?
Squirrel, Dancing & Buzz - The 14th!
Hary - Well I don't need to know.

FREAK ON A LEASH FACTFILE

At work, there was a new temporary worker in working with Squirrel, but Squirrel being of sound mind had sat him next to Destroy instead of next to himself. But still in earshot of the ridiculousness coming out of his mouth. Safe to say they won't be having him back next month.

Classic Quotes:

Most of these were made to Destroy who had the pleasure of being seated next to the Freak…

Goodhew: Francis Lee was caught speeding on the motorway. The policeman said to him "I'm afraid I am going to have to give you 3 points" to which Lee replied (In a dodgy gay accent provided by The Freak) "3 points, I haven't had 3 points all season"

Goodhew: Who do City play at weekend? Destroy: Birmingham. Goodhew: Oh you should beat them.

Goodhew: Name a singer who sings about Dogs. Destroy: Don't know, Who? Goodhew: Frank Sinatra Destroy: Oh right. I don't get it. Goodhew: Well in one song he says "Dooby, Dooby Doo" but it sounds like "Scooby, Dooby, Doo" Ho, Ho, Ho (Gimpish freaky laugh)

Goodhew: Who do City play at weekend? Destroy: Birmingham. Goodhew: Oh you should beat them.

Goodhew: Is your mum a weightlifter? Destroy: No, why? Goodhew: Because she raised a dumb bell like you.

Goodhew: Ding, Dong. Destroy: What? Goodhew: Ding, Dong, Colin Bell

Goodhew: Who do City play at weekend? Destroy: Birmingham. Goodhew: Oh you should beat them.

Goodhew: Red Rum walks into the bar and says to the barman, "Can I have a drink please" to which the barman replies, "Yea sure, hey we've got a drink named after you called Red Rum" (Think he got a bit confused with that one. Bless)

Goodhew: You like my jokes don't you Destroy.

Goodhew: Who do City play at weekend? Destroy: Birmingham. Goodhew: Oh you should beat them.

Goodhew: It's appropriate that's a bear isn't it (Referring to Destroy' M.C.F.C. cuddly toy on his desk.) Destroy: Why is it? Goodhew: Because nobody can bear to be a City fan.

Goodhew: Do you watch that Jungle thing? (I'm A Celebrity) Destroy: Sometimes, my girlfriend watches it. Goodhew: You should do that with everyone in the office. Make a jungle and put them all in it. Would be dead funny that would. Each week you can vote someone out, some places do that you know. (Yea, every fucking place you have been to votes you out you fucking weirdo!)

Goodhew: Who do City play at weekend? Destroy: Birmingham. Goodhew: Oh you should beat them.

The Tottenham Double

Friday 6th February - In another planned quiet night, Squirrel got back to Chez Didsbury, and announced to the audience of The Chemist, G Man and BB that he was meeting Hopalong for a couple in the Parrswood. Hopalong arrived from a stop at the Clocktower, and during their stay at the Parrswood, managed to cane Squirrel at pool. They jumped into a waiting taxi, and let a bloke with Alzheimer's share it, before getting out in Fallowfield, only for Hopalong to realise that he'd left his wallet in the car. However a call and some lying to the taxi firm saw its delivery back, and then allowed entrance to XS, where things got very messy, before kebab and home, where Ricky Organ was still up playing on his laptop.

Saturday 7th February - After a quiet day, during which Hopalong had gone out with Emerald, the evening came, and Ricky Organ was out with Plane. The Chemist was attached to the sofa, and Squirrel and G Man headed into Didsbury and the Dog and Partridge. Dodging rain they got to Fallowfield and the Great Central, where they met up with BB and after a few drinks there they headed into town with the intention of going to Funkademia. However the queue encouraged them to go in Font for a few first, and after a few in there they came out and headed back to Chez Didsbury. Once back Squirrel finished the tequila, while attempting a viewing of Tank Girl. Sleep came before the end of the film.

Sunday 8th February - A Sunday game, broke up a day of watching sport, and once back from five a side, an old favourite of the Sunday night film genre, The Wicker Man, was the evening's viewing.

Monday 9th February - It's at this point that you realise that perhaps this section should be written on a day-by-day basis, as at the end of a fortnight, events have blurred into one, and you can't quite pinpoint what happened when.

Tuesday 10th February - Same as above, but there was some football watched.

Wednesday 11th February - Football, both of the watched and played variety. G Man, after a half day from work, and a drinking session had to meet up with Mummy and Daddy G, whilst trying to appear sober while at Old Trafford.

Thursday 12th February - Squirrel did know this when he started writing this section, but he's forgotten now, no hold on, Crap TV and Ricky Organ to his next destination on his world tour, this time Nice.

Friday 13th February - Yeah of course we believe you Squirrel, you're not going out. With G Man off to Essex with BB for the weekend, The Chemist met Hopalong in the Parrswood, and were later joined by Squirrel after a late finish at work. The Chemist headed back after a couple, and Squirrel and Hopalong headed to the Clocktower, where they met up with a few of Hopalong's work colleagues, and the tequilas started. For a change on a Friday XS was the destination, where they saw Sally, and more tequilas followed, as did dancing, and then the obligatory trip to Abduls.

Saturday 14th February - Hopalong was out of the traps early to meet Emerald in the Parrswood to watch the derby game. Dylan struggled over to Chez Didsbury to watch the game after a heavy night in 42nd Street to find Squirrel quite happily eating the reheated remains of the previous night's kebab. Dylan headed home after the footie to recuperate before a night out. Ricky Organ returned from Nice and spent the evening with Plane. Squirrel headed to Fallowfield and the Great Central where he was joined by Morning and Dylan. After a few quiet ones, some more quiet ones followed in the Friendship, before tequila time was announced by entry to XS, where they again met Sally. Many drinks later saw Morning heading home, and at throwing out time there was mingerville.

Sunday 15th February - A quiet non-drinking day saw lots of football, and a strangely upbeat Sunday night film in Pirates of the Caribbean. Squirrel had been working at home all day sorting timesheets, and then was having a late-night shower when he came a cropper and slipped over. Ricky Organ had to help him out of the bath, a sight no one needs to see.

Monday 16th February - Squirrel sneaked off to Chorley for a date, and elsewhere the normal lounging thing was taking place. And the date didn't go as badly as many had for Squirrel recently. It was the first proper attempt at internet dating. The site being appropriately named as Loopy Love, probably based on the reasoning you would be needing to be a bit loopy to have a date with some on there.

Tuesday 17th February - G Man was hiding in his room with BB, The Chemist and Hopalong were out, presumed at the gym, and hours of MTV.

Wednesday 18th February - After 5-a-side, Ricky Organ, G Man, Dancing and Turkish met up in the Dog and Partridge for a few quiet ones to watch the England game.

Thursday 19th February - Ricky Organ's parents made an appearance and, in a bid, to fool the masses, he took some bottles to the bottle bank. G Man was out presumed with BB. Can't believe Spiderman was the film of the evening.

QUOTES OF THE FORTNIGHT

Ricky Organ - Is MC Hammer an MC?

Ricky Organ - I've worked in a gym, and they're right thick bastards that work there.

Blondie (Looking out of the window overlooking Lincoln Square) - No way is that saddo drawing a picture of Albert Lincoln.

Destroy (Talking about his elastic band ball) - It's like the child I never had. (Editor's Note - This was before it was kidnapped)

Blondie - I had a prawn curry last night and it was minging. It was really fishy.

Hopalong - You know if you have a mouse on your computer, what if you have more? Are they mouses or mice?
General mumbling - Mice
Hopalong - So if you have more than one sheep what do you call them? Sheeps?
Ricky Organ - No, just Sheep.
Hopalong - What about Fish, that's the same.
Squirrel - Fishes

Hopalong - Ha fishes, it's fish.

Ricky Organ - 5 loaves and two fishes.

Squirrel - That's what I was thinking.

Hopalong - Where's that from?

Ricky Organ - The Bible

Hopalong - Yeah, but Jesus was a complete retard, it's fish

Random Bloke (In The Parrswood) – Who would be your celebrity lookalike?

Hopalong – Dunno, although some have said I look like a fat Ronan Keating.

Random Bloke – Yeah, more like a very fat Ronan Keating.

Random Bloke's Mate – More like Ronan Eating.

When Irish Eyes Are Smiling

The Residents (including unofficial ones) have been served NOTICE TO QUIT Chez Didsbury, and must be out by May 1st.

Friday 20th February - Squirrel met Erine on the way home from work, and once back at Chez Didsbury there was a full house. Hopalong was suffering from a chest infection and was in his room. Erine was similarly unwell, and stayed in with Squirrel. Meanwhile, The Chemist, Ricky Organ, G Man & BB headed into Didsbury and to the Dog & Partridge, where after a few drinks, BB said she wasn't feeling too well either and with G Man they headed home where she became the latest to pick up the moniker of puke girl.

Saturday 21st February - Not much motion from most of the residents, with only G Man out at football where he met up with Baby G, who after Football, and along with another of his mates from Harrogate went to Ye Olde Cock Inn for some afternoon beers, with a brief stop and having picked up puke girl somewhere along the way they went for a curry in Rusholme, before heading to Font. Elsewhere it was Casino night at Dickie Boy's. Erine still being unwell stayed in leaving Hopalong, Ricky Organ, The Chemist, and Squirrel going, the usual pharmacy suspects including Iel were there, but it wasn't the most organised evening ever. Squirrel had to be Croupier for the roulette as no one else knew the rules. When people started leaving Squirrel and Hopalong made an escape, with Hopalong off to Emerald's, and Squirrel back home. Such was the life at the party both that The Chemist and Ricky Organ were sleeping, and when they woke, they thought it was a good idea for The Chemist to drive back.

Sunday 22nd February - More lounging, watching sport, and a film somewhere along the line, random people in and out all day, but such is life.

Monday 23rd February - Hazy recollections, so basically your guess is as good as mine, and probably better.

Tuesday 24th February - Football watching, except for The Chemist & The Quiet Man who went to the Didsbury celebrating The Chemist's birthday

Wednesday 25th February - Late 5-a-side. Some watching as well as playing

Thursday 26th February - Chorley for Squirrel to meet Erine and an early night.

Friday 27th February - Straight from Work, G Man & Topher went to Ye Olde Cock Inn, and after a quick drop off of G Man's car they headed into town and the Paramount where they met up with Squirrel. After a couple, a food stop at KFC was called for before a bus to Fallowfield and BB's fancy dress house party. After mingling and chatting, the first to disgrace themselves was Topher, with yet another bout of puking, this time while queuing for the toilets, soon after he passed out on the sofa, and almost in sympathy, Squirrel passed out on the chair opposite. They were woken up for the bus journey back to Chez Didsbury, however Squirrel kept trying to get on the wrong bus, and once on the right one refused to get off once in Didsbury, he then hid round the corner when it was kebab time. Meanwhile back at the party an outbreak of shagging in the toilet led to someone queuing to give up and shit on Oj's desk. Then to top things off there was a fight. Well there was also Squirrel managing to wake Hary's mum at 4am and 6am while pissed and lying on his phone sleeping in the lounge.

Saturday 28th February - Didsbury Dozen, who's fucking stupid idea was this? This will get messy was probably understatement of the year. First out was Dylan, with Topher in the pub at roughly the same time, Me Laird, Squirrel & Hary arrived at Ye Olde Cock Inn soon afterwards, and were joined by G Man & BB, then Dancing & Trebor and finally Wen, Zen & Enge. Double breakfast was the order of the day for Squirrel, and Me Laird wimping out of drinking at all in the first pub, before the call of next pub came. The Didsbury, boring warm beer, loss of most of agenda down the toilet, start of deviation from schedule. After leaving early there were a large number of people heading to the bookies, where they were joined by the somewhat slack Ricky Organ. The next pub was the Famous Crown, and Me Laird had no drink again. Next pub, just across the road to the Royal Oak, and at this early stage the scousers, Zen, Wen & Enge, were beginning to lag.

Deathly quiet. Next pub, Fletcher Moss, where there were revelations that Trebor used to be Wayout's lodger, and accusations that the party were students. Next pub, Pitcher & Piano, more lagging, again no drinking from Me Laird. Next pub saw the halfway point in The Nelson, which was fairly crowded by the locals, joined by Moyet. Next pub Clock Tower, lose Topher after he goes for kebab, and G Man wriggles out of drinking. Me Laird goes off to get his ex. Next Pub, Dog & Partridge, Starting to get messy, the scousers seriously starting to lag by this stage. Next pub O'Neill's lost G Man and BB for the rest of the evening on the way. Joined by Ant, The Quiet Man & Perhaps, last known point at which the scouse slackers were seen. Next Pub Hogshead, getting disjointed as Dylan, Trebor & Squirrel move into overdrive. Next pub Pear Tree, which Dancing manages to miss, The Chemist and Hopalong join the remnants of the survivors before they all head to pub fourteen on the list, missing the Station, which only Dylan, Trebor & Squirrel manage to negotiate. Trebor quite happily on the wine, Me Laird back out, now with his ex, rugby tackle by Hary on Ricky Organ on the way into the Slug & Lettuce, after Ricky Organ had held traffic up and shouted abuse at the female driver of a passing car. Squirrel fell asleep on a bar stool, and was subsequently ejected. The Chemist took exception to something Dylan said to him and left. Dylan, Hary & Squirrel head to Fallowfield. First stop in Fallowfield was XS, but contrary to popular belief there are some standards there, and there was no service, as they were too pissed. Undeterred by this hint and a half they'd had too much they staggered across the road into the Great Central, where, somewhat worryingly given the number of bouncers on the door, access was granted, and service was granted. Squirrel was ejected again for being too pissed. Hary noticed and after originally following him out went back in to get Dylan. They got back out to find that Squirrel had disappeared. (How the fuck does anyone lose Squirrel, he's not exactly incon-fucking-spicuous is he?) They went the wrong way & got slapping from scallies outside Orange Grove, and Hary got his phone nicked. Dylan wanders off home with a bit of a sore head. Hary finds Squirrel in Abduls (surprise surprise), and they get a bus back to Didsbury (and Squirrel got on the right one and got off without too much prompting as well) and walk back to Chez Didsbury. Ricky Organ is in gobby mood and spends the next half hour giving them shit.

Meanwhile The Chemist is headed to Drop Inn for the night. Hopalong, late to the party, goes to Fallowfield to catch up with the others only to find no sign of them as they'd all disappeared off home.

Sunday 29th February - Ricky Organ, Hary and Squirrel head for the nutritional brunch of Burger King, before Hary heads off back to Leeds. There is football on, and Plane comes round for the Sunday night film

Monday 1st March - Topher was off work still suffering from weekend. Squirrel was dumped by Erine for his general apathy. (It does need pointing out that on the first date Squirrel didn't recognise her, as she looked nothing like her profile picture. Then on the second meeting when she stayed at Chez Didsbury, when they went out for a walk, she was talking about getting married. And on the third meet up at her house in Chorley, she made him sleep on the sofa.) However straight from work he met G Man in Ye Olde Cock Inn for a couple before getting a curry at Sangam 2, and another couple in the Dog & Partridge.

Tuesday 2nd March - People out, people in, it's amazing how quickly time can go when you're sat round doing nothing.

Wednesday 3rd March - Late night football again meant a chance to watch football before playing and another late night.

Thursday 4th March - No 5th Avenue, though believe Squirrel when he says it was fucking tempting, just the same old same old, lounging and preparing for the weekend.

QUOTES OF THE FORTNIGHT

Next Pub!

Talking about Mexico when
Spiderwoman - That's near Africa.

Spiderwoman - When was Christmas Day
Destroy - 25th December

Hary - Who's this slag then?
Me Laird - That's my ex.

At a Fancy dress party, after all night dressed in bandages and sunglasses, the "invisible man" returns in normal clothes.
Squirrel - No mate, you looked better with the bandages on.

Insert Title Here

Friday 5th March - With the usual suspects showing no inclination to leave the Chez Didsbury living room, Squirrel wandered out to meet G Man and BB in the Dog & Partridge. After a couple in there they headed to Fallowfield, and decided that it would be a good idea to hit Karma. However, despite its sophisticated image, it is in fact scally central, and after a hasty drink they headed to the classier surrounds of XS, where they were going to meet up with Dylan, but unfortunately, he was on a temporary bar, after the previous week's excursion. Not long after Squirrel hit the dance floor G Man and BB sneaked off home, which led to an unsupervised Squirrel and dirty rounds. Kebab followed, but what route home is anyone's guess.

Saturday 6th March - Squirrel was rudely awakened by Mate ringing him wanting dinner time drinking on one of his rare excursions up to Manchester. It was at this point that Squirrel discovered numerous UDI's and clothes covered in mud (vague recollections of getting on the wrong bus, being in the middle of an estate in Sale, falling down the bank of a stream, and struggling to find a main road to get a taxi from). He managed to get to the Clocktower only to find that the venue had been changed to Ye Olde Cock Inn, and he got there just in time for the football and found that along with Mate, Hopalong, The Chemist and Dickie Boy were also in attendance, however there wasn't much drinking action going on. The early evening saw everyone leaving the pub, with Mate and Dickie Boy off out for the evening, and the others heading back to Chez Didsbury, just in time to see Ricky Organ and Plane heading off to the dags. Meanwhile G Man was heading to Elemental for a DJ set by someone he worked with.

Sunday 7th March - Sport was the order of the day, with the grand prix and football, and a non-Sunday night Sunday night film.

Monday 8th March - G Man and BB were at the Snow Patrol concert, and were the only movers.

Tuesday 9th March - Football watching for a change.

Wednesday 10th March - Playing football, another late start, and then late-night poker.

Thursday 11th March - What is it about the first Thursday of a fortnight? Squirrel can never remember what's going on. Probably football watching.

Friday 12th March - In a shock move, no one went out or did anything remotely interesting.

Saturday 13th March - With Ricky Organ down south somewhere, and G Man at BB's, Hopalong and The Chemist took the lead and headed to town, while Squirrel stayed in for the second night on the trot, this time however to annoy the neighbours by making full use of his decks for a few hours. In town the first stop for The Chemist and Hopalong was Teasers, and after a couple there they headed for the print works, and attempted Tiger Tiger, but were refused entry as Hopalong was too casual. Undeterred they headed for Lucid, and in shocker they managed to get in. On leaving Lucid they headed to the Casino (Viva Las Vegas), where unfortunately, due to new gaming rules, The Chemist (as a guest) was refused entrance. This didn't stop Hopalong, who used the 20-minute wait for a taxi to go and win £40.

Sunday 14th March - Derby day saw Hopalong out with Emerald. Squirrel headed to the Friendship to meet Kissme, who was a no show, and G Man was in corporate hospitality at the City of Manchester stadium, but had little to cheer about. The evening saw a Sunday night film, and a brief appearance from Ricky Organ, as he picked up some stuff on his way to spending the week at Plane's.

Monday 15th March - A quiet week started with Hopalong out and about and random flicking on TV

Tuesday 16th March - It continued with G Man out straight from work and then at BB's and more random flicking on TV.

Wednesday 17th March - Late night football was a killer, and kind of dampened the St. Patrick's Day spirit, and all that was left to do was watch late night poker.

Thursday 18th March - Basically to top a quiet week off, there was more quiet, strange that.

QUOTES OF THE FORTNIGHT

Talking about reasons for Blondie's tiredness.
Spiderwoman - That's a sign of Anaemia. Your iron could be low as well.

Squirrel - The Team With No Name played Parrswood Old Boys tonight.
Wen - We could do with them both losing.

When I'm

KIDNAPPING HORROR

Destroy's Elastic Band Ball was kidnapped over three weeks ago by someone calling themselves the Elastic Band Liberation Front. So far, they have sent him five ransom demands, and several postcards allegedly from the elastic band ball, which they are calling bandy. They also sent him stickers to wear saying "My name is Destroy. I'm an elastic band abuser. But I'm trying to change," which he had to wear for a week. He has done this and is now waiting for word.

Destroy is understandably gutted, having raised the ball from nothing when he first started work at Nat West as a teenager, and seeing it grow to its softball size as it was when it was kidnapped.

Therefore if anyone has information that can help in the solving of this terrible crime, please contact us at the earliest opportunity. All contact will be dealt with in strictest confidence. Thanks for your cooperation.

Friday 19th March - Ricky Organ, Plane and his sister were out for Zoo magazine in Yates trying to take pictures of fit women, which obviously wasn't going to happen, as Yates isn't a venue known for fit women, only women that are fit to drop. Then they headed on to Deansgate locks to cheat. G Man was straight out from work on another messy misadventure, with the Hogshead and the Pitcher & Piano being the Didsbury locations, before meeting BB and going to see Zero 7. Then it was a trip to Font, and BB finished the night off by regaining her puke girl title.

Saturday 20th March - Quiet, so much so it looked like there were new permanent covers on the seats in the Chez Didsbury lounge.

Sunday 21st March - See above.

Monday 22nd March - And again.

Tuesday 23rd March - And yet again.

Wednesday 24th March - Playing football broke the monotony, and The Chemist and Hopalong went to watch some at Squirrels. Talk about an old school blast from the past. The Chemist's wine (Holmes Place introduce a friend promotion) finally turned up, at which stage G Man owned up to having swiped and hid the original delivery. Which was a bonus all round as it meant two cases of wine instead of just the one.

Thursday 25th March - Something, or possibly nothing.

Friday 26th March - Ricky Organ headed off for the next episode in the lifestyles of the rich and famous, with him off for a conference at Sea World in Orlando for a week. Meanwhile Squirrel started on the baby early, and G Man and BB joined in, and after a few it was next destination Scubar. G Man knew one of the staff from Harrogate, and there were some messy drinks. Wandered up to The Garrett next and flyers were picked up for the final destination of the evening, 5th Avenue. Somewhat unsurprisingly things got very messy, and G Man's evening out was cut short after BB came back from the toilet to see him talking to a random bird on the dance floor and threw all her toys out of the pram. This left the now considerable worse for wear Squirrel to his own devices, and he managed to find his own way home, without any UDI's or food stops.

Saturday 27th March - This however led to still being pissed when he arrived for his early morning haircut, things didn't improve at the record fair, and after a sobering up session at pizza hut, he arrived back at Chez Didsbury with no idea what he'd bought. Meanwhile Hopalong was going upmarket for the evening and headed to Chester with Emerald.

Sunday 28th March - Loafing day, there has been more motion from the dead.

Monday 29th March - G Man went to stay at BB's, but managed to find time to have an altercation with Wayout before doing so. Needless to say Wayout is a cock, but it will be said anyway. The Chemist has the week off and is spending the time constructively by listening to classical music and drinking his wine.

Tuesday 30th March - Underground fire in Manchester meant that Squirrel, Garden, Spiderwoman, and Blondie were rushing around getting ready, and then driving down to Crawley to do some work. After some top-quality quotes, it turned out that Spiderwoman hadn't quite grasped the concept, that to pour wine, the lid needs to be removed.

Blondie found this highly amusing, until no more than five minutes later she managed to do the same thing. This in turn tickled Garden, who in trying to act out what they'd done, knocked her glass of wine over Squirrel. Furthermore it was discovered that Blondie and Garden are high new entries on the all-time lightweight list, with both being completely battered off two glasses of wine, so much so that Garden became the latest holder of the prestigious puke girl title.

Wednesday 31st March - After a series of calamities and various jollies five a side didn't happen, which left G Man watching England in the Friendship, though he wouldn't have seen much of the action as he had one eye out for the Ashton player that was in there as he cowered in the corner. Back in Crawley, Squirrel started on alcohol the second he got back to the hotel. Meanwhile the girls, were on a strict no drinking policy, or they were until after they'd had food and the football was well underway. Garden disappeared from the bar first, but she did have the excuse of Chip being there for the evening. After a couple of drinks the tiredness kicked in and Spiderwoman and then Blondie wandered off, leaving Squirrel in the bar, which just led to lots of beers and a late night.

Thursday 1st April - Not only had the fire been put out, but the computer lines had been fixed, which meant that Squirrel, Garden, Spiderwoman, and Blondie could head back to Manchester. Don't mention bar bills. Now then, is 5th Avenue a viable idea? Hell yes, not only is it a viable idea but Squirrel kops off with fit bird. Must be said it can be seen he'll be going back in the not-too-distant future.

QUOTES OF THE FORTNIGHT

Oh Yes. Besides the first weekend when The Chemist was on top form, but no record was kept, there have been the following.

Watching the Adidas advert
The Chemist - Is that really Muhammad Ali?
Squirrel - Yes.
The Chemist - Is that his daughter?
Squirrel - Yes
The Chemist - How did they do that?

Watching A Question of Sport on Friday evening, the day before the final round of six nations rugby games.

Sue Barker - Don't forget to watch the BBC's all-day coverage of the final day of the six nation's championship.

The Chemist - Surely if this is taped beforehand, they already know the scores to tomorrow's games.

Zen (on way home from 5 a side) - I'm going home to paint a rabbit.

The Chemist - What's the score in the Liverpool game? (they were playing Marseille)

Squirrel - 1 all

The Chemist - Have Marseille scored?

On way to Crawley, after opening window of car there is a strange smell, and a discussion about it. Then.

Blondie - No, That doesn't smell like shit, it smells like manure.

Not to be outdone on the journey, the fuel gage needle had just gone into the red and panic had set in.

Spiderwoman - Someone said that once the needle goes in the red you've got fifty miles left. . .. Or is it fifty gallons?

Retirement Age

Friday 2nd April - Squirrel dragged himself from the sofa in reception at work and spent the morning in somewhat of a daze, until a lunchtime drink with Destroy in the Hogshead brought him round. Not only that but actual plans for the evening had materialised, and so after a brief stop at Chez Didsbury, where the somewhat jet lagged Ricky Organ was suffering on the sofa, it was straight back out and off to meet G Man and BB in Sofa. However Sofa must have known they were coming and was shut, so instead they went in Troff, for a couple of drinks before heading to Rusholme, Shere Khan, curry and to meet up with Zen and Wen, who were having a joint birthday bash, and Pugh, Boots, Ly, Topher, Drew, Coke and Two Names, the other attendees. After a top curry, which, somewhat surprisingly didn't get that messy, it was off to Big Hands. Well, that was the plan, but in dawdling along they missed getting there before 11 and therefore there were a few reluctant parties willing to pay the £4 to get in, and so a change of destination was made, and it was across the road to the Oxford (which used to be the Hogshead). Despite Tequila madness from Squirrel, G Man, Zen, and Ly, it wasn't the most active place in the world, and the party split into two, with Squirrel, G Man, BB, Zen, Ly, and Boots heading to 5th Avenue. First to leave was Ly, though upon leaving he struck up a conversation with a Chinese midget and went back to hers in Ancoats. G Man was escorted from the premises by BB for the second week in succession, leaving Squirrel, Zen, and Boots as the ones there til the end. However upon exit they lost Boots, only for him to return five minutes later elated at scoring a big bag of weed for only a tenner. Back to Zen's for a smoke then, with a brief stop for food, during which Boots insisted on everyone leaving messages for random people in Australia. Just glad it was his phone bill. Zen managed to throw his food all over the worst gravel pit possible, but managed to retrieve all the items and put it back together to eat. Back at Zen's, Wen, Drew, and Pugh were still up watching Open University, and Boots skinned up, but the weed didn't look normal, it smelt of herbs, and after smoking had a pine smell and taste to it. There was the definite feeling he'd been ripped off. He wandered off home as everyone else crashed out leaving his phone.

Saturday 3rd April - Ly got to Zen's just after 8 after being ushered out of the Chinese midget's flat in the early hours. Everyone was up to watch the football. Boots arrived back round later looking for his phone as we all got to see his bag of pine needles he'd bought the night before. A trip to the bookies followed, with bets all round for the Grand National. Squirrel and Ly won with their horse speeding past Zen's in the final furlong. Wen had to return Ricky Organ's laptop and therefore gave Squirrel a lift back to Chez Didsbury, where G Man had also won on the national. After a quick shower Squirrel and Hopalong headed back to the Parrswood, where Hopalong had spent most of the afternoon. After Squirrel kicked Hopalong's ass at pool and they'd watched the boxing it was into Didsbury and a taxi to XS. Lots more drinks followed. Hopalong made Comi to be a Dirty Den look-alike. Squirrel pulled again, and then on leaving was pulled by another random. Hopalong was not in the mood to go anywhere, and refused to leave the kebab shop until Squirrel took his kebab and walked out. The same tactic was needed to get Hopalong to get out of the taxi and back to Chez Didsbury. Once food had been finished, Hopalong then decided he needed cigarettes, and made it as far as Fog Lane (with a stop to try and wake Wayout up), before giving up, as there were no taxis (Fog Lane is halfway to the garage). He came back and proceeded to fall asleep on the toilet.

Sunday 4th April - After a weekend like that it was a matter of taking it easy, and after Squirrel finished the remnants of his beer left the previous evening that's what happened. Football was watched. Ricky Organ saw Plane, Squirrel went to work, and Hopalong went into hiding. There was an attempt to watch a Sunday night film, but no one could be arsed to put a DVD into the PS2.

Monday 5th April - Busy little bastard time at work, but Monday night football calmed things.

Tuesday 6th April - As above, but the evening saw a magnificent Chelsea victory. The Chemist and Hopalong choosing to watch the match at the Didsbury.

Wednesday 7th April - Thankfully, football was cancelled, as the squad was a bit threadbare. Ricky Organ was at another lifestyles of the rich and the famous day, with team building and drinking in Crewe.

Thursday 8th April - Straight from work G Man was in Ye Olde Cock Inn, with Topher, and then managed to get into town and to Sinclair's to meet Squirrel. After a couple there it was a random crawl across town, taking in new venues of Sam's Chop House, The Crown, Seven Oaks, and The Overdraught on the way to 5th Avenue. However the pace of the evening got to be too much for a newly appointed lightweight G Man, and he wandered off towards Chez Didsbury getting back well before 1. Unperturbed Squirrel continued drinking and dancing til throwing out time, with the sunglasses making their first appearance of the year, and surviving the evening. A stop at Abduls wasn't that unexpected, but Squirrel's patience in waiting for a bus got to him, and he decided it was a good idea to get the next one coming, which meant he ended up in West Didsbury and a long walk home. Elsewhere Dylan was out at 42nd Street with his housemates, getting himself into a similar state.

Friday 9th April - Hopalong was up early to go to the gym, and G Man was up early to puke. The Chemist had gone back up to Newcastle the previous evening, and the non-motion of the house was jolted with Hopalong and Ricky Organ off to the driving range, where Ricky Organ's perseverance and accuracy led to a large part of the dividing partition breaking off. BB returned from Essex, which led to the reclusion of G Man for the rest of the weekend. In the evening only Ricky Organ was up for going out and headed into Didsbury and the Dog and Partridge with Plane.

Saturday 10th April - With Ricky Organ off to London, it left the deadly combination of Hopalong, Squirrel, and boredom, and sure enough shortly after 6 the temptation to do something was too much, and it was next stop Parrswood. After another ass kicking at pool for Hopalong, they headed to Didsbury and the Clocktower to watch the boxing, before heading into Fallowfield, where a couple of quick cheaper drinks were had in the Great Central, before heading to XS, where Squirrel had to turn his t-shirt inside out, cos it looked like a football top. Fortunately, common sense prevailed, and it was righted after a quick word. Things got messy, with tequila and Reefs joining the

Stella's in action, and a rare sighting of Sally, who is still not drinking. Closing time came too soon, which meant the normal Abduls and taxi route home.

Sunday 11th April - Severe lack of motion, which wasn't helped by the demotivational arrival of Ricky Organ late evening.

Monday 12th April - As above, with the added apathy of the return of The Chemist. An early night may have been the plan, but Sky's schedulers aren't helping.

Tuesday 13th April - Back to work, and the rare sight of Ricky Organ up before Squirrel had left for work. The evening saw G Man at Old Trafford, and The Chemist and Hopalong on a Gym and the Didsbury combination.

Wednesday 14th April - An early evening kick off left scope for other activities, and Ricky Organ and Turkish took advantage by going to the Dog and Partridge, where they managed to finish runners up in the quiz and therefore get some Jaffa cakes.

Thursday 15th April - One of those quiet days that may indicate a calm before the storm. However The Chemist did manage to make the posh Didsbury trilogy of the Hogshead, Pitcher and Piano and the Slug and Lettuce with The Quiet Man.

QUOTES OF THE FORTNIGHT

Destroy - In May, payday falls on the 27th for a change, not the Thursday. (Actually May 27th is a Thursday)

Destroy - If this was an office full of lads it'd be heaven!

G Man is about to get into his Honda to go to work.
Asian Neighbour - That's a nice car. If you were thinking about selling it, I'd be willing to buy it.

Hopalong is ringing the bell on Wayout's door, it's 3am.
Squirrel (from the doorway of Chez Didsbury) - What are you doing, he's not in, his car's not there.
Hopalong - Yes, he is, the doorbell's ringing.

Squirrel (to Boots) - Are you drinking that or are you letting it evaporate?

Boots - erm.

Squirrel - Jesus, you're nearly as bad at drinking as you are at football.

Taxi Driver - I'm Iranian

Hopalong - Uranian? You mean you're from Uranus. You're from another planet?

Squirrel - No mate, he said Iranian, meaning from Iran.

While watching The Sixth Sense

Ricky Organ - That dead girl was quite fit. (pause) A bit pale though.

The Clickety Click

Friday 16th April - G Man and BB picked a lovely time to go camping in the Lake District for the weekend, so you can basically blame them for the torrential rain all weekend. Meanwhile back at Chez Didsbury early evening drinking started pre football watching, with Hopalong and The Chemist out into Didsbury at half time to watch the second half in the Clocktower. Ricky Organ came back with Plane just as the match was finishing, and Squirrel then took the opportunity to join the other two in Didsbury. However neither of them had reception so Squirrel had to trawl through the Dog and Partridge, The Clocktower, and O'Neill's before finding them in the Hogshead. After a few more beers it was closing time for Didsbury, and the Chemist headed home leaving Hopalong and Squirrel to make the now familiar trip to XS. Yet again the bouncers thought they were being funny by saying it was full before letting them in. Time passed quickly, with some drinking, dancing, chatting to Sally, and Hopalong giving the cleaner from his work's sister his number. They are supposed to be twins, but it must be said the cleaner seems to have got all the teeth, which meant that the choice of her sister was a surprising one. The normal Kebab - taxi route home followed and another late crawl to bed.

Saturday 17th April - Most people were up early enough to put bets and get food, however Squirrel didn't manage to leave his pit until mid-afternoon. The arrival of Hary only minutes later with beer meant that Squirrel by passed food and started drinking again straight away. After a monumental struggle to get motion from the residents of Chez Didsbury, Hary finally managed to prise Ricky Organ, Hopalong and Squirrel out just after 7 to head into Didsbury and O'Neill's. Once there they met up with the crowd out for Cork's birthday which included Dancing, Moyet, Ant, The Quiet Man, Ory, Shan, Buzz, Artois, and some other random females that it was felt better Squirrel wasn't introduced to. After a few in O'Neill's then it was taxis into town and to Sinclair's Oyster Bar, where lots of Weiss beer was the flavour of the day. Everyone then headed over to the Printworks with the plan of getting into Lucid. Well, everyone except Squirrel, who in t-shirt, jeans and trainers had no intention of doing any such thing. He was having another beer and then heading for XS. However, little did he know he wouldn't be making the trip alone. Back in the queue for Lucid, Ricky Organ and Hary were having a play fight. Despite being told by bouncers to quit twice they continued and were ejected from the queue. They, along with the calming influence of Hopalong (Yes really!) headed to Waxy O'Connor's, where everyone apart from Cork (who had got in free with a borrowed press pass) had gone to as the queue for Lucid was stupid. However one of the bouncers had been the one that had asked Ricky Organ and Harry to quit earlier, and they were refused entry. Not only that but the Manager of the Printworks arrived on the scene to kick them off the entire complex. Hopalong managed to steer Ricky Organ away without him getting a beating (see quotes), as Harry gave telephone commentary to Dancing. They found Squirrel still drinking in Sinclair's and they headed out of town. Ricky Organ and Hary got to Rusholme and decided on food at Caspian. Squirrel and Hopalong headed for XS. Back in the Printworks Cork was throwing a strop cos no one had gone into Lucid and went and got everyone, except for Dancing who objected to shelling out a tenner, and so went home via Fallowfield for a kebab stop. In between early pints Squirrel changed Boy's phone to Italian, more drinks and dancing followed, with Squirrel getting off with the woman he'd done a few weeks previously. Meanwhile Hopalong was chatting up someone else, and come closing time it turned out that her and her guard dog mate were going back to Chez Didsbury, and they were seen by the passing Moyet and Artois as they tried to get a taxi. Once there, Hary and Ricky Organ were both found asleep in the living room. Squirrel opened the vodka (absolutely, positively no fucking need) and then proceeded to give the guard dog a tour of Chez Didsbury, including a detailed inspection of his room. And he struggled to get a radio station on his alarm clock, and the CD single of Queens Of The Stone Age "No One Knows" is not conducive mood music. And as Mr floppy was in effect and he had to resort to tongue action. The guard dog left later (without her mate (who had interrupted her and Squirrel), but not without a fit of histrionics) as Squirrel continued drinking vodka straight from the bottle.

Sunday 18th April - Hopalong was up first as his guest left. Everyone else was up and getting ready to go into Fallowfield for food.

They woke Squirrel just before 12, and he proceeded to horrify them by finishing the remains of the vodka. The Great Central was the choice for food with Hopalong, The Chemist, Ricky Organ and Squirrel all opting for the big fuck off mixed grill, and Hary somewhat bizarrely opting for a salad. Diet coke was the drink of choice, with one obvious exception, who was on the Stella. After food it was across the road to watch the football in the Friendship. Hary regained enough wits to attempt to drive back to Leeds, and at half time the rest headed back to Chez Didsbury, where they found that G Man and BB had got back and were attempting to dry their sodden tent. Somewhat amazingly Ricky Organ and The Chemist went to play squash. Meanwhile Hopalong was making the sofa his for the day, but was receiving constant torment from the mischievous Squirrel. Plane came round to see Ricky Organ in the evening and the start of the snooker championships saw the start of the watching of it.

Monday 19th April - A Sunday night film on a Monday, you better believe it, and it was a repeat showing of Irreversible. Meanwhile The Chemist and Hopalong were out doing the gym and The Didsbury double act again.

Tuesday 20th April - Ricky Organ was out with Plane for a while, and G Man was at Old Trafford, but overall, it was very much a lounging evening. G Man, who now has the keys to his flat, was to be found without BB for the first time in ages, and was last seen going to bed with the Argos Catalogue. No one realised they did lingerie.

Wednesday 21st April - The Chemist and newly single Hopalong headed for Didsbury as the rest of the residents headed for football. Squirrel got to see his new abode and G Man went to spend the night at BB's, after losing interest in the Argos catalogue. Hopalong and The Chemist arrived back after the Pitcher and Piano and The Pear Tree carrying kebabs, and then had an hour long pointless "discussion" with Ricky Organ about smoking.

Thursday 22nd April - Ricky Organ went out for a curry with Plane. Meanwhile G Man became the first to move out of Chez Didsbury, managing to fit all his worldly belongings in two cars. Squirrel moved some of his stuff too, as The Chemist and Hopalong had baby food while watching the football.

Friday 23rd April - Half past eight in the morning isn't exactly the time you expect people to start drinking, however it was just the time that G Man and his work colleagues did, and they were on a beer bus to Alton Towers for a very messy day, that by the end of it had left G Man in a speechless state not much after everyone else had gone out. Ricky Organ and Turkish had gone straight out with some other work colleagues and were getting totally ratted in Wilmslow. Meanwhile Hopalong and Squirrel, managed to get to the Parrswood before eight, and in a turnaround from recent weeks, Hopalong ended up kicking Squirrel's ass at pool. Next stop was the Clocktower, where Hopalong was trying to drum up participants for the Chez Kingsway housewarming the next day. After a few acceptances (the polite "yes, whatever, just go away now" ones) they moved on to Squirrels where they met up with Cabbage, Welsh Hard and a couple of others, before heading for the final destination of XS. Hopalong met up with Brook and Ditch (see previous Friday) and got a taxi back towards Didsbury at the end of proceedings, and left Squirrel to do the normal kebab and taxi run back to Chez Didsbury by himself.

Saturday 24th April - Everyone was up early, but to say that they weren't feeling tip top was somewhat of an understatement. Squirrel found he had left half his kebab on the sofa, but Hopalong threw it away before he could microwave and eat it. The moving process to Chez Kingsway started, which was hampered by the hung over / docile state of the movers and the fact that Ricky Organ had to get his car back from Wilmslow. A few trips followed, and then a nightmare trip to Tesco's for some of the worst kind of pissed up shopping. Then mid-afternoon, G Man managed to reverse and hit another car at a set of traffic lights. By all accounts it was at a funny angle. The "party" started with the arrival of both Hary and Shan over from Yorkshire, directed by Squirrel, and they were soon joined by Turkish and his mate Singo, who had been out drinking in Didsbury all day. Basically not a great deal happened. The Quiet Man and Dialy came over for a few hours. Asset came later for a couple of hours, and Hopalong went to the Gateway to meet Brook and Sitch and bring them back, only for them to take him off to Stockport where they went to Sam's and Pure. Back at the "party," Hary was less than impressed with the mood and turnout, and was providing the only entertainment, by wearing sunglasses (a normal Squirrel characteristic), abusing people, and bringing up the classic get together conversations of animal porn, wanking mirrors, and cocks through letterbox. Hopalong arrived back from Stockport with the words, "good things come to those who wait" ringing in his ears, and everyone was crashed out before 3.

Sunday 25th April - Shan felt the need to be up before 8 and out to go surfing, and Hary felt that it was time to start watching films. A triple header of football followed, with Hary heading back to Leeds halfway through. Squirrel eventually wandered back to Chez Didsbury. Meanwhile the evening saw Hopalong out with Brook again, with stops in Didsbury, and the Dog and Partridge in Heaton Mersey.

Monday 26th April - A bit more stuff moved out of Chez Didsbury, but nothing exciting going on.

Tuesday 27th April - See above for details. The only difference is that G Man went to Ikea for a couple of small items, but ended up spending nearly £200. That's what happens when you take women shopping with you.

Wednesday 28th April - An early kick off in the football would only mean one thing, and that's a Hit The Bar outing to the Dog & Partridge to do the quiz. G Man headed home to see what kind of disaster area BB had turned Chez Woodheys into while doing DIY and Zen went home to calm down, leaving Ricky Organ, Dancing, Turkish and Squirrel to go to the pub where they were joined by The Chemist, Moyet, and a couple of other randoms. Needless to say, but going to say it anyway, they won the quiz.

QUOTES OF THE FORTNIGHT

Squirrel (To Hary as he walks into Chez Didsbury wearing check shirt) - Nice Tablecloth

Hary (To Chinese bird) - The Chinese only use chopsticks cos they never got round to inventing the spoon.

Hary (Again, about young couples buying houses) - Yeah, their combined wages would be enough to get a mortgage, but at 23-24, she's going to be childbearing age, and they're not going to afford it then.

Bouncer at Waxy O'Connor's (To Ricky Organ with a supreme piece of personality recognition) - You're a cunt.
Ricky Organ (Somewhat unadvisable retort) - You're a balding cock.

Hary (Yet again, in a somewhat confused State) - It was like that with the rugby team as well. They were full of Ra Ra. (pause) Henry's

Tin (Spiderwoman's other half while arguing over who a presenter is on TV) - That's Clive James, the one who did Tarrant on TV

Destroy (On arriving at work after cycling in) - I'm sweating like a paedophile in Mothercare.

It's after 5-a-side and Squirrel has told Zen about his ex-wife faking a death cert to get his vinyl out of storage to sell it.
Zen (Genuinely & without the slightest hint of sarcasm) - Was it an amicable split?

G Man - So what did you think of the flat then.
Squirrel - It's tip top mate, I'm just not sure about the colour of the bathroom.

CHEZ DIDSBURY - AN OBITUARY

The end of an era is upon us. With effect from 12.30 this Saturday, May 1st 2004, the world that has been Chez Didsbury officially comes to an end. It seems a world away from Saturday 29th September 2002 when the four residents, G Man, Hopalong, Ricky Organ and Squirrel moved in. Surerandomality hadn't even been thought of then, and people still had their original names. The residents are moving to new locations, with Hopalong, Ricky Organ and The Chemist (Long time temporary resident) moving to the new Chez Kingsway location, and Squirrel and G Man moving to their new Chez Woodheys location. What follows is a brief synopsis of the life and times of Chez Didsbury.

First day there laid the groundwork for what would follow. Stuff was moved in, with the help of various people, and Squirrel came out from the shower exclaiming, "This ain't no instamatic muthafucker!" to a room with all the residents, The Chemist, Mate, The Quiet Man, and Hopalong's dad in it. People had fun and games finding their way back that first night, and it was the first of regular occasions where people crashed over, with people stopping over ever week for the first 10 weeks. Since then: -

Fry ups housewarming party, Darth Maul pulling pants, FIFA 2003, eyebrow shaving, Crying At The Discotec, poker schools, if you can't reach it - use a crutch, MTV, chess, chillies, G Man's birthday carnage, Gold, dartboard, tequila roulette and the Christmas party, non-residents cooking Christmas dinner, Boxing Day shit films, The Getaway, more guests, fajitas, weights bench, Hawk days, the baby, getting locked in the bathroom, child invaders in the garden, football playing, smoothies, Swiss furniture rearrangement, Sunday night films, first temporary residency, worm boy, speaking pikey, frying pan on a string, guests without alarm code = alarm going off, SARS isolation, second temporary residency, air gun, fuse box terrorism, monkey mating, barbecues, garden party, bouncy castle, fugal sticks, Absinthe, more guests, casino on line, third (short term) temporary residency, and start of long term temporary residency, Vice City, condemned boiler, hedgehogs, improved levels of laziness, sleeping in chairs, International King Of Sports, play fights and holes in walls, golf, pizzas, new Thursday night sleeping arrangements, couple's night's in, Tekken Bowling, puking in suitcases, Tiger Woods, late night poker watching, decks, Scrabble and Sinatra, packing cutlery, mini pool, Friday night carnage, holes in doors, Britain's hardest, eviction notice, even more guests, tension, Seven Nation Army, cleaning, packing, leaving.

That only scratches the surface. There have been some great times, some shit times, laughs, tears, lunacy, lounging, and a supporting cast of literally tens, but the one thing you can say is it's never been boring, so please, wherever you are and whatever you are doing, remember that on Saturday at 12.30pm, raise a glass, drink a beer, and shed a tear for the passing of Chez Didsbury.

Edgar Allan Poe Tales

Thursday 29th April - Fun time started early this fortnight, with all the sensible people managing to avoid getting dragged out with the storm that is Squirrel. First stop was Sinclair's, before a quite sensible food stop at El Macho, where although the idea of food was sensible, the cocktails that accompanied it weren't. Hopalong was meanwhile in The Crown with Brook, and couldn't be tempted into town, and instead headed into Stockport. Squirrel meanwhile continued with stops at the Overdraught and The Garrett (where there was a decent Live band), before the destination of 5th Avenue was reached, Closing time saw a stop in Fallowfield for a Kebab, and a half 3 arrival at the deserted Chez Didsbury, where he managed to leave the front door open until he woke to go to bed at 6.

Friday 30th April - The removal and clean up squad of Hopalong, The Chemist and Ricky Organ arrival at Chez Didsbury to find Squirrel throwing pieces of a broken-up wardrobe out of the bathroom window. After much action they headed back to Chez Kingsway for the night. With no one else going out after doing removals from Chez Didsbury, Squirrel met Dylan, Sofi, and Trick in Sofa, and then headed to 5th Avenue for a lot of vodka - red alert combinations. While on the dance floor someone started on Dylan, who, quite harshly, got thrown out. 3 o'clock saw Squirrel, Sofi and Trick get a Taxi back via Chorlton as they argued, and then to Fallowfield for the obligatory kebab stop, with the arrival time at Chez Didsbury being 4.30.

Saturday 1st May - The end of an era came and went in a quiet whimper as the last items were removed from Chez Didsbury and the keys given back. It was very much a day of moving as Garden and Chip moved out of their flat as well. G Man and BB were putting laminate flooring down, hampered by Topher, and by the time Squirrel was coming back from town, they had given up and were in the Frog & Railway. After a few they headed to the Crown for a couple more, before heading back to Chez Woodheys to get changed before heading out for the evening. Within 5 minutes of getting back, and of Squirrel living there, the neighbour was round complaining about the volume of the music. Even for Squirrel that is some kind of record. They headed for a curry at Sangam 2, though Topher preferred to get some kind of takeaway, and they met back up in the Famous Crown. After a quick drink there they headed to the Slug & Lettuce, to meet up with Dancing, Moyet, Trebor, Cork, and others. Meanwhile Hopalong & The Chemist were also in Didsbury, visiting the Dog & Partridge, The Hogshead, and the Pitcher & Piano. At midnight with everyone else going home, Squirrel headed for XS, and his usual Saturday night liaison, and on the way home thought it was a good idea to walk from Parrswood centre back to Chez Woodheys.

The End

Well it is of this book. There was going to be an epilogue of what happened afterward Chez Didsbury to the five residents. But as I pulled the information together to write this book, I found there was so much stuff covering the next six months that there is plenty of scope for a second book following the further adventures of these miscreants.

That book will follow in due course, and hopefully it will not take the seven and a half years this tome took me to finish from having the idea and writing the first chapter until finalising it, editing it, and getting it published.

Not only that, but there are likely to be a whole host of spin off books which will cover the other pieces included in Surerandomality over the years. I like to keep myself busy.

How this book came to be written

I suppose congratulations are in order. You made it to the end, and are now trying to wonder how the events of twenty years ago have come to be written.

Well, I fell into writing by accident. I hadn't realised how much I wrote when I lived in Manchester, I was in too much of an alcoholic haze at the time to know just how much I had done.

But it was all there (well a good proportion of it anyway), in e-mail archives. In writing other bits and pieces over the years, it finally wriggled its way into my brain to write about those times in Manchester. And so, slowly it was all collated, but I felt it was going to be a bit out of context without going through how everyone met, so needed to write the lead up to the shared house, which is what took the time as it required dredging memories, and as I did, little things popped up and so that section grew.

And then it was finished. Almost. There was the long arduous task of changing everyone's name and trawling through changing every reference to any person mentioned. It required a spreadsheet as there are well over one hundred people, some of which I really have no memory of, but they were mentioned in the original e-mails.

I didn't even try to get this traditionally published, it's too personal and would have required so many edits and rewrites it would have been another ten years before anything came out if at all.

About the author

Kevin Rodriguez-Sanchez is a writer who lives somewhere in deepest darkest West Sussex. When he is not writing, he is thinking about writing, or coming up with new ways to procrastinate about doing any writing.

To keep up to date with what else he has published, and his social media channels, follow him on one or more of the below.

Website: - https://www.onetruekev.co.uk/
E-mail: - KRS@onetruekev.co.uk
X: - @kevin_rod_san
Facebook: -
https://www.facebook.com/KevinRodriguezSanchezAuthor/

Watch out for the follow up to this tale, coming sometime in the next year. And for various spin off books from the Surerandomality files over the next eighteen months.